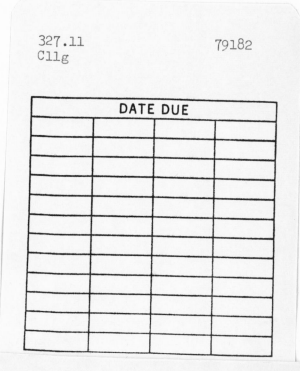

DATE DUE			

STUDIES IN INTERNATIONAL SECURITY

*

STUDIES IN INTERNATIONAL SECURITY: 16

GUNBOAT DIPLOMACY

Political Applications of Limited Naval Force

⬤━◗●◖●◗●◖━⬤

James Cable

1971

PRAEGER PUBLISHERS

New York · Washington

for

THE INSTITUTE
FOR STRATEGIC STUDIES

BOOKS THAT MATTER
Published in the United States of America in 1971
by Praeger Publishers, Inc., 111 Fourth Avenue,
New York, N.Y. 10003

© 1971 by James Cable

Library of Congress Catalog Card
Number: 76–165526

Printed in Great Britain

To
VIVECA

Patient Victim
and
Principal Inspirer
of
GUNBOAT DIPLOMACY

CONTENTS

PREFACE

This book would never have been born without the aid of two illustrious midwives. The Diplomatic Service granted the author a sabbatical year and the Institute for Strategic Studies received him as a Research Associate. Neither bears any responsibility for the results, least of all for the opinions expressed in this book, which are those of the author alone. Both have earned his gratitude by their tolerance.

The facilities of the Institute for Strategic Studies, the stimulation of its rigorous intellectual climate, the advice and help of its staff, the opportunities afforded for argument with experts, the books for which the Institute's long-suffering Librarian ransacked the country: all these fuelled and encouraged the author's efforts.

Numerous naval officers, both serving and retired, British and foreign, have tried to save the author from the worst consequences of his unseamanlike ignorance, but cannot be blamed for those errors which still remain. Nor can Professor Bryan McL. Ranft of the Royal Naval College at Greenwich, though he has been constantly helpful.

The author's greatest debt is naturally to other writers, whose books and articles have been individually acknowledged in footnotes and in the bibliography. Many of these books might, however have escaped the author's attention but for the generosity of various libraries, some of them not normally open to the public, who allowed him to browse among their shelves or even, greatly daring, lent him books. He is particularly grateful to the libraries of

The American University of Beirut
Cambridge University
Foreign and Commonwealth Office
Institute for Strategic Studies
Ministry of Defence, Whitehall
National Maritime Museum
Royal Institute of International Affairs
Royal Naval College, Greenwich
Royal Naval Staff College, Greenwich
Royal United Services Institution

US Naval HQ in London
Westminster City Reference Library
Weybridge Public Library

In West Brompton, alas, regulations are stricter and the author
was unable to wander among the doubtless interesting shelves of the
Admiralty Library.

Finally thanks are due to the Trustees of the National Maritime
Museum at Greenwich for permission to quote from manuscripts in
their possession and to Mr Pearsall, the Custodian of Manuscripts,
for finding them. Transcripts of Crown-copyright records in the
Public Record Office appear by kind permission of the Controller of
H.M. Stationery Office. The Naval Historical Branch of the Ministry
of Defence were kind enough to answer a number of questions and
the Editor of the Naval Review increased the author's indebtedness
to his invaluable publication by permitting reference to some of his
articles.

INTRODUCTION

We have no more reason to believe that the days of
gunboat diplomacy are over than to believe that the
threat of force will not be used on land and in the air.

Millar[1]

GUNBOAT diplomacy is most familiar, but will never be employed in these pages, as a term of abuse, a metaphorical
epithet for almost any kind of attempt by one government to exert an
unwelcome influence on the policy of another. It is often applied to
situations involving no threat or use of naval force, sometimes even
to disputes in which the only pressures employed are economic or
diplomatic.

This degeneration of a phrase that was once exactly descriptive
stems from the belief that gunboat diplomacy is a technique as obsolete as the vessels that used to sustain it. Both are vaguely supposed
to have vanished with the passing of Victorian imperialism, the first
under the pressure of altered political attitudes, the second in response to the advance of naval technology. Indeed, even naval officers
are sometimes unaware that the 1969–70 edition of *The Military
Balance*[2] credits the Chinese People's Republic with 300 gunboats,
that the United States had to develop new types of gunboats for use
off the coasts and in the rivers of Vietnam and that, on 8 July 1969, a
Soviet gunboat was reported by the Chinese Government to have
shot at Bata Island in the Heilung Kiang (Amur) river 'in a frenzied
way'.[3]

Not every use of gunboats, however, can be regarded as gunboat
diplomacy, nor is it essential that the warships employed should
actually bear this name. Gunboats, which are almost as old as the
naval gun, have assumed many different forms in their long history
and have been employed on many different tasks, most of which are
outside the scope of the present work.[4] We shall not be concerned
with their employment in the conduct of war or for coastal defence
or on such routine operations as police, anti-smuggling or fishery
protection duties in the territorial waters of their own state. The
purpose of this book is to consider the recent and future applications
of limited naval force as one of the instruments of foreign policy.

The concept of limited naval force is one which requires, and will

receive, a more extended definition. This, in turn, will be supported
by an analysis of some of the many instances of gunboat diplomacy
during the last fifty years[5] so as to bring out more clearly not only the
nature and scope of gunboat diplomacy, but also the theoretical
principles which might be regarded as determining its efficacity. Both
the theory and the practice of the past, however, will be examined
primarily for the lessons these offer for the future. This is not a work
of history, not even of the relatively under-recorded history of limited
naval force since 1918, but of speculation. The question to be ex-
plored is how, in the years to come, the principal naval powers might
wish, or be able, to exploit their naval resources in furtherance of
their foreign policy. What does analysis of the past suggest as the
future rôle of limited naval force? Against whom might this be
exerted and what indications can be discerned of readiness for its
employment?

If this is not a history, neither is it a manual of naval strategy or
tactics, which will be considered only in their relation to the achievement of political and diplomatic objectives. Above all, this book is
not concerned with naval warfare, for any kind of war, particularly
in the second half of the twentieth century, constitutes the failure of
foreign policy and the abandonment of diplomatic expedients.
Limited naval force, as it will be considered in the present work, is a
peace-time technique or, if employed during an actual war, one confined to the exertion of pressure on allies or neutrals.

Even this restriction still leaves an elastic field for inquiry.
Neutrality has always tended to be disputed or disregarded when this
suited the purpose of belligerents, but the difficulty of distinguishing
between the state of war and the state of peace has increased still
further since 1946. The foreign offices of the world, or their legal
advisers, were so impressed by the Nürnberg Judgment that not one
of the many wars[6] of the last twenty-five years was ever declared: a
dubious triumph for international law, but an unmitigated nuisance
to diplomatic historians. To describe gunboat diplomacy as a peace-
time expedient thus offers only an uncertain and provisional ceiling
to the domain of limited naval force, not a substitute for the more
elaborate definition to be attempted in the first chapter. Nuclear
exchanges are clearly beyond the scope of our inquiry and so are most
aspects of the Second World War or the conflicts in Korea and
Vietnam, but subtler tests are needed to discriminate between
coercive diplomacy and undeclared war in the doubtful zone that lies
beneath such heights of violence.

Such tests are not, unfortunately, to be found in the nature and
number of the warships concerned or even in the duration of their

employment. The political applications of limited naval force range all the way from the single gunboat that merely drops her anchor in alien territorial waters (as did s.m.s. panther at Agadir in 1911) to the use of as many as eighty-eight assorted warships in active hostilities in the Baltic from December 1918 to May 1921. Nor is gunboat diplomacy normally exercised only by warships at sea: the landing of sailors, marines, soldiers and supplies is a common attribute, while it is nowadays more difficult to imagine circumstances in which this expedient could be employed without at least potential air cover. The subject matter of this book will not, therefore, be confined to purely naval operations, but it will exclude all threats or uses of force in which the availability of warships does not play an essential and, in most cases, a predominant part. Gunboat diplomacy can comprise much more than the mere arrival of a gunboat to reinforce the representations of an Ambassador or Consul, but it must not be divorced from the seas that have always sustained it.

That they have done so, even in the recent past, may seem a proposition easier to establish than the likelihood of their doing so in the future. The sea is increasingly regarded as no more than a protective covering for the operations of missile-firing submarines; diplomacy as an anachronism offering no useful alternative to the modern techniques of deterrence or subversion. These are objections that will have to be stated and tested throughout the present work, but a preliminary outline may help to clarify the nature and scope of the ensuing argument. Technically, it is contended, the obstacles to naval operations on an unfriendly coast have steadily increased from the virtual zero of 1850, when an invulnerable British fleet blockaded Greece and seized Greek shipping,[7] to such a level that, on 21 October 1967, an Israeli destroyer patrolling at least ten miles off the coast of Egypt could be destroyed at long range by only four missiles.[8] Politically, the once respectable practice of coercing maritime countries not enjoying the protection of a Great Power has become an outrage against sovereignty and a threat to peace, though this moral stigma is perhaps less important than the increased powers of resistance which even the weakest states derive from the growth of nationalism and political organization.

It is to assist in the erosion of these objections that 1918 has been selected as a starting point for the analysis of earlier applications of limited naval force. By then mines, torpedoes, submarines, coastal artillery and even aircraft[9] were already hampering the operation of warships in coastal waters and the concept of the nation-state had taken firm root well beyond its nurseries in Europe and North America. The half century that followed 1918 thus possesses a degree of contemporary – and future – relevance not enjoyed by earlier periods. If instances of gunboat diplomacy towards the end of this era prove comparable with those at the beginning, it becomes arguable that this technique has already been successfully adapted to changes in the international environment and is capable of further evolution in future.

This is a capacity less easily deduced from the actual composition of contemporary navies or official statements of their purposes. The strength and shape of a navy at any given moment are often as much the result of chance as of design and one can seldom expect to find anything approaching Admiral Fisher's reconstruction of the Royal Navy at the beginning of the century, when gunboats were deliberately and avowedly sacrificed to battleships and the navy's diplomatic capacities were reduced to augment its readiness for major war. Warships, moreover, are such flexible instruments of coercion that even these drastic and controversial reforms left considerable scope for the continued use of limited naval force by successive British governments. Changes in the order of battle of the world's navies thus offer only partial indications of their prospective employment.

These indications are most inadequately supplemented by official statements, which are constrained to a hypocritical ambiguity by the desire simultaneously to satisfy the prevailing political cant and the professional aspirations of naval officers. Given the pejorative overtones attached to gunboat diplomacy in the second half of the twentieth century, its absence from the public speeches of Ministers of Defence is scarcely surprising. Their omissions, however, are often remedied by third parties and the functions of one navy may occasionally be best deduced from the more outspoken comments of apprehensive rivals. This indirect evidence is particularly useful in the case of navies whose slender past achievements in gunboat diplomacy create no initial presumption of their readiness to undertake such tasks in the future. For instance, when the same month produces a similar assessment of Soviet naval capacities, albeit in very different language, from two such normally incompatible sources as the United States and China, there is no need to share the preconceptions of either to find their coincident opinions of interest. It was in June 1969 that the American Center for Strategic and International Studies declared that:

In the broad field of diplomacy a Soviet naval intervention force could become a credible, flexible tool previously unavailable to Kremlin planners.[10]

and in the same month that the New China News Agency proclaimed that:

> The gunboat policy pursued by the Soviet revisionist renegade clique is essentially the same as that of Tsarist Russia. . . . Soviet revisionism is stepping up the construction of ocean-going naval vessels, carrying out far ocean activities by its Navy and making global naval reconnoitring, thus threatening the security of some Asian, African and Latin American countries.[11]

The Soviet Union is by no means the only naval power whose capacities and policies permit such deductions, but, if the pace of naval innovation during the last decade were to be matched during the next by a corresponding fertility in the political techniques of intervention, some of the most interesting pages in the future history of limited naval force might turn out to be written in Russian. This is a possibility which will thus receive particular consideration in the final section of the present work.

In its navigation of the relatively uncharted waters of the recent past, no less than its groping into the mists and shoals of the future, this book must steer an inevitably controversial course, but one objection ought to be anticipated, if it can scarcely be avoided. This book attempts to assess the effectiveness of limited naval force in terms of its ability to achieve the results originally intended by the initiating government. It does not question the purposes of such governments. This treatment of force merely as a tool – and its measurement only as a lever – implies no moral judgment. Gunboat diplomacy can be described as an infringement of national sovereignty or as the maintenance of international law and order; as aggression or as self-defence. Such distinctions are irrevelant in a book concerned with means rather than ends and, if we are to believe the greatest of all authorities on the application of Force, probably possess little intrinsic meaning:

> the exercise of this force may be considered both as resistance and impulse: It is resistance in so far as the body, for maintaining its present state, withstands the force impressed; it is impulse in so far as the body, by not easily giving way to the impressed force of another, endeavours to change the state of that other. Resistance is usually ascribed to bodies at rest and impulse to those in motion: But motion and rest, as commonly conceived, are only relatively distinguished; nor are those bodies always truly at rest, which are commonly taken to be so.[12]

B

NOTES

[1] T. B. Millar, *The Indian and Pacific Oceans: Some Strategic Considerations*, Adelphi Paper No. 57, Institute for Strategic Studies, London, May 1969.

[2] *The Military Balance 1969–70*, Institute for Strategic Studies, London.

[3] *The Times*, 9 July 1969.

[4] See Anthony Preston and John Major, *Send a Gunboat*, Longmans 1967, for the earlier history.

[5] See also Appendix.

[6] Estimates vary with the preconceptions of their authors, but some put the total as high as fifty. See, for instance, C. & S. Mydans, *The Violent Peace*, New York, Atheneum, 1968.

[7] To enforce the claims for compensation of Don Pacifico, a British subject resident in Athens.

[8] According to the Israeli commander, the missiles were fired by Egyptian naval craft in Port Said Harbour, which was $13\frac{1}{2}$ miles away. See article 'Aftermath of the Eilath' by Robert D. Colvin, *USNIP*, October 1969.

[9] A German aircraft had bombed and damaged the Russian battleship SLAVA as early as 1915, *The Soviet Navy* (ed.) M. G. Saunders, London: Weidenfeld & Nicolson, 1958, p. 50.

[10] *Soviet Sea Power*, Special Report Series, The Center for Strategic and International Studies, Georgetown University, Washington, D.C.

[11] NCNA broadcast in English from Peking, 14 June 1969.

[12] Definition III, *The Mathematical Principles of Natural Philosophy*, Sir Isaac Newton, translated from the Latin by A. Motte and published by Benjamin Motte at the Middle Temple Gate in 1729.

Chapter One

DEFINITIONS

'When I use a word,' Humpty Dumpty said, in rather
a scornful tone, 'it means just what I choose it to mean
– neither more nor less.'
'The question is,' said Alice, 'whether you *can* make
words mean so many different things.'
'The question is,' said Humpty Dumpty, 'which is to
be master – that's all.'

Carroll[1]

MORE bathers have heard of the jelly fish, even seen it, than
could depict its shifting outlines, translucent as the sea in which
they merge and blur, or grasp the slipperiness of its floating substance. Gunboat diplomacy is equally familiar and no less amor-
phous. Its scope and nature are not easily discerned: they resist the
simplicity of a single, *a priori* definition. Instead the subject must be
enveloped and, step by step, isolated from its fluid and shadowy
environment. This process of definition by elimination is necessarily
arbitrary. In the absence of any consensus of received opinion doubt
and disagreement are not merely permissible but justified. It is the
need to fix a starting-point, not its self-evident validity, that demands
precision, even pedantry, at the outset of an inevitably speculative
venture across the horizons of the future. The more categorical the
statements that follow, the more they will need, but for the avoidance
of tedious repetition, will not receive, the perpetual qualification:
'for the purposes of this inquiry'.

If, therefore, we begin by asserting that gunboat diplomacy is an
instrument of governments, this is not to ignore the rôle of limited
naval force in the hands of those who seek to overthrow or to coerce
their own régime. When the cruiser AURORA trained her guns on the
Winter Palace[2] the political consequences were momentous and
enduring, but this was a revolutionary act, not an exercise of gunboat diplomacy, which is the exclusive prerogative of those already
in effective control of the state.

The threat or use of naval force by governments in the repression
of their own subjects – as the British Government menaced the
strikers of Liverpool with the guns of H.M.S. BARHAM and H.M.S.
RAMILLIES in 1926[3] – is equally beyond the scope of the present work.
Gunboat diplomacy is something that governments do to foreigners.

15

This is a proposition which must be interpreted with some care and with more regard to the realities of a situation than its appearances. If a political organization commands the powers of a government and behaves as one in relations with other governments, its legitimacy is a secondary consideration. If it acts in the furtherance of a dispute involving other nation–states, the international character of its action is not necessarily diminished if this takes place entirely within the national territory and is ostensibly directed only against its own nationals. For instance, when Admiral Muselier seized the islands of St Pierre and Miquelon on 24 December 1941, Gaullists could regard this as a mere assertion of domestic authority, Pétainists as an act of rebellion. In either view, in a simplified or purely legalistic interpretation, this was a dispute among Frenchmen. In reality, of course, it was nothing of the kind. The only significant opposition came from a foreign government, that of the United States, who had rejected Admiral Muselier's prior request for their concurrence and suggested a Canadian intervention instead. This was not simply because the United States Government then recognized Marshal Pétain as the ruler of France: their disapproval would scarcely have been diminished if the situation had been reversed, if Vichy warships had seized power in a Gaullist island. Indeed, one of the motives of American policy – deriving partly from the mystique of the Monroe Doctrine – was to freeze the political status of French territories in the Western Hemisphere and to prevent any change of allegiance for the duration of the war. What was at issue was not which French Government should control France – St Pierre and Miquelon were the merest grains of dust in those scales – but the right of any French Government to disregard the suzerainty temporarily claimed by the United States over French territory in the Western Atlantic. General de Gaulle was the virtual government of France in this instance, because he could and did assert the independence and authority of his own nation–state in a dispute involving a foreign government.

One of the advantages of this otherwise rather unusual instance of gunboat diplomacy is that its exceptional characteristics facilitate more precise definitions. The nature of the initiating authority, the nationality of the ostensible victims and even the territorial jurisdiction at the point of action are all shown to be secondary to the crucial question: was force applied in the furtherance of a dispute between different nation–states? Here it clearly was. The free French had originally sought the concurrence of the British, Canadian and United States governments for the assumption of authority over St Pierre and Miquelon and, when this was refused by the United States

Government, proceeded clandestinely to assemble a naval force capable of seizing the islands before American opposition could take a more concrete or effective form. But for American opposition, indeed, naval force might have been unnecessary: the Vichy governor capitulated in twenty minutes and a plebiscite produced an overwhelming Gaullist majority.[4]

To establish an act of force as an instance of gunboat diplomacy, therefore, one minimum qualification is that this should have occurred in the furtherance of a dispute between different nation-states. Such a dispute may be directly and explicitly between two governments or one government may usurp the prerogatives of another in circumstances that imply a conflict between nation-states even in the absence of inter-governmental dispute. For instance, during the year 1927 British warships used or threatened force on the rivers or in the territorial waters of China on at least twenty occasions. Only a minority of these incidents involved any direct or open disputes with the Chinese Government: the purpose generally being to rescue or protect British subjects whose safety was menaced by riotous mobs or rebels. It is arguable, therefore, that the Chinese Government might themselves have wished to take similar measures if they had enjoyed sufficient authority in the areas concerned and that British warships were, in a sense, acting in lieu of the Chinese Government rather than against them. This is, however, a dubious argument, not merely on the facts of these particular incidents, in which the prior approval of the Chinese Government was seldom sought and never regarded as an essential condition for action, but also on grounds of general principle. When force is used by one state within the territorial jurisdiction and against the nationals of another, this creates the presumption of a dispute between nation-states and that presumption cannot be rebutted merely because the government of the second state have consented to or even actually requested forcible foreign intervention. Whatever the legal or moral merits of particular cases, governments do not acquiesce in, let alone invite, foreign coercion against their own nationals on their own territory unless they have already lost some of their domestic authority and, therefore, forfeited the exclusive claim to represent their own nation-state. Nor do foreign governments take such action without regard to their own national interests or without exciting a degree of sympathy with the victims of coercion among the nationals of the other state. British warships never went into action in Chinese waters without leaving the impression on at least some Britons and some Chinese that a dispute existed between Britain and China. It would thus be equally plausible to contend that any use or threat of force against foreign nationals within the territory of their own state implies the existence, at least in embryo, of a dispute among nation–states.

It may, however, be simpler and less controversial to free ourselves from dependence on such subtleties by expanding our preliminary definition of the political conditions for gunboat diplomacy. *Prima facie*, therefore, any use or threat of limited naval force, otherwise than as an act of war, may constitute an instance of gunboat diplomacy if it is committed either in the furtherance of an international dispute or else against foreign nationals within the territory of their own state.

With these words, however, we can no longer postpone the most difficult and controversial stage in the process of definition by elimination: when and why is the use of force in international disputes not an act of war? The intractability of this question can, of course, be reduced by discarding a whole category of meanings: we are not concerned with the criteria whereby international lawyers endeavour to assert that particular uses of force are only permissible in a state of war or, if applied in time of peace, could be held to justify a resort to war. For our immediate purposes an act of war is either the use of force against an alien enemy during an existing war or, alternatively, one which, although committed in time of peace, has the result of producing a state of war. Peace and war, however, have become regrettably hard to distinguish. Almost everyone would agree that, from the moment Israeli aircraft attacked Egyptian airfields in the early morning of 5 June 1967 until the cease-fire took effect on the evening of 10 June, there existed a state of war between Israel and Egypt. But when, and on what criteria, could those two countries be said to have been at peace? Israel, after all, suffered more casualties at Arab hands after the cease-fire, even if at a much slower rate, than she did during the Six-Day War itself. Many Arabs would answer that they have been at war with Israel ever since the foundation of a state whose existence they have never admitted and some Israelis would agree that war, if intermittent, has at least been latent and endemic for the whole of these twenty-one years. Yet, even if this contention were more widely accepted outside the Middle East, how is this state of affairs to be distinguished from that which has existed for almost the same period between China and the United States? For twenty years these two nations have neither recognized one another, nor been in diplomatic relations nor permitted any normal intercourse between their respective citizens. Their regular forces met and fought an undoubted war in Korea; there have since been minor clashes on the high seas; there has been an almost uninterrupted exchange of recrimination, abuse and attempts to inflict minor injury. For two decades there has been a state of mutual hostility, but was it war?

Indeed, the more one considers actual cases, the more one is driven to the reluctant conclusion that the peaks of undoubted war and demonstrable peace are separated by a valley of uncertainty where the classical definitions offer no guidance that is either absolute or precise. 'An act of violence intended to compel our opponents to fulfil our will'[5] includes an Arab bomb in a London store; 'armed conflict between nations'[6] almost justifies those journalists, who in 1958, talked of Britain's 'Fish War' with Iceland.

On the other hand there is one criterion which, though neither objective nor exact, might offer some assistance. This is sometimes described as the profit motive. In theory, at least, there are two broad categories of motive which might prompt a government to employ violence against foreigners. One is positive: to gain something for the initiating state. The other is negative: to injure the foreigners or their state. In total war these two motives become one and the same: injury to the enemy is regarded as inherently advantageous and cost-effectiveness as the touchstone for choosing to inflict one kind of injury rather than another. In extreme cases hurting the foe may seem desirable even in the absence of any conceivable advantage: despatching the last missiles from a country already irretrievably destroyed in a nuclear holocaust. In limited war the restraints are greater and more various: many possible methods of injuring the enemy will be rejected if these entail incidental disadvantages. Poison gas may not be used, privileged sanctuaries allowed, third powers permitted to assist the enemy. But there will still be a presumption – even if this can now be more easily and more often rebutted – that the enemy's loss is automatically our gain. In peace, on the other hand, the likelihood of injuring foreigners does not provide a self-sufficient motive for employing violence against them. On the contrary, it may even be a disincentive. Those advocating the use of force are thus compelled to argue that the result will either bring positive advantage to the initiating state or else prevent it from suffering otherwise predictable loss. In peace, governments have to explain why they have injured foreigners; in war, why they have not.

Any attempt to identify wars by reference to the state of mind of the participants has obvious inconveniences in practice. It may even appear more than a little absurd. After all, if tanks grind across frontiers, shells fall on cities and men of different nationalities kill one another in repeated and protracted conflict, what need is there of sophisticated and psychological analysis? Yet all these things happened in Hungary in 1956 and nobody called that a war; none of them occurred in 1939 on the Western Front, where everyone believed that Britain and France were at war with Germany.

The truth of the matter is that war and peace can be defined in many different ways, each appropriate to a different purpose, but that no single definition is likely to satisfy all purposes or to be immune from the challenge presented by particular situations difficult to accommodate within the framework of a general definition. To suggest, therefore, that war is a violent conflict between states in which policy is determined by the desire to inflict injury rather than the hope of positive advantage, is to set up a yardstick for only one dimension of a multi-faceted complex. Nevertheless, it may be more useful when attempting to distinguish between the diplomatic and the warlike character of a particular act of force, to inquire its purpose – as this was seen both by the initiator and by the victim – than to count the forces involved, the shots fired or the casualties sustained. From 1840 to 1949, for instance, few years passed without British warships employing armed force in Chinese waters, but it would be as misleading to regard this as a hundred years' war between Britain and China as it would be to ignore the occasions on which this pattern of coercive diplomacy was broken by outright acts of war.

For our purposes, therefore, an act of war is the use of armed force against or in a foreign state for the primary purpose of injuring that state, whether as part of an existing policy of injuring the other state as and when opportunity serves or to initiate such a policy or, and this is a new and important point, without regard to the risk that the reaction of the victim state will go beyond mere self-defence to a reciprocal adoption of injury rather than profit as the prime motive for policy. In other words, an act of war may either continue an existing war, be deliberately intended to start a war or liable to provoke the victim into starting one.

An act of coercive diplomacy, on the other hand, is intended to obtain some specific advantage from another state and forfeits its diplomatic character if it either contemplates the infliction of injury unrelated to obtaining that advantage or results in the victim attempting the infliction of injury after the original objective has been either achieved or abandoned. Coercive diplomacy is thus an alternative to war and, if it leads to war, we must not only hold that it has failed: we may even doubt whether it ever deserved the name.

Governments, no less than reasonable men, must be presumed to intend the predictable consequences of their acts and, if the seizure of St Pierre and Miquelon had led to war between the United States and the Free French, Admiral Muselier would have been hard put to it to maintain his honoured place among the successful practitioners of gunboat diplomacy.

His actual success was, of course, entirely dependent on the use of warships, American opposition making it impossible to mount an expedition from bases near enough for aircraft and German submarines preventing unescorted merchant vessels from crossing the Atlantic. There is no need, however, for so exacting a test in order to determine that any particular instance of coercive diplomacy was also one of gunboat diplomacy. It is enough that the actual choice fell on the use or threat of naval force and that, even if other means were available or employed in addition, the presence of warships played an essential part. This part must, however, specifically relate to at least the potential use of force to resolve a particular dispute. When US warships appeared off Santo Domingo on 19 November 1961, they did not actually do anything, but US representatives ashore made it quite clear that they might intervene if the surviving relations of the dictator Trujillo failed to facilitate the establishment of a government acceptable to the United States by leaving the Dominican Republic.[7] The visible presence of warships was thus a threat of naval force and, therefore, an instance of gunboat diplomacy, which mere naval visits are not if, as so often happens, their only political purpose is a general reminder that the government concerned possess a navy.

This incident usefully illustrates the lower boundary of our subject – a threat, however delicate and discreet, that naval force might actually be applied in support of specific diplomatic representations. The upper edge, as we have seen, falls short of the brutal, if sometimes uncertain, threshold of the act of war. The earlier description of gunboat diplomacy as the application for political purposes of *limited* naval force will nevertheless require further elucidation of that often ambiguous epithet. Though of the greatest importance, this may nevertheless be reserved for the next chapter. Having explained who uses gunboat diplomacy and against whom, having distinguished this expedient from naval action in revolution, repression and war, having at least outlined the upper and lower limits of its operation, we can now repeat, with only minor modification, our earlier definition:

Gunboat diplomacy is the use or threat of limited naval force, otherwise than as an act of war, in order to secure advantage, or to avert loss, either in the furtherance of an international dispute or else against foreign nationals within the territory or the jurisdiction of their own state.

NOTES

[1] Lewis Carroll, *Alice Through the Looking Glass*, Nonesuch Press 1939.

[2] On 25 October 1917, when the threat of bombardment and the use of her sailors ashore led to the capitulation of the Kerensky Government to the Bolsheviks (historians are not agreed whether the cruiser actually fired live rounds or not).

[3] Julian Symons, *The General Strike*, The Cresset Press 1957, p. 53.

[4] Vice-Admiral Muselier has written his own, first-hand, account in Chapters 22–24 of *De Gaulle Contre le Gaullisme*. See also Bibliography for other relevant books.

[5] Clausewitz, *On War*, English translation, Pelican Classics 1968.

[6] Alastair Buchan, *War in Modern Society*, Watts 1966.

[7] See John Bartlow Martin, *Overtaken by Events*, Doubleday & Co. N.Y., 1966.

Chapter Two

PRINCIPLES AND PRECEDENTS OF LIMITED NAVAL FORCE

Limited is a victim of SLIPSHOD EXTENSION. . . .
a lazy habit of treating LIMITED as a convenient
synonym for many more suitable and more exact
words . . . to limit is to confine within bounds.

Fowler[1]

I Definitive Force:[2] ALTMARK and PUEBLO

AT twenty minutes to four in the cold darkness of the morning of
14 February 1940, a Norwegian coastguard rang up the curtain on one of the classic dramas of gunboat diplomacy, perhaps the purest instance in recent times of the definitive use of limited naval force in isolation from all other means of pressure.

As the morse stuttered to and fro, the accustomed routine was methodically applied '*Et ukjent skip war kommet in på Frohavet fra sjøen*'[3] – an unknown ship had come in from the sea to enter the Frohavet, the stretch of water that divides the Froan islets from the mainland and constitutes the northerly approach to Trondheim. The news was confirmed by the coastguard station at Tustna and the torpedo boat TRYGG sailed from Kristiansund on yet another of the routine investigations by which the Norwegian Navy were accustomed to uphold the neutrality of their country in those early months of an undoubted but still dormant European war. Her report that afternoon was reassuring: the unknown ship was a tanker bound for Germany from the United States; she had conformed with the requirements of Norwegian neutrality by dismounting her anti-aircraft guns; she had no passengers on board; her name was ALTMARK.

But Admiral Tank-Nielsen, the Norwegian area commander, was a stickler for detail. TRYGG had reported ALTMARK as an armed merchant ship, but had not provided satisfactory answers to all the seventeen questions specified for such vessels in article 21 of the relevant standing instructions.[4]

Two further visitations, this time by the torpedo boat SNØGG, in the evening of the 14th and the morning of the 15th, still failed to satisfy the Admiral, who put to sea himself in the destroyer GARM and, at 1 o'clock in the afternoon of the 15th sent his Chief of Staff

on board ALTMARK, which had meanwhile been continuing her south-
ward journey through Norwegian territorial waters under the escort
of SNØGG. By 4.15 that afternoon both the Norwegian Commander-
in-Chief in Oslo and Mr Bull, the Secretary General of the Norwegian Ministry of Foreign Affairs, had received Admiral Tank-
Nielsen's initial report. It was brief, but it revealed the reason for his
stubborn persistence. Three words of muted brass were enough to
mark the first entry of this essentially Wagnerian drama's *leitmotiv:*
'*Antakelig fanger ombord*' – probably prisoners aboard.

Admiral Tank-Nielsen was more than meticulous, he was alert and
farseeing. Over a month earlier he had spotted a story in the Oslo
newspaper *Aftenposten* that the German naval auxiliary ALTMARK
was expected to cross the Atlantic with 400 British prisoners en route
to Germany. He had immediately addressed a special circular to his
command calling attention to this report. By one of those mis-
chances familiar in all navies – and other organizations as well – this
circular never reached the commanders of TRYGG and SNØGG. But it
explains Admiral Tank-Nielsen's reluctance to accept the repeated
denials, as relayed to him by his subordinates, of ALTMARK's captain:
'no passengers; there are no persons on board who belong to the
armed forces of another belligerent country, nor are there civilians
of a belligerent country'.

It explains his demand to inspect the ship and, when this was
refused on the grounds that ALTMARK was a State ship flying the
Reichsdienstflagge, his decision that, without inspection, ALTMARK
might not traverse the waters of the Bergen defended area, a decision
that would have required her to follow a course only just inside Norwegian territorial limits. The Admiral's attitude was not determined
by *Aftenposten* alone: his Chief of Staff had heard and seen for
himself, as Oslo was informed later that evening, SOS signals from
ALTMARK's fo'c's'le and noted the efforts of the crew to hide them by
working the winches and slamming the deadlights.

But Admiral Tank-Nielsen was also a prudent and circumspect
officer, careful not to let his personal sympathies over-ride the obligations of discipline and responsibility. He neither disregarded the legal
force of Captain Dau's refusal of a search nor sought to present his
superiors with a *fait accompli*. His decision – to refuse passage
through the defended area – was a compromise that neatly avoided
any direct clash on the delicate central issue, which he nevertheless
indicated to his superiors with a concise clarity: '*Antakelig fanger
ombord.*'

There is no suggestion in the Norwegian documents[5] that these
three ominous words were discussed between the Commander-in-

Chief, Admiral Diesen, and Mr Bull before the latter went off to change for his dinner at the Brazilian Legation. Their conversations had turned on the right of naval auxiliaries (as opposed to actual warships) to passage through the defended area, on the signal of protest dispatched by ALTMARK's captain and on the desirability of speeding this ship on her way before detection by the British gave rise to an awkward situation. At 5.30 that afternoon Admiral Diesen telegraphed his order: 'Let the vessel pass in her capacity as a State ship. Escort.'

At 6 he told Admiral Tank-Nielsen by telephone that his order covered passage through the defended area. At 10.30 Admiral Diesen was able to reassure the German naval attaché, who had telephoned to complain of the delays imposed on ALTMARK, that the vessel was again on her way south. The closing note of Act One was quietly reassuring: '*Han takket.*' – He thanked me.

Across the North Sea, the stage hands were still setting the scene for the next Act. The British Admiralty had long been acutely aware that ALTMARK was on her way home with British prisoners transferred to her from the pocket battleship ADMIRAL GRAF SPEE, but there had been no news of ALTMARK's whereabouts since December 1939 and no one knew that dirty weather had enabled her to elude British patrols in the Iceland–Faeroes passage during the night of 12/13 February. It was thus a most unpleasant surprise to learn, on the evening of 15 February,[6] that ALTMARK had not merely gained the shelter of Norwegian territorial waters, but had progressed as far as Bergen by noon that day. At 25 knots, of which speed the British believed her capable, not many hours of steaming – and most of those in Norwegian territorial waters – now divided her from the potential shelter of German air cover. Immediate decisions were clearly needed and at ten minutes past midnight the curtain went up for the Second Act. Captain Vian, then patrolling northwards from the Skagerrak in H.M.S. COSSACK with four other destroyers and the cruiser ARETHUSA under his command received the signal: 'ALTMARK your objective. Act accordingly.'[7]

Admiral Forbes, the Commander-in-Chief of the Home Fleet, was as concise in his signals as Admiral Tank-Nielsen, but perhaps a trifle less explicit. Captain Vian, after all, had not been sent out to look for ALTMARK, but for German iron ore ships. His presence off the Scandinavian coast was coincidental. He did not even know what ALTMARK looked like and, on finding a picture of two ships in an old copy of the *Illustrated London News*, unfortunately chose the wrong one as his intended victim.[8] Curiously enough it was Admiral Diesen's order of the previous evening which helped him to correct this error. Even at 3 o'clock[9] on the afternoon of 16 February visibility was poor south of Stavanger, where the Norwegian coast sheds its islands and begins an eastward curve towards the country's southern tip and the entrance to the Skagerrak. Without the conspicuous – and significant – presence to seaward of the escorting FIRERN, even that sharp-sighted officer of H.M.S. ARETHUSA might have not identified ALTMARK as, hugging the coast, she slipped through the gathering dusk. But ARETHUSA closed to read the name on ALTMARK's stern and to be reported, with her accompanying destroyers, by FIRERN as five British cruisers. The full cast was now assembled on the stage and we may skim over the largely irrelevant moves before the next curtain – the torpedo boat SKARV taking over escort duties, the exchange of signals (often mutually incomprehensible) with the British warships, their unsuccessful attempts to stop ALTMARK or detach her from her Norwegian escort, ALTMARK's flight into Jøssingfjord closely followed by SKARV, by the newly-arrived torpedo boat KJELL and by two British destroyers. Act Three began only at 5 pm, when Captain Vian responded to protests against British violation of Norwegian neutrality by informing KJELL's commander of his orders from the British Admiralty[10] to liberate 400 British prisoners on board ALTMARK. This time it was the full orchestra that blared out the *leitmotiv* first introduced by Admiral Tank-Nielsen twenty-four hours earlier.

When KJELL's commander had replied that he knew of no prisoners, had rejected a proposal for a joint inspection of ALTMARK and had demanded British withdrawal from Norwegian territorial waters, there followed a pause. The two British destroyers left Jøssingfjord to join their consorts on guard outside the three-mile limit; two more Norwegian warships joined KJELL and SKARV inside; ALTMARK lay motionless against the ice, as close to the shore as she could get. COSSACK's telegraphists worked frantically at their keys, but the Norwegian commander's wireless was blanketed by the mountainous sides of the fjord: amid all his other pre-occupations he could only obtain instructions by rushing ashore to find a telephone. He got through to the local defence HQ at Kristiansund, who confirmed the standing orders on the upholding of Norwegian neutrality: he was to go on protesting, but not to resort to force.

The orders elicited by Captain Vian's signaller, orders personally drafted by Mr Churchill after he had obtained the Foreign Secretary's concurrence by telephone, were rather more elaborate:

Unless Norwegian torpedo-boat undertakes to convoy ALTMARK to Bergen with a joint Anglo-Norwegian guard on board and a joint escort, you should board ALTMARK, liberate the prisoners and take possession of ship pending further instructions. If Norwegian torpedo-boat interferes, you should warn her to stand off. If she fires upon you, you should not reply unless attack is serious, in which case you should defend yourself using no more force than is necessary and cease fire when she desists. Suggest to Norwegian destroyer that honour is served by submitting to superior force.[11]

The finale is too well known to require recapitulation in detail. At 11 pm COSSACK re-entered the Jøssingfjord, her searchlights blazing. When KJELL's commander went on board to reiterate his protests, he was informed by Captain Vian that his orders required him to liberate ALTMARK's prisoners with or without Norwegian consent. British and German ships crunched together, the boarders went in, a few shots punctuated the brief scuffle and at thirty-five minutes past midnight, COSSACK was steaming out of Jøssingfjord with 299 British subjects supernumerary to her proper complement. Churchill's careful conditional clauses had not, it seems, been needed,[12] though we shall have to return to them later. Instead this opera closes on the chord first struck by Admiral Tank-Nielsen:

COSSACK had meanwhile manœuvred herself on to ALTMARK's port bow and now there appeared a crowd of people – presumably prisoners – 'Antakelig fangene'. . . .[13]

This drama was introduced to these otherwise prosaic pages as a classical example of the use of limited naval force. This is a phrase demanding elucidation. To the victims of any kind of force the epithet 'limited' often presents a more controversial appearance than it does to the wielders of force. It is nevertheless arguable that, for practical purposes, force may objectively be regarded as 'limited', provided certain conditions are met. The first of these is that the act or threat of force should possess a definite purpose of which the extent is apparent to both sides. On the night of 16 February 1940, both British and Norwegian naval officers understood that no more was intended than the release of British prisoners from a German ship. Admittedly the Norwegians were sceptical of the existence of these prisoners (KJELL's commander was one of the many unfortunates who had never received Admiral Tank-Nielsen's circular), but they did not question the intentions of the British, only the evidence on which these intentions were founded.[14]

So far as they were concerned, the challenge presented by Captain Vian was radically different from that offered seven weeks later by the entry into Oslofjord of the German cruiser BLÜCHER. She was sunk outright because her undeclared intentions seemed to represent an unlimited threat – not to the letter of Norwegian neutrality, but to the independence of Norway. Both decisions, incidentally, were taken by naval officers alone;[15] Norwegian Ministers in 1940 were seldom available at moments of crisis and the Minister for Foreign Affairs left the capital to address the Trondheim Students' Union just two hours before COSSACK re-entered Jøssingfjord. As a general rule, however, it will be convenient, in the absence of evidence to the contrary, to assume that the decisions, intentions and reactions of responsible officers and officials were broadly representative of those of their governments. In the heat of action Captain Vian may not have used all Mr Churchill's words, but he did make clear the limited intentions of the British Government.

Secondly, the purpose of those employing force must not only be recognized as limited, but also as tolerable. This is a vaguer and more difficult concept. The purpose is obviously unwelcome or the use of force would scarcely be necessary. But there is a difference between the kind of result that can, however reluctantly, be accepted under duress and the circumstances in which, to use an increasingly outmoded cliché, 'I would rather die'. The use of force is not limited if its purpose is likely to be regarded by the victim as demanding an unlimited resistance.

This is naturally not a criterion of general or absolute validity: different peoples at different periods and in differing circumstances have reacted very variously to otherwise similar challenges. What affronts are tolerable and which call for desperate resistance is a question requiring separate study and an individual answer in every particular case. That same year of 1940, for instance, elicited from the various peoples of Europe a remarkable range of responses to the single stimulus of German invasion. Broadly speaking, however, a tolerable result is one which, in the eyes of the victim, is less undesirable than resort to war. This was clearly the view taken of the liberation of the ALTMARK's prisoners by all the responsible Norwegians involved.

This reference to the extent of the resistance likely to be evoked by an act of limited force leads us from the political to the military conditions of this expedient. The force employed must be regarded by both sides as capable of achieving its specific purpose. If COSSACK, for instance, had not been expected to reach ALTMARK and to return with the prisoners, then Churchill's order of 16 February, unless it had been a mere gamble, would have implied a readiness to follow an initial failure by the employment of more extensive force. Before the attempt the choice was between abandoning the prisoners and offending Norway by their rescue: after an unsuccessful attempt the option of avoiding Norwegian anger would no longer have existed and its adverse consequences could only have been aggravated by either of the alternative courses which would then have remained: to accept defeat or to seek victory through more extended hostilities. Whether or not the latter course then led to actual war, it would have involved the use of force for objectives, and to an extent, which the British Government could not have defined in advance. Both would have depended on Norwegian reactions which would no longer have been predictable, or perhaps even directly related to the original cause of dispute.

A government embarking on an act of genuinely limited force should thus have a reasonable expectation that the force initially employed will be sufficient to achieve the specific purpose originally envisaged without regard to the reactions of the victim, whose options are thus confined to acquiescence or a retaliation which can only follow, and not prevent, the achievement of the desired result. In such cases the use of force is not merely limited, but also definitive: it creates a *fait accompli*.

It is, however, important that the probability of immediate military success should be equally apparent to the victim. If ALTMARK had been capable of effective defence, or under the protection of shore batteries, or if the escorting Norwegian warships had been strong enough to sink COSSACK out of hand, the problems confronting the Norwegians would have been different. Neither Churchill's suggestion 'that honour is served by submitting to superior force' nor the Norwegian proviso that violations of neutrality were not to be resisted 'against a considerable superiority of force'[16] would have applied. Indeed, if it had seemed likely to be successful, Norwegian resistance could have been justified by other arguments than those of honour or compliance with the regulations. Suppose that, instead of a cruiser and five destroyers, a single weak warship had entered Norwegian territorial waters and had there been sunk, thus allowing ALTMARK to reach Germany before the arrival of British reinforcements, the *fait accompli* would then have confronted not the Norwegian, but the British Government with a situation which they might resent, or even seek to revenge, but which they could no longer undo. The sword of limited force would have been turned against British breasts, to face them with a choice between ineffective protest and an unwanted war.

As events actually fell out, however, the Norwegians had no doubts regarding British ability to achieve their limited objective without regard to Norwegian reactions. Indeed, thanks to FIRERN's mistaken report of five cruisers, they may even have over-estimated their opponents' strength. The choice presented to them was thus between a relatively painless acquiescence and the certain casualties of a futile attempt at resistance, casualties which, by arousing an emotional demand for retaliation, might then have exposed Norway to the prospect of greater suffering in a wider conflict.

The desire to avoid casualties or suffering may, however, seem less compelling, if these have already been inflicted. In such cases a fourth test is often suggested to establish that the force is actually limited. This is the more familiar and, conventionally, the more important condition, that the force employed should manifestly be the minimum needed to achieve the desired result.

In applying this test it is naturally important to distinguish between force and violence. The fact that more force – in the shape of five additional warships waiting outside the Jøssingfjord – was available than was actually employed to liberate the ALTMARK's prisoners did not detract from Churchill's insistence on the use of minimum force. From the standpoint of the victim the greater the force available to the opponent, the stronger become the arguments for his own acquiescence. But, when this force is employed in actual violence against the victim, this may produce both an emotional and a rational reaction in favour of resistance. If COSSACK, for instance, before boarding ALTMARK, had taken the militarily defensible precaution of torpedoing KJELL, this would have further reduced the chances of successful intervention by the remaining Norwegian warships, yet made it more likely that even the coolest and least berserk of their commanders would have felt bound to attempt it. In doing so he would have been responding to a different duty in a new situation: instead of adopting an attitude of prudent restraint towards the violation of neutrality, he would have been reacting to an act of war, an infliction of injury not obviously related to the achievement of what he had previously assumed to be a limited and tolerable objective. On the other hand, if KJELL had suffered damage, or even casualties, from a collision with COSSACK while attempting to bar the way, there would have been much less reason for any fundamental change in the Norwegian attitude, either then or afterwards.

An act of force may thus forfeit its limited character if the damage inflicted during the actual operation seems to the victim to be disproportionate, because the excess of violence may suggest the existence of hostile intentions not confined to the achievement of an immediate and limited result. Even if the conclusions drawn by the victim do not increase the effectiveness of his resistance to the actual operation, they make it more likely that he will retaliate. Therefore, when limited force is employed as an alternative to war, it will often be desirable to make this clear to the victim by accepting military risks that would never be run in war: allowing the victim to fire first and even suffering his fire without replying. If the immediate objective can be achieved whatever happens, it becomes more important for the assailant to avoid the infliction than the incurring of casualties.

Unfortunately this ideal combination of maximum force and minimum violence – a force which the victim cannot hope to withstand, but a violence he can expect to survive – is not always feasible. Even when limited force is used definitively – to remove the cause of dispute rather than to persuade someone else to do so – the infliction of damage and casualties may be a foreseeable, even an inevitable, feature of the operation. The victim's capacity for resistance may be so great, for instance, that only a surprise attack will secure the objective or this may be a fort that must actually be destroyed. In such cases it is not resistance (which must be overwhelmed) that has to be avoided, but retaliation and it does not necessarily follow that this will best be achieved by minimum violence. The infliction of any casualties or damage is bound to arouse anger and it will largely depend on the circumstances, and on the national characteristics of those concerned, whether the resulting desire for revenge will be diminished by the argument that the assailant could have caused even more suffering than he actually did. It may sometimes even seem desirable to increase the level of violence, so that the inevitable resentment is accompanied and balanced by fear. The most that can be ventured as a general proposition is that, if violence is confined to the time and place of the actual operation, this will tend to reinforce the idea of its limited character, whereas preparatory or diversionary attacks will suggest a general hostility more akin to the start of a war. The level of violence in the actual operation, on the other hand, is difficult to measure by any standard acceptable to both sides, who can seldom be expected to agree on its necessity. If, as in the ALTMARK incident, the victim suffers no violence at all, this may usefully reinforce his readiness to believe that the objective was limited and tolerable. Otherwise the concept of minimum violence is probably more useful after the event – to the lawyers and propagandists who must assert or deny its justice – than it is to those who, in the heat of conflict, endeavour to distinguish between limited force and acts of war.

This was a distinction established with exceptional care and clarity in February 1940, but the liberation of ALTMARK's prisoners is a classic case of gunboat diplomacy rather than an entirely typical one. The friendly relations between Britain and Norway, the similar traditions and political outlook of the two peoples, even the fact that most of the Norwegians directly involved could speak English: these unusual features made it much easier for the British to explain the limited character of their operation and much easier for the Norwegians to believe British assurances. Although there was a war on, in spite of the mutual suspicions engendered by earlier disputes regarding Norwegian neutrality, notwithstanding the importance – for both sides – of the issues now at stake, there was throughout this operation an exceptional degree of mutual comprehension, confidence and forbearance. It is not very usual to find a victim (Captain Halvorsen of KJELL) testifying to his assailant's courtesy: 'the conversation (with Captain Vian) was throughout conducted by both sides in a polite, but firm manner'.[17]

Any such comment would have been inconceivable in a later instance of the definitive use of limited naval force: the seizure, on 23 January 1968, of the U.S.S. PUEBLO off the coast of North Korea. This incident, however, is less remarkable for its lack of amenity than for the success with which North Korea exploited a local and momentary advantage against a victim otherwise incomparably more powerful. Gunboat diplomacy is traditionally a weapon employed by the strong against the weak and this somewhat exceptional instance thus demands careful analysis to establish whether it resulted from a chance combination of circumstances unlikely to be repeated or whether it can be fitted into a theoretical framework of more general application, even if this framework then entails some modification of the principles tentatively derived from the rather different ALTMARK episode. This is not an easy task. Our evidence of even American intentions and assumptions is fragmentary, while those of the North Koreans can only approximately and tentatively be deduced from their actions and public statements. These last offer a particularly uncertain guide. To Western ears the vocabulary of Communist diplomacy – except on those occasions when peaceful co-existence is hymned in the glutinous vibrato of an early Wurlitzer – resembles the gamelan orchestra: it includes only the instruments of percussion. The sheer stridency of abuse is so deafening that courage often contributes more than expertise to the detection of those trifling reductions in pitch or volume that may signify restraint or a readiness to compromise. The interpretation that follows is thus necessarily conjectural.

The background, however, is clear enough. Relations between North Korea and the United States had long been devoid of sympathy or mutual understanding. Neither would feel inhibited in the conduct of an immediate dispute by any recollection of past friendship or hope of future goodwill. Lack of contact made each inherently liable to misinterpret the other's intentions and, when they erred, to do so by exaggerating the extent of the opponent's hostility. Perhaps this was particularly true of the United States Government, for there was no equivalent in North Korea to the wealth of information published to the world by the American press and radio. American interpretations were thus necessarily based on only a fraction of the corresponding data available to the North Koreans and were, in addition, liable to distortion by a factor from which the Koreans, who only had to concentrate their efforts at analysis on the United States Government, were immune. In Washington the actions of Asian Communists had traditionally been explained as the response to directives from Moscow or Peking. Even if this assumption had been valid – and it is arguable that often it was not – there was obviously added scope for confusion and misinterpretation in trying to relate specific actions or statements to the patterns of behaviour characteristic of not one, but three, centres of decision.

Thus, when the North Korean radio broadcast on 9 January 1968,[18] an attack on the activities of American electronic surveillance vessels off the coast of North Korea, there may have been at least two good reasons for not taking this seriously. Firstly, it was the practice of the North Koreans to denounce everything done by the Americans, so that any significant message was easily obscured by the volume of indiscriminate abuse. Secondly, Americans and Russians had established a pattern of mutual tolerance of espionage outside their respective territorial waters. Any expectation that the North Koreans would violate these conventions thus demanded either the admission that they were capable of pursuing independent policies or else the assumption that the Russians had wider and more sinister motives for permitting such a breach. It was the latter notion which, after the event, seemed to come more naturally to the Americans, who meanwhile failed to react to the admittedly imprecise warning they had received.

On 23 January 1968, therefore, PUEBLO was placidly carrying out her accustomed task of electronic surveillance at a point that, in the light of North Korean signals intercepted by the Americans, was almost certainly just outside the territorial waters of North Korea. For all practical purposes she was unarmed, her crew were not trained in self-defence, she was not escorted and no arrangements had been made for her protection or rescue. Her commander and his superiors relied entirely on the immunity conferred by international law, an essentially European concept that had been little applied, and less imitated, in Asian waters. This illusory confidence was scarcely ruffled when, about noon, she was located, challenged and identified by a North Korean patrol vessel. This visitor, however, was not content with shadowing PUEBLO. Reinforcements were summoned and the luckless American vessel soon found herself surrounded by four patrol craft escorted by two fighter aircraft. She was again summoned to heave to and, when she ignored the signal, was fired on till she complied and, now obedient to further directions, followed her assailants towards the coast before being boarded and taken into Wonsan as a prize. There she remained, while her crew had to endure a barbarous captivity for eleven months until the US Government, having unsuccessfully attempted a variety of other expedients, finally purchased their release on the terms demanded from the outset by the North Koreans: 'all you have to do is to admit military provocations and aggressive acts committed by your side, apologize for them and assure this table that you will not recommit such criminal acts'.[19]

Bearing in mind that no satisfactory evidence exists of North Korean motives, two interpretations are possible of this remarkable story. The first is that the North Koreans recklessly committed – perhaps even on the initiative of a relatively junior commander – a potential act of war and that they only escaped its consequences because of a fortuitous combination of American weariness with hostilities in Asia, American uncertainty about the intentions of China and the Soviet Union, and American humanitarian concern for the lives and liberty of PUEBLO's captive crew. Mr Rusk, after all, early described the incident as 'in the category of actions that are to be construed as acts of war';[20] American warships and military aircraft effected a threatening concentration against North Korea; reservists were called up; the Security Council convened. That all these gestures expired in empty air; that North Korea escaped all retaliation and achieved her full objectives; that events finally demonstrated this to have been an act of limited force: these, it may be argued, were the chance results of a desperate gamble in circumstances so favourable that they could scarcely be repeated, could not usefully form the basis for more general deductions and hardly qualify for inclusion in the annals of gunboat diplomacy.

Another interpretation is that the factors which made the United States willing to wound but afraid to strike were not beyond the wit of North Koreans to foresee and that, in deciding to impose their will on a Super-Power, they were taking a risk they had calculated in advance. If this was indeed a deliberately planned operation, we must presume – even if we have no Korean equivalent of Churchill's order of 16 January 1940 to rely on – that the objective, the method and the obstacles to be expected had been formulated in advance. The objective seems obvious – though it has been disputed: to put a stop to PUEBLO's espionage, to capture her secrets and, by this example and by exploiting her crew as hostages, to deter the United States Government from replacing this vessel by any other with similar tasks. If this assumption is correct, then the North Koreans intended both an act of definitive force – the removal of PUEBLO – and one of purposeful force – inducing the United States Government to desist from this type of espionage in future. These were defined and limited objectives.

They were not, however, initially clear to the United States Government. This was partly due to the apparently constitutional inability of the North Koreans to explain themselves in a manner comprehensible and convincing to American ears. The signal they may have desired to convey, whether in the broadcast warning of 9 January or in General Pak's statements of the 20th[21] and 24th, was swamped by the background noise of seemingly irrelevant and ambiguous abuse. But their failure probably owed something to the obsessive American belief that all Communist actions were centrally directed from Moscow. On this view it was inconceivable that the Soviet Union, which had long practised seaborne electronic espionage on the largest scale, should jeopardize American tolerance of these activities by permitting an act of violence on the high seas unless this had some purpose far wider and more sinister than mere counter-espionage. As a result the American press, no doubt reflecting official speculation, canvassed the wildest hypotheses: this was the opening move of a new Korean war, a Soviet probe of American resolution, a gambit to reduce American pressure on North Vietnam. The idea that the North Koreans objected to being spied on and had acted independently to rid themselves of this nuisance was often mentioned only to be dismissed. Even President Johnson spoke of the incident as the culmination of 'a stepped-up campaign of violence against South Korea and American troops' that might be intended 'to divert South Korea and US military resources from the Vietnam war'.[22]

These speculations may have been far-fetched – the doctrine of total control from Moscow had already taken some battering in Asia – but their prevalence demonstrates the extent of the North Korean failure to communicate to their victim the limited character of their objective. Perhaps they did not try very hard, because they believed that a further war in Asia would, in any case, prove less tolerable to the United States than the actual results of their action and that the United States would not retaliate on mere hypotheses unless these were confirmed by further and concrete acts of violence by North

Korea. Such a calculation could reasonably have been based on the assumption that no middle course was open to the United States between all-out war and concessions to obtain the release of the crew. Indeed, the crucial weakness of the American position was the predominance over most other considerations of their anxiety to preserve the lives and obtain the liberty of these hostages. It is this factor which, at first sight, seems to differentiate the PUEBLO affair from that of ALTMARK and to make of the former an isolated case difficult to fit into the general pattern of gunboat diplomacy.

This may be a misleadingly superficial analysis. The exploitation of hostages is an expedient regularly employed against governments sensitive to the welfare of their individual nationals and there is no reason to expect its use to be less frequent in the future than in the recent past.[23] When employed in connection with an act of limited force it serves the purpose of rendering acquiescence by the victim's government relatively less intolerable than other courses of action unlikely to preserve the lives or secure the liberty of the hostages. Moreover, on this issue the North Koreans took greater pains to make clear the limited character of their objectives. Although the first definite indication that PUEBLO's crew would be released if the United States admitted their fault, apologized and promised that there would be no repetition seems to have been given only on 31 January,[24] this was surely implicit in General Pak's statement of the 24th. It is at least arguable, therefore, that the North Korean conduct of this operation, when allowance is made for the hostile and mutually uncomprehending relationship between assailant and victim, can be interpreted as presenting a rough approximation to the principles derived from the ALTMARK incident. The North Koreans did have a defined and limited objective, which they did, however inadequately and unsuccessfully, endeavour to explain before and immediately after their act of force. They had reason to regard the results of their action as less intolerable to the Americans than war and they exploited their seizure of hostages to provide an additional incentive to American acquiescence. They could be confident that their military resources were adequate to create a *fait accompli* which the Americans could neither prevent nor undo and which would confront the United States Government with a choice between acquiescence and an escalatory retaliation. During and after the operation, they refrained from unrelated acts of force (which had been frequent during the preceding fifteen months) and they may even be said to have used the minimum violence of which they were capable in the actual operation itself. The opening of fire and the infliction of four casualties by a superior force that had surrounded a defenceless ship may reasonably be ascribed to mere nervousness and incompetence on the part of assailants who must surely have been ordered to secure vessel, crew and secrets intact. This view receives some support from General Pak's subsequent pretence[25] that the unarmed PUEBLO had carried 'large quantities of weapons' and had fired first. These lies may have been prompted by the consciousness that more violence had been employed than was in fact necessary. They were not essential to his main thesis that PUEBLO had been captured within territorial waters.

This is a conjectural interpretation, but it is not an impossible one. It would, however, be straining conjecture too far to argue either that the Koreans consciously acted on these principles or that their tenuous compatibility with the actual unfolding of events enables us to claim the PUEBLO affair as a further instance of the validity of the ALTMARK principles. On the contrary, a better conclusion might be that not all the principles deduced from the almost ideal case of ALTMARK are equally important in every case. In that instance a major, if secondary, preoccupation of the British Government was to preserve Anglo-Norwegian friendship, a purpose which found no echo twenty-eight years later in Pyongyang, but which necessarily demanded greater precautions. The North Koreans had only to consider how to avoid American retaliation, for which purpose their exploitation of the hostages may have seemed a sufficient means of rendering acquiescence less intolerable than any alternative course. It may thus be preferable to treat an act of force as possessing a limited character if it has a defined objective of which the achievement is expected to evoke only a limited response and to regard the ALTMARK principles as aids to predicting that response rather than indispensable elements of a definition. Provided the North Koreans expected to achieve their objective without retaliation, their failure, even their refusal, to communicate to their victim the limited character of this objective would not require the exclusion of the PUEBLO operation from the category of acts of limited force, something that could only be justified if their objective had been too far-reaching for achievement without war or if they had envisaged war as a likely and acceptable result. The glaring differences between the ALTMARK and PUEBLO incidents are partly attributable to the very different character and mutual relationship of assailant and victim, but also to the distinction between the purely definitive nature of the force employed in the ALTMARK affair and the transition from definitive force, which captured PUEBLO, to purposeful force, which wrung concessions from the US Government. But these differences are less important than the underlying similarity: in each case limited naval force was successfully employed to achieve, without retaliation or other consequences undesired by the assailant, a defined objective scarcely attainable by any other means.

What is more, in spite of the twenty-eight years and the major changes in the technology of war and the structure of international relations that divide one incident from another, a comparison of the ALTMARK and PUEBLO affairs suggests that the potential efficacy of gunboat diplomacy has actually increased. The greater elegance and smoothness of the Royal Navy's operation should not blind us to the fact that their objective was easier and their victim potentially far less formidable than those of their North Korean successors. The British merely liberated some prisoners in the face of ineffectual and even half-hearted protests by a far weaker state; the North Koreans seized an American naval vessel in international waters, stopped American seaborne espionage against their country[26] and used the hostages they had taken to extract significant and humiliating concessions from a Super-Power.

Acceptance of this view, however, demands an answer to one obvious question. If the efficacy of gunboat diplomacy had not merely survived, but increased, why was the strongest naval power in the world unable to use this expedient against North Korea? There are two explanations: one particular and technical, the other political and of more general application.

The first is paradoxical. Gunboat diplomacy is the weapon of the strong against the weak, but strength is to be measured not by potential power, but by the ability to apply appropriate force about the point at issue. By this yardstick the North Koreans were stronger and had used their naval forces which, though relatively insignificant, were on the spot, to create a *fait accompli*. Long before any of the innumerable ships of the US Navy could reach North Korean waters, the hostages were aboard a train rattling into the interior of the country.[27] The tactical situation was thus entirely different from that obtaining in 1926, when the Royal Navy rescued British prisoners (at considerable cost in casualties) from two merchant vessels captured by the Chinese at Wanhsien high up the Yangtse, or in 1949, when H.M.S. LONDON and H.M.S. BLACK SWAN failed in their attempt to rescue H.M.S. AMETHYST, then aground under artillery fire in the same river.[28] In both those cases the location of the captives was known and accessible to nearby British warships. To liberate PUEBLO's crew, however, the Americans would have to emulate the exploits not of the Royal Navy, but of Otto Skorzeny, whose successful rescue of Mussolini in 1943 was facilitated by precise intelligence not available to the United States Government in 1968.

The second explanation is that, when an act of definitive force has created a *fait accompli*, any reaction by the victim can only take the form either of purposeful force – inhibited in this case by concern for the safety of the hostages – or of retaliation. The latter operates in a different moral and military climate: tension has already been aroused by the initial act of limited force, the assailant is on the alert and prepared to resist any counter-attack, the entire corpus of international law and morality exerts a vague but, on Western governments, sometimes efficacious disapproval of the whole concept of retaliation: above all, retaliation is liable to assume the character of an act of war and thus incites the apprehension and mobilizes the dissuasive energies of allies, of international organizations, and of large sections of public opinion, both within and beyond the borders of the victim state. All these factors combine to support the argument that, however infuriating, outrageous and immoral the original act of limited force, mere retaliation would be fruitless, dangerous and even wicked. This is not necessarily a valid argument, nor one which invariably prevails, but it probably exercised considerable influence on the United States Government, whose acquiescence cannot be attributed to any flaw in the concept of gunboat diplomacy as an instrument for the furtherance of foreign policy.[29]

In its definitive form, therefore, we may provisionally conclude that limited naval force, where this is employed, as in the case of PUEBLO, to seize the property or nationals of the victim, or, as happened in Zanzibar in 1964, to rescue the nationals of the assailant,[30] or in the creation of other kinds of *fait accompli*, has lost none of its ancient effectiveness in recent years as long as the assailant is able to support an informed resolution with appropriate naval force at the decisive point and the critical moment. The capture of PUEBLO, however, though itself an act of definitive force, was subsequently exploited by the North Koreans to extract concessions from the United States Government and it is to this purposeful application of limited naval force that we must now turn our attention.

II Purposeful Force: Corfu and Kuwait

Limited naval force is employed purposefully in order to change the policy or character of a foreign government or of some organized group whose relationship to the assailant is, for practical purposes, substantially that of a foreign government. In its purposeful application force does not itself do anything: it induces someone else to take a decision which would not otherwise have been taken: to do something or to stop doing it or to refrain from a contemplated course of action. This is a less direct and hence a less reliable expedient than definitive force, which itself removes the cause of dispute, because purposeful force depends for its success on a choice made by the victim. Once the North Koreans decided to attack PUEBLO, there was no option open to the United States Government which could have been exercised to prevent the capture of the vessel and her crew, but the subsequent exploitation of the hostages only succeeded because President Johnson decided that their lives and liberty were worth the concessions demanded, a choice he was not compelled to make.

There are, however, many situations in which the desired result can only be achieved with the co-operation of the victim. If a safe is to be opened, for instance, definitive force can be used to seize a key or blow the lock, but a memorized combination can only be obtained if force – or some other inducement – convinces the holder that revealing it has become the least disadvantageous course still open to him. On this analogy the most direct application of purposeful force is to the leaders of the victim state or organization. They may be induced by personal threats or violence to take the desired decisions or they may be removed and replaced by others able and willing to do so. Such methods have been successfully applied in recent years (Czechoslovakia in 1968, Hungary in 1956) but seldom by the use of limited naval force. In principle, however, there is no reason why warships should not become the instruments of future gambits of this kind against a government with a coastal capital. The parachutists (again under the command of the resourceful Otto Skorzeny) who seized Admiral Horthy in 1944 and replaced him with Hungarian leaders more amenable to German wishes,[31] might be emulated, in some capital nearer the sea, by helicopters operating from one of the carriers now maintained, in one form or another, by all the leading naval powers. The obstacles would be political rather than technical: the danger of intervention by other powers, the risk of a nationalist revulsion among the people of the victim state. Although there are many governments accessible to naval kidnapping, there are relatively few whose forcible replacement would have no repercussions liable to prevent their successors from being able to give effect to the desired decisions. The possibility will receive further consideration when our attention is turned to the future, but, in the absence of recent and authentically naval examples, we need only note, at this stage, that the application of force to the persons of foreign leaders is purposeful, rather than definitive, because it still leaves their followers with a choice whether or not to acquiesce in the decision taken under duress by their old leaders or their new replacements.

Failing direct action against foreign leaders, another possibility is the employment of limited naval force to promote or assist a seemingly indigenous political manœuvre, revolt or *coup d'état* intended to alter the policy or character of the victim government. In 1933 and again in 1961 the visible presence of US warships off the coast assisted the respective US Ambassadors to obtain the desired changes in the governments of Cuba and the Dominican Republic[32] and it is not difficult to imagine circumstances in which more extended forms of intervention would be appropriate.

On the whole, however, the political developments of recent decades have been unfavourable to the use of foreign limited force against governments as opposed to their states. The number of intrinsically vulnerable governments – those without a centralized administration or the ability to count on a degree of popular support against foreign intervention – is steadily declining. Most modern nation–states are hydra-headed: remove one set of leaders and another, equally obnoxious, may replace them. Overt intervention – and limited naval force is necessarily overt – is liable to generate a reaction, not only among the people of the victim-state, but also from other governments. Even if the victim has no powerful foreign protector, the modern doctrine of absolute national sovereignty may generate a degree of embarrassing international sympathy for a government evicted by foreign violence. This may not be important – if the force available is sufficient – but it constitutes a disincentive that has probably reinforced the contemporary tendency towards increasing reliance on other methods: covert assistance to indigenous movements anxious to replace the obnoxious government or overt force which, without attempting the eviction or personal coercion of the leaders, induces them to change their policy by altering the balance of national advantage in the options open to them.[33] The potential naval contributions to subversion – and its prevention – will be considered subsequently: what now concerns us is the rôle of limited naval force in convincing a foreign government that new circumstances require them to take altered decisions.

Such force can sometimes be applied directly to the cause of dispute. During the Spanish Civil War, for instance, the Italian Government wished to prevent other countries from sending aid to the Spanish Republicans and, from August 1937 onwards, Italian submarines were intermittently employed, without their use in this rôle being officially admitted, to sink ships bound for Republican ports. Because Italy had insufficient submarines and did not wish to risk an open rupture with other Powers this practice was not fully effective, though it did constitute both a deterrent and an impediment to the supply of arms and equipment to the Republican forces. So far as

British ships were concerned, these sinkings were discontinued when the British Government countered with their own threat of limited naval force: that submarines found submerged in the area patrolled by British destroyers would be sunk.[34] In principle, however, the more nearly that purposeful force can be related to the actual cause of dispute, the more likely it is to achieve the objective while retaining its limited character.

The patrol maintained off Beira since 1966 by the Royal Navy[35] may not be a particularly effective way of stopping oil from reaching Rhodesia, but it does seem to have prevented its importation by this particular route and to have done so without any of the direct confrontations with dissenting governments that other methods might have entailed. When a particular course of action can demonstrably be prevented, a reasonable government will not wish to persevere in an unattainable objective. It is no coincidence that one of the traditional conditions in international law for the recognition by neutrals of a naval blockade is that the blockade should be effective.

Limited naval force, however, can only be directly applied to disputes in which the sea or the use of navigable waters is an intrinsic element. British warships may protect British trawlers fishing in Icelandic waters or assert the right of innocent passage through territorial straits; the US Seventh Fleet may throw a defensive girdle around Formosa; the Soviet Mediterranean squadron may interpose its warships between Port Said and the Israeli Army on the opposite bank of the Suez Canal: none of these navies could directly influence the outcome of a purely terrestrial dispute. The elephant is not vulnerable to the crocodile until his trunk dangles near the water's edge.

In its indirect applications, however, the influence of limited naval force can be extended to disputes far beyond any high water mark. This is mainly achieved by damage infliction, which need not be directly related to the actual cause of dispute. Instead injury is threatened or performed until the victim purchases immunity by the desired concessions. Methods employed in the past include blockade, harassment of shipping, the capture or sinking of vessels flying the victim's flag, coastal bombardment, the occupation of islands or coastal areas, the landing of punitive expeditions and, of course, the seizure and exploitation of hostages. In its more extreme forms damage infliction comes close to war and – when the reactions of the victim have been wrongly estimated – sometimes develops into war, as happened when the United States tried to end the insurrection in South Vietnam by inflicting damage on the North. In the nineteenth century, when a fleet at sea was almost invulnerable to anything but a stronger fleet, the use of limited naval force for damage infliction often allowed an assailant to put pressure on his victim with impunity, but both political and technological developments have since impaired the effectiveness of this expedient. As its future usefulness is not necessarily exhausted, a brief examination of one of the classic cases of modern times – the Corfu incident – may serve to illustrate the principles involved and the extent to which these require adaptation to the different environment of the later twentieth century.

On 27 August 1923, General Enrico Tellini, the Italian President of the Commission of Delimitation appointed by the Conference of Ambassadors (on which Britain, France, Italy, Japan and the United States were represented) to mark out the frontiers of Albania, was ambushed and murdered, together with those of his staff who had accompanied him, in a wood at Zepi. This was in Greek territory, though not very far from the Albanian border, and the General was on his way to a meeting of the Commission at the time of his death. For reasons that need not concern us the Italian Government decided, with very little evidence to support their view,[36] that the Greek Government were morally responsible for this murder and should be required to make reparation to Italy. On the evening of 29 August the Italian Minister at Athens accordingly presented a note demanding an apology, the presence of all members of the Greek Government at a funeral for the victims in Athens, naval honours, an investigation, capital punishment for the culprits, 50 million Italian lire and military honours for the corpses on their final embarkation for Italy. A reply was required within twenty-four hours.

A conciliatory answer was received from the Greek Government within the time-limit specified, but this did not accept all the Italian demands. On 31 August, therefore, Mussolini dispatched a personal message to all Italian diplomatic missions abroad, which was communicated to the Greek Government that afternoon:

> To the just demands formulated by Italy following the barbarous massacre of the Italian Military Mission committed in Greek territory, the Hellenic Government has replied in terms that correspond in essence to the complete rejection of the same.
> Such an unjustified attitude places upon Italy the necessity of recalling the Hellenic Government to a sense of its responsibility.
> I have therefore communicated the order for the landing on the island of Corfu of a contingent of Italian troops.
> With this measure of a temporary character Italy does not intend an act of war but only to defend its own prestige and to manifest its inflexible will to obtain the reparations due to it in conformity with custom and international law.

The Italian Government hopes that Greece does not commit any act that may modify the pacific nature of the measures.[37]

At three o'clock that afternoon Captain Foschini of the Italian Navy landed on the Greek island of Corfu and informed the local authorities that the Italian Fleet, commanded by Admiral Solari, were on their way and would carry out the occupation of Corfu in thirty minutes' time. Unless a white flag was raised by 4 o'clock to signify the surrender of the island, bombardment would begin. It did. Thirty-five shells were fired, killing sixteen people and wounding about fifty, before the white flag appeared. Militarily this shelling was unnecessary and contrary to Mussolini's orders, but it did not prevent the occupation, without resistance from the Greeks, of Corfu and the adjoining islands, an occupation successfully maintained until 27 September, by which date the Greek Government had complied with every one of the original Italian demands, which had meanwhile been endorsed by the other four governments represented in the Conference of Ambassadors and presented to the Greek Government by that organization as their own. The Council of the League of Nations, to which Greece had appealed, took note of the intervention of the Conference of Ambassadors and welcomed their success in reaching a solution.

A number of interesting points emerge from this singular story. First of all, limited naval force had achieved complete success for Italy in a manner which no other expedient could have. The rôle played by the Conference of Ambassadors was essentially a moderating one – they induced the Italian Government not to press some of their supplementary demands, the payment by Greece of the cost of the Italian operation, for instance, and they smoothed the way for Greek surrender by giving an international veneer to Italian pressure, but they would never have endorsed the demand for 50 million lire except as the only means of terminating the occupation of Corfu. The almost simultaneous repudiation of responsibility by the Swiss Government for the murder in Lausanne of a Soviet diplomat, V. V. Vorovsky, suggests the likely fate of unsupported diplomatic representations.[38]

Secondly, the Italian conduct of the operation conformed closely (if the incompetence of the Italian Admiral is excepted) to the ALTMARK principles. The objective was defined, limited and tolerable; it was carefully communicated to the victim (the phrase 'Italy does not intend an act of war' is particularly noteworthy); the forces employed were manifestly capable of achieving their purpose without regard to Greek reactions and actions of violence unrelated to the operation were avoided.

These are factors obviously still relevant today, but there are other aspects of this episode for which it might seem difficult to find a recent, or imagine an imminent, parallel. To begin with, no Great Power was seriously prepared (though the British Government made tentative and ineffectual gestures) to support Greece. In these days of bipolarity, when most small states expect to appeal to one Super-Power against coercion either by the other or by a lesser Power, this may seem an unlikely contingency. Yet, is it so different from the ineffectual condemnation of intervention in Hungary in 1956, in Cuba in 1961, in the Dominican Republic in 1965, in Czechoslovakia in 1968? Or, if it be objected that, even in 1923, Italy scarcely ranked as a Super-Power, were Scandinavian objections then any more futile than Afro-Asian reactions to the use of force by Israel in 1967, 1968 and 1969? In 1923 France had her reasons for extending diplomatic support to Italy as, in a more recent era, the United States had for backing Israel, or the Soviet Union North Korea. The international kaleidoscope has shifted, but it is the patterns that are new, not their character. The combination of a relatively strong Italy, whom no one particularly wished to quarrel with, and a relatively weak Greece, whom no one felt especially bound to defend, is one that could still be reflected in the future.

On the other hand, the inability of the Corfiotes to defend themselves against the Italian Navy and their ready, if reluctant, acceptance of the inevitability of Italian occupation (the Prefect of Corfu was authorized by a meeting of government officials to 'bow before superior force')[39] might find fewer parallels today, when otherwise weak states (Albania in 1946,[40] Egypt in 1967) can devise effective counters to naval operations off their coast or organize irritatingly vigorous popular resistance to an otherwise effective military occupation (Vietnam ever since 1965). They can, but they do not always do so: the US Navy operated with impunity off the shores of the Dominican Republic; there has been no militarily significant resistance to Soviet occupation of Czechoslovakia. Exceptional circumstances are nowadays required for the successful exercise of limited force, but so they were in 1923. There were not many other countries against which Mussolini could then have executed a similar coup.

One factor of importance in the Corfu episode does, however, seem to have disappeared, at least temporarily, from the contemporary scene. This is the degree of responsibility which nation–states were then expected to assume for the safety and immunity within their territory of diplomatic representatives or international emissaries, even of ordinary foreign nationals. The Italian view that the Greek Government had a duty to guarantee the personal safety of 'all legally accredited missions in its territory' and the opinion of the Conference of Ambassadors that 'every State is responsible for crimes and political outrages committed on its territory' did not pass unchallenged by the international lawyers – what opinion ever will? – but they commanded acceptance from many members of the League of Nations otherwise critical of Italian conduct. At the very outset of the dispute, and before Italian intentions were known, the French Government proposed that the Powers represented in the Conference of Ambassadors should 'reserve to themselves to present eventually any demands for sanctions and for reparations that will appear necessary to them' and the final exaction of the indemnity of 50 million lire was justified by the Conference of Ambassadors on the ground that '*les coupables n'étaient pas encore découverts*'. 'The right of the Conference to reparations for the murder of General Tellini was never questioned during the settlement of the crisis.'[41]

The contemporary maltreatment, almost always with impunity, of Ambassadors, diplomats and international representatives – of which the murder on 17 September 1948 in Jerusalem by Jewish terrorists of Count Folke Bernadotte, the Mediator appointed by a special assembly of the United Nations, is only the most notorious among many instances[42] – shows how far international standards have since altered. This change – and the absence of any recent reaction of the Corfu variety to similar provocations – probably constitutes a source of more unalloyed satisfaction to coastal dwellers than to the smaller number of people likely to be charged by their governments or by international organizations with the conduct of such dangerously invidious missions.

Borrowing the words of a more illustrious author, 'I leave it to be settled by whomsoever it may concern, whether the tendency of this work be altogether to recommend paternal tyranny or reward filial disobedience.'[43] The only moral that need be pointed here is that, thanks to the use of limited naval force for damage-infliction, the Italian Government successfully exacted, in spite of a climate of international opinion much less indulgent than the Conference of Ambassadors, all the considerable concessions they had originally demanded. In similarly exceptional circumstances, though doubtless from different motives, other governments might still emulate Mussolini's exploit against victims incapable of coastal defence, unwilling to contemplate popular resistance and devoid of resolute allies. So far, however, the Corfu incident remains a unique example of the extent to which damage-infliction by limited naval force can be carried without provoking war or any international complication capable of detracting from the complete success of the assailant in all his original demands.

Instead, therefore, of seeking any direct parallel from a later decade, we must content ourselves with examining an instance in which the purposeful use of limited naval force was equally extensive and just as successful, but in which force was applied directly, defensively and without any element of damage-infliction.

On 25 June 1961, the government of Iraq, then headed by the violent and impetuous General Kassem, broadcast over Baghdad radio an announcement that they regarded the neighbouring state of Kuwait as an integral part of Iraqi territory. This was followed the next day by a note to diplomatic missions in Baghdad setting out the historical arguments for the Iraqi claim and by reported movements of Iraqui troops in the Basra area near the Kuwait border. On 26 June the government of Kuwait announced their intention of defending the national territory and on 30 June they formally requested British assistance under the Anglo-Kuwait treaty concluded some ten days previously. The British Government responded the same day by announcing their intention of taking 'normal precautionary measures' 'in the face of a declared threat to this small independent State of annexation by a more powerful neighbour'. On 1 July H.M.S. BULWARK, a Commando carrier hurriedly summoned from Karachi, landed 600 marines, while tanks were put ashore from a tank-landing ship which had been carrying out normal training manœuvres in the Persian Gulf. These initial contingents were rapidly reinforced by sea and air and altogether forty-five warships (including two other aircraft carriers) were concentrated for this operation. A defensive perimeter was established five miles from the Iraqi border and, although further Iraqi troop movements were reported, the presence of British forces successfully deterred any actual attack. In an inconclusive debate in the Security Council the British representative gave a categorical assurance that British troops had no aggressive intentions, would only be employed in combat if Kuwait were attacked and would be withdrawn as soon as Kuwait considered the threat of invasion had ceased. British action was criticized by Ceylon, Egypt and the Soviet Union. Subsequently, however, Egypt joined other Arab states in expressing support for the independence of Kuwait and in providing a contingent of an Arab League force to replace British troops in the defence of Kuwait. With the agreement of the Kuwait Government a phased British withdrawal began on 19 September and was completed on 19 October. After renewed declarations by General Kassem of his intention to 'liberate' Kuwait, minor British naval movements were announced on 26 December, but the threat did not materialize and no British forces were actually landed. Although relations with Iraq remained tense until General Kassem's overthrow in February 1963, Kuwait's independence was not again menaced and was formally recognized by Iraq on 4 October 1963.

The success of this straightforward and bloodless operation[44] needs no further emphasis, but three comments are appropriate. The first is that, in spite of the numerically more important participation of the Army and the Royal Air Force, the naval contribution was crucial. The presence of tanks at the outset was essential and these could only be landed from ships, while the air direction facilities provided by the carriers were equally important. The smooth success of the actual operation has often obscured the fact that, in the early stages of their concentration, British forces were barely sufficient to withstand a determined Iraqi attack: without the Navy the risk might have been too great to run.

The second comment is that the ALTMARK principles again applied, although, once again, the visible presence of the Navy may have been essential to convince the Iraquis that the available British force was sufficient to attain the defined, limited and tolerable objective stated in the Security Council by Sir P. Dean.

Finally, although this British use of purposeful force enjoyed the political advantages of a prior request from Kuwait and the general unpopularity of the then Iraqui régime, it should be noted that there was initially no general consensus of international approval for British action. If this had been deferred and if an Iraqi invasion had meanwhile taken place, there would presumably have been the usual general disposition to acquiesce in and condone the *fait accompli* and to deprecate any attempt to disturb it. Both the political and military obstacles to British intervention would then have been so much greater that this might never have been attempted and, if it had, could only with difficulty have been confined to the use of limited force.

This necessarily speculative comment serves to bring out a point of much wider relevance: 'a resort to force is more likely to meet with acquiescence if it is immediate in its application, instantaneous in its effect and appropriate in its nature'.[45] The need for an instantaneous effect – the creation of a *fait accompli* – applies primarily to definitive force and has already been considered, as has the desirability of using only *appropriate* force, but the importance of immediate application has hitherto been insufficiently emphasized. Yet it is one of the most essential criteria for the successful use of limited force, not only in the particular cases so far mentioned, but in most others. There are relatively few victims so unfortunately circumstanced that, if given sufficient notice of the intended use of force against them, they cannot organize enough defence, mobilize enough foreign supporters or stimulate a popular resistance capable of inflating the proportions of the original dispute and jeopardizing the ability of the assailant to confine his action within the bounds of limited force. Hence the frequency of surprise tactics or twenty-four-hour ultimata in gunboat diplomacy and hence, too, the failure of General Kassem, whose tanks could have motored into Kuwait in a matter of hours – if only they had started in time.

III   Catalytic Force: From the Baltic to Beirut

So far we have been concerned with the use of limited naval force to achieve objectives defined in advance: to liberate prisoners, seize a ship, extract precisely formulated concessions, deter a foreign government from an expected course of action. But force is often applied for vaguer purposes. A situation arises pregnant with a formless menace or offering obscure opportunities. Something, it is felt, is going to happen, which might somehow be prevented if force were available at the critical point. Advantages, their nature and the manner of their achievement still undetermined, might be reaped by those able to put immediate and appropriate power behind their sickle. These are situations peculiarly favourable to the exercise of limited naval force. Warships can cruise for long periods awaiting the moment most auspicious for their intervention. As long as they remain on the high seas they are not committed. Even after they have intervened, they can easily be disengaged and withdrawn. Air forces and armies, unless they enjoy the advantages of an adjacent frontier, are cumbrous instruments, dragging a long tail behind their teeth, ill-adapted to the tactics of tip and run, to the limited, tentative, noncommittal probe. A ship, a squadron, a fleet can as well float off one coast as another.

Of course, even for navies, the circumstances must be suitable. No American squadron could today be advised to cruise off the Russian coast in readiness to exploit an anti-Communist rising and to pick up whatever plums might best suit the tastes of the United States. Yet this is very much what the British did in the Baltic – and elsewhere – from 1919 to 1921.

The situation, admittedly, was unusual, but, in international affairs no less than in anatomy, it is the exception that is the rule. The Baltic is normally the preserve of the limitrophe powers and, ever since the eclipse of Swedish imperialism, had been contested between Germany and Russia. After the conclusion of the armistice of 11 November 1918, both these states were temporarily incapacitated by defeat and civil strife. The sea and its shores were open to the influence of their lesser inhabitants – and of outside Powers. In Russia the seizure of power by the Bolsheviks was hotly contested by a clutch of generals and admirals each with their ragtag-and-bobtail of miscellaneous supporters; in East Prussia the locally undefeated German armies were trying, under ambitious leadership, to snatch compensating advantages from the disaster that had overtaken their comrades on the Western Front; the long repressed nationalism of Estonians, Finns, Latvians, Lithuanians and Poles was hissing and seething. With the ice cracking and the bergs plunging in all directions anything might happen and the British Government concluded that the chances of an outcome favourable to British interests would be improved by the presence of a British naval squadron in the Baltic.

For many months that was about all they did decide. When Rear-Admiral Sinclair sailed for the Baltic in command of a light cruiser squadron and nine destroyers, his orders could scarcely have been vaguer: 'to show the British flag and support British policy as circumstances dictate'.[46] He was, admittedly, furnished with a supply of army weapons and authorized to give these to the Estonian National Council (who had earlier requested British assistance) and to the Latvian authorities to facilitate their defence against the Bolsheviks, but his instructions regarding Russia were as confused as the policy of the British Government. It was the Admiralty, and not the Foreign Office, who told him that 'a Bolshevik man-of-war operating off the coast of the Baltic Provinces must be assumed to be doing so with hostile intent and should be treated accordingly'.[47]

The trouble was that, throughout the period of our story, three mutually incompatible policies were open to the British Government, whose inclination towards first one, then another, was determined less by the intrinsic merits of each than by the rivalry within the British Cabinet of Churchill and Lloyd George and by the gradual unfolding, around the brackish waters of the Baltic, of events neither foreseen nor determined in Whitehall. There was a case for backing one or more of the White Russian leaders against the Bolsheviks – but this meant ignoring the claims to independence of their subject Baltic peoples; there were arguments for assisting the movements of national liberation of Estonians, Finns, Latvians, Lithuanians and Poles – but this outraged the imperialism of the anti-Bolshevik

Russians; there was a view, insignificant at first, but increasingly influential as the months went by, that Lenin and his blood-stained henchmen were going to win and ought not, therefore, to be irretrievably alienated. Until this last opinion was finally established by the force of events long after the conclusion of the Baltic episode, the presence of British warships seemed to offer British policy a wider range of options.

To begin with Admiral Sinclair interpreted his mission, as did his successor, Rear-Admiral Cowan, exclusively in terms of the first and second of these conflicting objectives. Having landed arms for the Latvians and Estonians, British warships shelled Bolshevik troops near Narva on 13 December and, when attacked at Reval by the Red Fleet on 26 December, captured two of their destroyers. Subsequently action had to be taken both against German troops (whose leaders wanted to make the Baltic states a German protectorate) and against dissident Latvians. On 29 December H.M.S. CERES opened fire on barracks containing mutinous troops 'with excellent effect'.

In January 1919, when Rear-Admiral Cowan took over command, the previous orders were amplified: 'British interests,' he was told, 'may be summed up as follows: to prevent the destruction of Estonia and Latvia by external aggression.' He interpreted these orders liberally: on 9 February naval gunfire drove the Bolsheviks out of Windau; in April he rescued Latvian Ministers and ships from the Germans; in May, admittedly, British support was refused to Mannerheim's plan for a Finnish advance on Petrograd, but in the same month the Bolshevik fleet was chased back to harbour from the Estonian coast and German troops shelled by H.M.S. EREBUS.[48] It is scarcely surprising that, in March, the Admiralty should have protested to the Cabinet: 'It is essential, if our naval force is required to undertake operations of war, that it should do so in pursuance of a definite and coherent policy.'[49] Admiral Cowan's spectacular interventions were, after all, subsidiary to the main political and military struggle ashore, where the raw and scanty troops raised by Estonia and Latvia had to rely on the sporadic and dangerously self-interested assistance of German and White Russian forces in order to resist a Bolshevik invasion that came by land and not by sea. As British troops were not to be employed, some of Admiral Cowan's help had to go to these doubtful allies and it would have been convenient to know which he should prefer, against whom and to what extent. Above all, was he or was he not to lend himself to the attempted overthrow of the Bolshevik régime in Russia itself?

Nobody actually replied, as happened on a more famous occasion, 'je n'en vois pas la nécessité', but it was not until 4 July that HM

Government decided that 'a state of war did exist between Great Britain and Bolshevist Government of Russia', a decision which they then nullified by not announcing it. These ambiguities seem to have worried Admiral Cowan less than they did the Admiralty. Admittedly it was after the non-declaration of war that he bombed the Red Fleet in Kronstadt harbour and later sank two of their battleships in the same base, but he had sunk a cruiser in Kronstadt as early as 17 June and his consistent strategy of neutralizing the Red Fleet seems to have been endorsed, sometimes reluctantly, rather than initiated by a divided Cabinet, whose belated decision may, however, be thought to provide some legal basis for the institution of a blockade of Petrogad on 10 October. Meanwhile, for all the vigour and effectiveness of British naval operations, the British Government continued to hedge their bets: the White Russians, the newly independent Baltic peoples, the German military adventurers, were all in turn encouraged, restrained or exploited. Even the Bolsheviks, though more often attacked, occasionally received emissaries as well as bombardments.

Gradually, however, there emerged the conviction that British interests would best be served by avoiding involvement in the struggle for power within Russia, concentrating instead on the maintenance of the newly-created Baltic States. To writers in this field it can only be a source of gratification to find that the view which ultimately prevailed was first enunciated by the author of 'The Twenty Years Crisis' and 'Conditions of Peace', then a Third Secretary in the Foreign Office: E. H. Carr. In April 1919, he had minuted:

> It is most undesirable that General Yudenitch (Commander of the White Russian North-Western Army) should be in any way encouraged to interfere in Finland or Estonia or to make either of these countries a base for offensive operations against Petrograd . . . the result . . . would probably be the sweeping of Estonia, and possibly Finland, by Bolshevism.

Ullman[50] from whom this quotation is taken, records that reaction within the Foreign Office was uniformly approving and Carr's minute may perhaps be regarded as the first crystallization, by the customarily implicit and instinctive process, of British policy. Even though this objective was never formulated, the effect was to establish the existence as independent countries of Estonia, Finland, Latvia and Lithuania, a result beneficial to British interests and one which could scarcely have been achieved without the application of limited naval force to neutralize the otherwise preponderant Red Fleet, to supply the Baltic armies, to support their coastal operations, to deny, as necessary, the use of the sea to Russians and Germans, and to hearten and assist Estonians, Latvians and Lithuanians against their two more powerful opponents. Page[51] repeatedly emphasizes the crucial importance of British naval assistance and only Finland could perhaps have dispensed with it.[52]

On 2 February 1920, Estonia, on 30 June Lithuania, on 11 August Latvia and on 14 October Finland, were able to sign treaties with the Soviet Union establishing peace and the recognition of their independent sovereignty. In 1921 British naval forces were finally withdrawn from the Baltic, their long uncertain mission accomplished. Altogether 238 warships had been employed, the number in the Baltic at any one time varying between twenty-nine and eighty-eight. Seventeen ships, including one light cruiser, were lost (mainly to mines) and 128 naval officers and men were killed; twenty-six French, fourteen United States and two Italian warships served under Admiral Cowan at one time or another, but were less heavily engaged).

These were extensive operations, and, if we accept as the objective that which ultimately emerged rather than anything which might have been envisaged, though never authoritatively formulated, at the outset, considerably more successful than simultaneous adventures against the Bolsheviks elsewhere on the periphery of Russia. But was this the exercise of limited naval force or was it an undeclared war?

Both views are arguable and the justification for preferring the former may be sought in the arguments of Chapter One: this was not a conflict between states in which policy was determined by the desire to inflict injury rather than the hope of positive advantage. The British Government wanted, with varying degrees of conviction, to change the Russian régime: they had no desire to injure Russia. Indeed, their readiness to assist the Baltic peoples was constantly inhibited by their reluctance to commit themselves, until a very late stage, to the detachment of provinces from the Russian Empire. The Baltic episode, though here treated in isolation, was part of a pattern of behaviour – it can scarcely be called a policy – that had originated during the war against Germany and had stemmed from the desire to keep Russians fighting Germans. As time passed and circumstances changed, so motives proliferated and conflicted, but war with Russia was never one which the British Government were prepared to admit to the British people. At most they were intervening in a civil war; in the Baltic they were fishing in troubled waters and with rather more success than in the Barents, the Black, the Caspian or the Japanese Seas.

British ability to undertake this remarkable adventure (in which, incidentally, no fleeting reflection of the ALTMARK principles can be discerned) depended on two particular features of the unusual state of affairs that followed the armistice with Germany: a disposable surplus of British naval capacity and the absence of rivals capable of effective opposition.

The new nations of the Baltic differed from Britain only in their more grandiose conceptions of the scope and aims of British assistance; the German adventurers could not count on the backing of even their own defeated state; Russia was torn and distracted by civil war; the remaining Western Powers favoured and even abetted British intervention.

The one real opponent – the new Bolshevik régime – was neither capable of responding to British acts of force by escalation to a wider war nor, in all probability, desirous of adopting a course likely to encourage and strengthen their Russian rivals. British success in confining so violent and protracted an intervention within the bounds of limited naval force was thus due to the exceptional advantages offered by an unusual situation and cannot be ascribed to any special expertise in the conduct of gunboat diplomacy. In most other circumstances operations which, as the British Government themselves recognized, involved what would normally be considered acts of war, would have led to actual war.

This brings us to the distinctive feature of the Baltic episode and to the main justification for choosing such an exceptional and even marginal instance of gunboat diplomacy for extended analysis. This is the first example we have considered in which the assailant could afford to ignore reactions by his victim, the risks of retaliation and the possible repercussions elsewhere. Mussolini in 1923 was not particularly concerned about the Greeks, but the possibility of British intervention was worrying; Churchill did not want to alienate the Norwegians even if their hostility was likely to prove ineffective. In the Baltic, however, the only real restriction imposed on Admiral Cowan was the persistent refusal of the British Government to contemplate the landing of British troops. This effectively limited both the extent of British involvement and the ability of the victims to inflict injury on British forces, but the ban was imposed for entirely British reasons and not with any idea of persuading the victims that British objectives were limited and tolerable. It follows, therefore, from this extreme case, that the circumstances of the victim are no less important than the intentions of the assailant in determining whether a particular intervention can be confined within the bounds of limited force or whether this must assume the character of an act of war.

In 1956, for instance, Britain and France jointly employed force against Egypt in a way that can only be described as catalytic: 'to bring Nasser to his senses'[53] the objective initially stated by Eden, scarcely qualified as purposeful. But the reason why this operation failed – and the reason for placing it beyond the shadowy line that divides gunboat diplomacy from an act of war – did not reside merely in the weaknesses of its planning and execution. The original conception of the British Government certainly neglected some of the principles earlier suggested as important to the establishment of an act of force as limited, but greater efforts were made than in 1919, even if they did not succeed, to impress on the victim the limited and tolerable character of British objectives. Force was more tardily applied than in 1919, but its effect might have been expected to appear sooner. Even the resources available were greater, both absolutely and in relation to the area of their deployment. But the circumstances of the victim were utterly different: instead of an internationally friendless régime struggling for its very life against half a dozen domestic rivals Britain had attacked an established leader enjoying full national support and the favour of numerous and important foreign governments. If the sword failed, it was be- cause it fell on thicker armour, not because it was wrongly wielded or because weapons were out of favour.

This is a version of the lesson of Suez which is not universally accepted. Some argue that Britain was revealed as militarily too weak ever again to undertake such operations; others that modern notions of absolute national sovereignty have finally discredited limited force as a viable alternative to war. These are points to be examined more fully in a later chapter, but the story of Kuwait goes some way to- wards disproving the first contention while the PUEBLO episode quite refutes the second, the evidence of these two instances being in no way invalidated by the sympathy and potential support on which Britain could rely in 1961 and North Korea in 1968. Britain was still more fortunate in 1919 and even Mussolini, in 1923, received im- portant backing from France. There is nothing new in the elementary proposition that gunboat diplomacy is more likely to succeed when the assailant enjoys these advantages and that only exceptional cir- cumstances will ever permit the successful use of limited force against stronger or better supported victims. What matters is whether or not the passage of time and the evolution of international relationships have consistently reduced the frequency of opportunities – which have always been relatively rare – for the successful employment of limited naval force.

At this stage it is worth emphasizing that political change is a con- tinuing, and not very predictable, process: the pattern revealed when we look backwards from 1969 may be scarcely recognizable in 1979;

yesterday may offer better precedents than today for the situations of
tomorrow. During the twenties and thirties, for instance, the use of
limited naval force on the Baltic model to rescue new nations from
the wreck of a shattered empire, was hardly conceivable. In 1950,
however, when China's situation reflected Russia's in 1919, and
Japan's that of Germany, the intervention of the US Seventh Fleet
was no less effective than Admiral Cowan's. Formosa, which owed
her independence, as did Estonia, Latvia and Lithuania, to naval
midwifery, has already preserved it almost as long, not through any
repetition of Soviet quiescence in the Baltic between 1920 and 1939,
but because the US Navy have continuously interposed their shield
of limited force between Formosa and the irredentist fury of a
resurgent China.

For all its intriguing parallels with the Baltic episode, the defence
of Formosa was nevertheless a straightforward example of the purposeful use of force and, for our next instance of the catalytic mode,
we must return to the Mediterranean, where, before two years had
dried the ink on the lessons of Suez, Nasserist Arab nationalism was
again the victim, but this time in circumstances sufficiently altered to
permit a genuinely limited use of naval force.

This was an operation in which the relationship between objective
and outcome is as complex and controversial as it was in 1919: the
American intervention of 1958 in the Lebanon. Not the least of its
difficulties is its intricate involvement with Lebanese politics, a
mystery which only a Lebanese historian could – and when a few
decades have quelled the passions this year still inspires – perhaps
one day will expound. Meanwhile the uninitiated can best envisage
the situation confronting the US Government in terms of three con-
centric circles. The innermost was the Lebanon itself, where President Chamoun strove to maintain Christian ascendancy and the
traditionally pro-Western orientation of his country – perhaps also
to prolong his own personal rule – against the increasingly violent
opposition of discontented Moslems, Arab nationalists, leftists and
those more moderate Lebanese who, for a variety of reasons, preferred a more flexible policy of adaptation to the altered circumstances of a new era. The middle circle was the Middle East, in which
Nasser, far from displaying any gratitude for American help at the
time of Suez, seemed to Washington to be whipping Arab nationalism
into adventures ever more adverse to American interests. And, in the
outermost circle, the spectre of advancing Soviet imperialism, to
which Eden had vainly pointed in 1956, soon seemed so real to President Eisenhower that, on 7 March, the celebrated 'Eisenhower
Doctrine' was endorsed by the United States Congress.[54]

When the Lebanese Government, on 16 March 1957, accepted American material aid and declared their readiness to defend Lebanese political independence, their opposition to outside interference in Lebanese internal affairs and their determination to co-operate with the United States in resisting the menace of international Communism, they gave to all three circles a common centre. President Chamoun had publicly committed his country in the Cold War, he had defied President Nasser's leadership and, by making any stand at all, he had alarmed as many Lebanese as his choice either delighted or outraged. Egyptian indignation and the apprehension excited among even Christian Lebanese were increased by two further developments during 1957. At the end of April the US Sixth Fleet arrived off Beirut in avowed readiness to assist King Hussein of Jordan, who had just overcome an attempted *coup d'état* of allegedly Egyptian, Syrian and even Soviet inspiration. And in July the Lebanese parliamentary elections produced a majority capable, when they came to elect a President in 1958, of giving Chamoun a further six-year term. The Lebanon was agitated and divided and her dissensions were actively inflamed from Egypt and from neighbouring Syria. Then, on 1 February 1958, the Lebanon's two Arab enemies proclaimed their fusion in the United Arab Republic of Egypt and Syria. Although this achievement was to prove ephemeral, its announcement and President Nasser's visit to Damascus on 24 February were as exciting to Moslems and Arab nationalists in the Lebanon as they were alarming to those who already despaired of maintaining Lebanese independence against the advancing tide of Nasserism. Over 300,000 Lebanese made the pilgrimage to Damascus and the taxi-fare from Beirut reached five times its normal level.[55] On 28 March rioting broke out in Tyre and other Moslem districts, on 9 May it was repeated in Tripoli where the US Information Office was burned down, and on 12 May in Beirut. When the Syrians attacked the Lebanese frontier post at Masnaa, disembowelling and castrating the five Lebanese customs officers they found there,[56] fighting was widespread, the chief leaders of the revolt being Moslem politicians and the Druze feudal chieftain and fellow-traveller Kamal Jumblatt. President Chamoun was supported by the police and by many of the Christians, the Lebanese Army preferring to hold aloof from a conflict calculated to divide its own ranks as much as it did the nation.[57]

The origins and nature of the civil conflict thus summarily described will be long disputed, but President Chamoun was in no doubt that he was facing a '*coalition des forces communistes et de celles de la République Arabe Unie*',[58] the very contingency for

which the Eisenhower Doctrine had been designed. On 11 May the
US Ambassador was asked whether his government were prepared
to assist the Lebanon, on 13 May the US Sixth Fleet and HQ
Second Provisional Marine Force (Task Force 62) were alerted, on
14 May President Chamoun was told that the Sixth Fleet would
stand by and on 18 May the Commander of the Sixth Fleet and of
Task Force 62 (whose HQ had by then reached the Mediterranean)
began the planning of Operation Bluebat.[59] This assumed as the
enemy most likely to be encountered – if, indeed, there was any
opposition at all – the Syrian First Army, which was credited with
40,000 men and 200 tanks.

There followed a pause, in which both Americans and Lebanese
seemed to have second thoughts about their first impulsive reaction.[60]
On 21 May the Lebanese Government appealed to the Arab League
and on 22 May to the Security Council. The first of these bodies
was unable to reach agreement, the second decided on 11 June (the
representative of the Soviet Union abstaining) to send a group of
observers to the Lebanon to prevent the illegal infiltration of men,
arms or materials of war. On 3 July the Secretary-General, who
had himself visited Beirut, announced that no mass infiltration could
be detected, a report received with considerable scepticism by both
the US and the Lebanese Governments.[61] Meanwhile the civil war
continued, as did requests from the Lebanese Government for various
forms of American assistance. These caused considerable perplexity
in Washington, where the US Government, though anxious to uphold
the validity of the Eisenhower Doctrine, wished neither to over-ride
the United Nations, for which they had professed such respect in
1956, nor to involve themselves needlessly in what, as their Embassy
in Beirut warned them, might turn out to be primarily an internal
conflict susceptible of eventual resolution by one of the mysterious
compromises in which Lebanese violence so often ends. Even President Chamoun, though formally authorized by the Council of Ministers on 16 June to seek military assistance from friendly powers,
continued to shrink from an irrevocable step which, as he was well
aware, would no longer be welcome in Washington and, as occasional
successes against the rebels sometimes encouraged him to hope,
might still not be essential. On 1 July the US Sixth Fleet relaxed its
state of alert, most of its ships were dispersed to Italian ports and
only the 6th Amphibious Squadron with the 1st Marine Battalion
Landing Team aboard remained at sea. There was no such relaxation
in the Lebanon, where pitched battles were fought in the hills and the
rebels turned an entire quarter of the capital into an armed camp,
whence they sallied forth to kidnap or assassinate rivals, to blow up

their houses and to attack official buildings. Arms – and probably
men as well – were freely imported across a frontier largely controlled by the rebels, who were continuously encouraged by broad-
casts from Cairo and Damascus. These activities were countered to
the best of their ability by the supporters of Chamoun and, though
the good sense of the Lebanese people (and the occasional interventions of the Lebanese Army) kept the level of violence well below
that of civil wars in other countries, as many as 3,000 Lebanese were
to be killed during the six months the conflict lasted.

Whether the fighting would ultimately have burnt itself out in
compromise or whether, in the absence of any counterpoise, it would
have grown under Egyptian and Syrian pressure to proportions incompatible with the continued survival of an independent, pre-
cariously united, but genuinely prosperous Lebanon, we shall never
know. On 14 July chance (though in Beirut and Washington it then
appeared as the most sinister of designs) intervened: a revolution
broke out in Iraq, the King, his family and his pro-Western Ministers
were massacred, the British Embassy was destroyed, Moscow and
Cairo radios rejoiced at the fall of the reactionaries, the Lebanese
rebels were excited to frenzy and, in Chamoun's words,[62] *'une grande
peur s'était en revanche emparée des milieux attachés à un Liban
paisible et indépendant. Leur moral, longtemps mis à dure épreuve,
atteignait subitement les limites de la débâcle.'* President Chamoun
took only two hours to make up his mind: at 9 a.m. he asked for
American military assistance with twenty-four hours.[63] The response
of the United States Government was equally prompt: at 2 p.m.
President Chamoun was told that help was on its way and by 30
minutes past midnight (Beirut time) Admiral Holloway, command-
ing the operation,[64] had been ordered to start landing his marines by
3 p.m. on the 15th.

To the dismay of the US Ambassador, whose wireless link with
the Sixth Fleet had broken down and who had been given insufficient
time to reconcile the startled and indignant Commander-in-Chief of
the Lebanese Army, General Chehab, to the prospect of American
intervention, the Admiral was only four minutes late. The landing
craft grounded on the dingy sands of the remote and unfashionable
bathing beach at Khaldé, the marines charged inland past the Coca-
Cola stalls and cooked-meat sellers, across the road and up the
dunes to secure the international airport of Beirut, some miles south
of the city proper. The advance into the city was delayed for negotiations with the Lebanese Army, but the following evening a further
contingent of Marines, preceded by the US Ambassador in his car
with his dog and a somewhat reluctant General Chehab as passenger

and mediator, secured the harbour, the bridges on the Tripoli road at the opposite extremity of Beirut and the US Embassy. On 20 July the first airborne reinforcements arrived and by the end of the month ten thousand Americans were holding a twenty-mile perimeter around Beirut. The force reached its peak of nearly 15,000, including a regiment of tanks, on 8 August; one marine battalion was re-embarked as a floating reserve on 14 August; withdrawal began on 14 September and was completed by 25 October. In spite of occasional confrontations with indignant Lebanese officers (who had initially wished to resist the landing) and one or two exchanges of shots with the rebels, the Americans were never called on to fight, encountered no significant opposition and had only one man killed at Lebanese hands. Although shortage of tanks and essential items of equipment during the first few days worried American commanders ashore, there was ample air cover from the carriers of the Sixth Fleet (altogether fifty warships were involved) and no real reason for military concern, though American naval commentators have rightly emphasized that, as at Kuwait, only a naval landing could have met Chamoun's deadline:

> It was five days after the landing, in full force, of seaborne Marines from 18-knot transports, before the first lightly-armed airborne troops reached Lebanon and that only after delicate and uncertain negotiations, in a tug-of-war against Communist political pressure, for overflight permissions from each country in the paths of the transport planes.[65]

What were the objectives of this imposing operation (which cost the United States 200 million dollars)[66] and what did it in fact achieve?

There is no certain answer to either question and any conjecture is necessarily controversial, because the situation that provoked American intervention was never as clear-cut as, in the lurid glare from Baghdad, it briefly appeared at the moment of decision. In the message to Congress that preceded the arrival of the first marines on Khaldé beach, President Eisenhower appeared to accept in its entirety the thesis, which had hitherto been questioned in Washington, of President Chamoun:

> It is clear that the events which have been occurring in Lebanon constitute indirect aggression from without, and that such aggression endangers the independence and integrity of Lebanon.

In the same message he explained that:

US forces are being sent to the Lebanon to protect American lives and by their presence to assist the government of Lebanon in the preservation of Lebanon's territorial integrity and independence.

In another statement issued on the same day President Eisenhower added a phrase with which the reader will by now have become familiar:

These forces have not been sent as any act of war.

All these statements – and many other explanations and qualifica-- tions have been omitted – provided an objective for American inter- vention that was limited and tolerable and entailed a minimum use of force, but was not, perhaps, very precisely defined. Indeed, the words 'by their presence to assist' might almost be the motto for the catalytic, as opposed to the purposeful, use of force: a threat existed, all the more acute because it was formless, and the outcome seemed likely to be more favourable with the Marines than without them.

There was a further consideration, which President Eisenhower put to his Special Representative in the Lebanon, Mr Robert Murphy, on the following day:

sentiment had developed in the Middle East, especially in Egypt, that Americans were capable only of words, that we were afraid of Soviet reaction if we attempted military action. Eisenhower be- lieved that if the United States did nothing now, there would be heavy and irreparable losses in Lebanon and in the area generally. He wanted to demonstrate in a timely and practical way that the United States was capable of supporting its friends. . . . My oral instructions from the President were conveniently vague, the sub- stance being that I was to promote the best interests of the United States incident to the arrival of our forces in the Lebanon.[67]

Once again, a clear case of catalytic force and a remarkable echo of British instructions to their Baltic admirals forty years previously. Although no one said so, US Marines had not landed in pursuance of a defined objective: their purpose was to hold the situation and to gain time in which the United States Government could decide what their objective should be.

The tentative and exploratory character of American intervention was not generally appreciated and it is misunderstanding of this point that still bedevils so much analysis of the actual American achievement. Most Lebanese, for instance, whichever side they were on, imagined that the Americans had come to crush the rebellion

E

and restore the authority of President Chamoun. When US forces placidly continued to man their perimeter, while Mr Murphy helped to negotiate a compromise favourable to the rebels, many Christians denounced American betrayal and loss of nerve;[68] many Moslems and Nationalists rejoiced at American failure. Mr Murphy's instructions, however, had mentioned only 'the best interests of the United States' and these were well served by the actual settlement – once this had been adjusted by a last-minute counter-revolt of the Christians. It was this final factor which caused many Lebanese – a nation more solicitous of, than grateful for, foreign assistance – to argue, once the dust had settled, that this had always been an internal dispute needlessly complicated by an American intervention in panic response to irrelevant events in Baghdad. This must always remain a conceivable hypothesis, though the intemperate reactions to American intervention of Egypt, Iraq, Syria, and above all, the Soviet Union, scarcely support it. If this was no more than a domestic squabble, why did Mr Khruschev, not content with the customary fulminations and with breaking the windows of the American Embassy in Moscow, find it necessary to tell President Eisenhower on 19 July that American intervention had brought the world 'to the brink of catastrophe'?

When everything was over, when Khruschev's demand for an immediate Summit Conference had expired in the sterility of diplomatic exchanges, when hurriedly arranged Soviet manœuvres (including those of the Black Sea Fleet) had failed to shake American resolution, when American forces, which had never found it necessary to resort to violence, had withdrawn in their own good time and a new Lebanese President had settled down with a Coalition Government to rule a more tranquil, but still independent country of substantially unaltered social structure, neither of the two extreme conclusions suggested at the outset was entirely valid. Not everyone in the Lebanon agreed 'that the United States was capable of supporting its friends', but were the Kremlin equally convinced that 'the time has passed when the fire of colonialist gunboats and the landing of armed detachments can crush the uprisings of oppressed peoples?'[69] In the innermost circle the eventual resolution of the Lebanese crisis might seem curiously unrelated to the activities of the US Sixth Fleet, but elsewhere governments had been forcibly reminded that, as long as the Soviet Navy were confined to the impotence of manœuvres in the Black Sea, it was not the Americans who 'were capable only of words'.

The lesson was learnt. Eleven years later a somewhat similar crisis erupted in the Lebanon. Once again armed interlopers crossed the frontier to exacerbate internal dissension, once again the pressure of external events threatened the unity, the social and political structure and the international alignment of the Lebanon. As always the radios of the Middle East vomited their diatribes, as usual the Lebanese turned wistful, but no longer very optimistic, eyes towards the varied sources of potential assistance. This time, however, no one in Washington contemplated intervention; no one in Moscow found it necessary to threaten global war. The Sixth Fleet was no longer alone. In the faintly ambivalent words of Rear-Admiral Navoitsev on 17 May 1969: 'the presence of the Soviet Navy in the Mediterranean is a most important factor for stabilization in that troubled area of the globe'.[70]

IV Expressive Force: DEUTSCHLAND to DEDALO

The last and least of the uses of limited naval force in furtherance of the objectives of foreign policy is the expressive, in which warships are employed to emphasize attitudes, to lend verisimilitude to otherwise unconvincing statements or to provide an outlet for emotion. Its distinction from the threat of purposeful force, on the one hand, and from mere flag-showing, on the other, is as vague and uncertain as the usual result of its employment. Yet the task must be attempted, because the expedient is more common than it is valuable.

On 3 August 1936, for instance, just twenty-five years after PANTHER's arrival at Agadir, the German pocket-battleship (*Panzerschiff*) DEUTSCHLAND and the torpedo-boat LUCHS visited Ceuta in Spanish Morocco. The German Admiral went ashore and lunched with General Franco and the German Consul from nearby Tetuan, who duly reported: 'the visit is considered direct support of the Nationalist uprising of General Franco'.[71] The point had been made, though the reasons for making it so flamboyantly remain somewhat obscure. The German transport aircraft that were already ferrying Franco's troops to Spain had actually given him the backing that DEUTSCHLAND's visit only symbolized and that Hitler was otherwise still at pains to conceal. Perhaps the dramatic gesture of DEUTSCHLAND's appearance seemed an irresistibly appropriate sequel to a decision Hitler had taken at Bayreuth after a performance of *Die Walküre*.[72]

Ambiguity is a recurrent feature of acts of expressive force, but the significance of this one was that it did not constitute a threat of purposeful force – there was no suggestion of German naval intervention at that stage[73] – yet, because it was related to the specific objective of emphasizing German support for Franco, it was more than a mere reminder of German naval might. If it was useful, it was presumably because it conveyed a message with emphasis but without precision or commitment.

Not all naval messages are so clearly distinguishable from the threat or use of purposeful force. When the Netherlands Government announced, on 5 April 1960, the dispatch of the aircraft carrier KAREL DOORMAN and two destroyers to New Guinea, the intention was presumably to deter Indonesia from attacking that island colony. As a threat of purposeful force, however, the announcement might have been more effective if made after the ships had arrived. As it was, the message was ill-received, not only in Indonesia itself, but in other countries due to be visited *en route*, and probably did more harm than good. But the incident could be assigned either to the purposeful or to the expressive category.

On the other hand, when H.M.S. BERWICK initiated the Beira patrol[74] on 9 April 1966, by stopping the Greek tanker MANUELA, this was a purposeful use of limited naval force: to prevent oil from reaching Rhodesia. Yet, as the months went by and the evidence accumulated that Rhodesia was now importing oil by other routes, the purposeful character of the Beira patrol began to wear a trifle thin and its expressive function may now be the most significant.

Similarly, when President Johnson sent the Seventh Fleet to the Sea of Japan after the capture of PUEBLO in 1968, this was a clear threat of purposeful force against North Korea. When President Nixon repeated the manœuvre after the destruction of an American aircraft in 1969, the events of the previous year had stripped his bluff of credibility: he was merely assuaging American indignation by a gesture of expressive force.

The same year, however, witnessed a rather more elegant and classical employment of this gambit, in that very Western outlet of the Mediterranean that seems almost consecrated to the expressive use of naval force. Changes in the Spanish Government having prompted newspaper speculation that the claim to Gibraltar might no longer be so vigorously pressed, the Spanish carrier DEDALO and twelve other Spanish warships arrived in the Bay of Algeciras and dropped anchor in sight of the Rock. Once again a point had been made without the embarrassment of words. The British retort was as taciturn and equally traditional, almost blatantly so: when the Spaniards arrived, a match was being played ashore – between the football teams of H.M.S. EAGLE and H.M.S. HERMES.[75]

The reader must excuse these frivolities. In its expressive mode limited naval force resembles the ceremonial and representational aspects of ordinary diplomacy: equally rich in anecdotes, equally unproductive of identifiable advantages, equally dear to the romantic schoolboys who become politicians, diplomats and naval officers. Such practices may legitimately be recorded, and their principles analysed, without too nice a regard for their utility: they are inherently likely to continue.

NOTES

[1] *Fowler's Modern English Usage*, second edition, O.U.P. 1965.
[2] Use of local force to create or remove a *fait accompli*. See Grant Hugo, *Britain in Tomorrow's World*, Chapter 5, Chatto & Windus 1969.
[3] *Innstilling Fra Undersøkelsekommisjonen av 1945*, Bilag I, Oslo 1947.
[4] Reidar Omang, *Altmark-Saken 1940*, Gyldendal Norsk Forlag Oslo 1953.
[5] The whole of this section is based on, and the quotations taken from, Reidar Omang op. cit. and the *Instilling* of 1945.
[6] Intelligence reports from Bergen, confirmed later by aircraft of Coastal Command RAF, were the first definite reports of her location since the previous December and these reached C-in-C Home Fleet at 1710 on 15 February. See also S. W. Roskill, *The War at Sea*, Vol. I, pp. 151–3.
[7] Sir P. Vian, *Action This Day*, Frederick Muller 1960.
[8] *Ibid.*
[9] Norwegian time.
[10] He may have been stretching a point here, as he does not appear to have received specific instructions at this stage, but Admiral Forbes was doubtless rightly confident that a generous and informed interpretation would be given to his order: 'ALTMARK your objective.'
[11] Vian op. cit.
[12] It was one of the incidental Anglo-Norwegian controversies arising from this incident whether or not Captain Vian had ever uttered the first clause of his instructions. See *Correspondence respecting the German Steamer* ALTMARK *Command 8012* of 1950, H.M.S.O. London.
[13] Captain Halvorsen's report in *Reidar Omang* op. cit.
[14] Captain Halvorsen's report in *Reidar Omang* op. cit. Captain Halvorsen asked Captain Vian: 'If there are no prisoners on board ALTMARK – what then?' and received the reply, 'That will be a mistake from my government's side.' Doc. 89 in *Reidar Omang* op. cit.
[15] In the latter case Army officers were also involved, though the Commander of the Norwegian patrol vessel POL III was the first to take action and shore-based naval torpedoes dealt the *coup de grâce*. See J. L. Moulton *The Norwegian Campaign of 1940*, Eyre & Spottiswoode 1966.
[16] Article 17 of *Alminnelig Instruks for Sjøforsvarets Sjefer under Nøytralitetsvern*. See *Reidar Omang*.
[17] *Reidar Omang* op. cit., doc. 26.
[18] 'The US imperialist aggressors have lately gone so far as to infiltrate boats carrying espionage and subversive elements', *New York Times*, 25 January 1968.
[19] Statement by Major-General Pak Chung Kook, the North Korean delegate, at the meeting of the Military Armistice Commission at Panmunjon on 24 January 1968, *New York Times*, 26 January.
The document finally signed by the American Major-General Gilbert H.

Woodward on 23 December 1968, included the following paraphrase of General Pak's original terms:
'The government of the United States of America, acknowledging the validity of the confessions of the crew of the u.s.s. PUEBLO and of the evidence produced by the Representative of the Government of the Democratic People's Republic of Korea to the effect that the ship, which was seized, by the self-defense measures of the naval vessels of the Korean People's Army in the territorial waters of the Democratic People's Republic of Korea on January 23 1968, had illegally intruded into the territorial waters of the Democratic People's Republic of Korea, shoulders full responsibility and solemnly apologizes for the grave acts of espionage committed by the US ship against the Democratic People's Republic of Korea after having intruded into the territorial waters of the Democratic People's Republic of Korea, and gives firm assurance that no US ships will intrude again in the future into the territorial waters of the Democratic People's Republic of Korea.'
By a procedure of which Mr Rusk said, 'I know of no precedent in my nineteen years of public service', the signature of this document was preceded by an oral statement in which General Woodward declared its contents to be at variance with the facts, which his signature could not and would not alter, *Washington Post*, 23 December 1968.

[20] In testimony to the House Foreign Affairs Committee on 24 January 1968. *Keesings Contemporary Archives*.

[21] 'At the 260th meeting of this commission held four days ago, I again registered a strong protest with your side against having infiltrated into our coastal waters a number of armed spy boats . . . and repeatedly demanded that you immediately stop such criminal acts.' General Pak on 24 January, *New York Times* of 26 January 1968.

[22] Televised address on 26 January as reported by *International Herald Tribune* of 27 January 1968.

[23] By a curious coincidence one of the most extended examples of the use of this technique had been given by the government of South Korea which had exploited many hundreds of Japanese hostages to secure concessions from the government of Japan between 1953 and 1959 (see Appendix). The government of South Korea did not, however, venture to extend this technique to the Soviet Union and denied that their naval vessels had, as charged by the Soviet Union, made an unsuccessful attack on the Soviet survey ship UNGO off the Korean coast on 28 December 1959.

[24] *The Times*, 1 February 1968.

[25] In the statement of 24 January previously quoted.

[26] 'The Pentagon never admitted it publicly until the plane was lost, but all ship surveillance of the North Korean coast was discontinued after the PUEBLO was seized.' *Christian Science Monitor*, 21 April 1969.

[27] Lt. Murphy's account in *Christian Science Monitor*, 17 June 1969.

[28] See Appendix.

[29] For an analysis of American problems in the PUEBLO affair see Grant Hugo, *Appearance and Reality in International Relations*, Chapter 2, Chatto & Windus 1970.

[30] See Appendix.

[31] In fact the German Minister had persuaded Horthy to surrender and leave the Palace a few minutes before Major Skorzeny's men arrived on 16 October 1944, but the threat of armed German intervention was a critical undercurrent to all the complexity of Hungarian intrigues in this confused

episode. See C. A. Macartney, *October Fifteenth: A History of Modern Hungary 1929–1945*, Part II, Chapter XVIII, Edinburgh University Press 1956.

[32] See Appendix.

[33] Although governments engaged in disputes frequently proclaim that their quarrel is only with the leaders, not the people, of the opposing state, there is, in practice, a distinct tendency to regard ordinary people as more legitimate victims of violence than politicians. The British Government, for instance, always rejected proposals for the assassination of Hitler.

[34] See Appendix.

[35] See Chapter 4.

[36] See James Barros, *The Corfu Incident of 1923*, Princeton University Press 1965, where it is argued that the unknown assassins operated without the knowledge or complicity of the Greek Government, who did their unavailing best to clear up the crime.

[37] Quoted in Barros op. cit.; the last paragraph, which referred to the Ambassadors' Conference, has been omitted.

[38] See Barros op. cit. to whose book, which is by no means partial to Italy, this account is heavily indebted.

[39] Barros op. cit.

[40] It was actually in the Corfu Straits, between the Greek island and the Albanian mainland, that H.M.S. VOLAGE and SAUMAREZ were badly damaged by an Albanian minefield. See Appendix.

[41] Barros op. cit.

[42] Israel did express regret and pay the small sum demanded in compensation by the UN (Sweden having waived her claims) for the murder of Count Bernadotte, but Arab governments in whose territory UN officials were killed did not even reply to the Secretary-General's letters and 'no satisfaction has been received for any claims addressed to the Arab States'. Rosalyn Higgins *United Nations Peacekeeping 1946–67: The Middle East*, O.U.P. 1969.

[43] Jane Austen, *Northanger Abbey*, Everyman Edition.

[44] This account is mainly based on press reports.

[45] Grant Hugo, *Britain in Tomorrow's World: Principles of Foreign Policy*, Chatto and Windus 1969, Chapter 5.

[46] See G. Bennet, *Cowan's War*, Collins 1963; S. W. Page, *The Formation of the Baltic States*, Harvard 1959; Richard H. Ullman, *Britain and the Russian Civil War*, Princeton 1968.

[47] Stephen Roskill, *Naval Policy Between The Wars*, Vol. I, Chapter 3, Collins 1968.

[48] David M. Mercer, 'The Baltic Sea Campaign', article in *USNIP* September 1962.

[49] S .W.Roskill op. cit.

[50] Op. cit.

[51] Op. cit.

[52] Though Finnish representatives in London emphasized to Lord Curzon as late as 7 May 1919 the apprehensions entertained by the Finnish Government of a Russian naval attack. See p. 170 of Stig Jägerskïold, *Riksförestàndaren Gustaf Mannerheim 1919*, Holger Schildts Förlag Helsingfors, 1969.

[53] 'We must be ready, in the last resort, to use force to bring Nasser to his senses', Eden to Eisenhower 27 July 1956, Antony Eden *Full Circle*, Cassell 1960, p. 428.

[54] This authorized the President 'to employ the armed forces of the US as he deems necessary to secure and protect the territorial integrity and political

independence of any such nation or group of nations requesting such aid against overt armed aggression from any nation controlled by international Communism'.

[55] Fahim Qubain, *Crisis in Lebanon*, Middle East Institute Washington 1961.

[56] These unhappy victims thus paid for their zeal in intercepting a consignment of arms on the previous day.

[57] Although most Moslems tended to support one side and most Christians the other, this was not a straightforward religious conflict. President Chamoun retained the loyalty of his Moslem Prime Minister and of Kamal Jumblatt's principal Druze rival, while a number of Christians initially co-operated with the rebels.

[58] Camille Chamoun, *Crise au Moyen-Orient*, Paris-Gallimard 1963.

[59] See *Marines in Lebanon 1958*, Marine Corps Historical Branch G3 Division, Washington 1966.

[60] Though the US Ambassador had told Chamoun on the 14th that he should appeal to the Security Council and seek diplomatic support from other Arab governments – Robert McClintock – 'The American Landing in Lebanon', Article in *US Naval Institute Proceedings*, LXXXXVIII, No. 10, October 1962.

[61] Robert Murphy, President Eisenhower's special envoy to the Lebanon, says that the UN observers operated only in the daytime, leaving the frontier open at night. *Diplomat Among Warriors*, N.Y. Doubleday 1964, Chapter 27.

[62] Chamoun op. cit: Chapter 29.

[63] Formally this and the original request of 11 May were addressed to Britain and France as well, but it was understood that the response would be American, British forces being earmarked for Jordan and French committed in Algeria. Chamoun thought the Sixth Fleet was too far away and allowed them forty-eight hours, asking for interim British and French help within twenty-four. See McClintock op. cit.

[64] As C-in-C. Specified Command, Middle East.

[65] Heinl, *Soldiers of the Sea*, US Naval Institute 1962. The author might have added that, when the transport planes did arrive, they landed at an airport first secured by seaborne marines. The same was true of Kuwait in 1961.

[66] Murphy op. cit.

[67] Murphy op. cit.

[68] So have some Americans, notably Miles Copeland in his interesting *The Game of Nations*, Weidenfeld & Nicolson 1969. Undoubtedly the US Government could have imposed a settlement more favourable to American interests, but could they then have withdrawn and avoided further intervention?

[69] Soviet statement of 17 July 1958.

[70] Article in *Moscow News*, No. 20, 1969.

[71] Documents on German Foreign Policy, Series D, Vol. III, Doc. 27 H.M.S.O. 1951.

[72] On 26 July, see Hugh Thomas, *The Spanish Civil War*, p. 228, Eyre & Spottiswoode 1961.

[73] In *Spain and The Great Powers* Puzzo suggests that DEUTSCHLAND's presence also prevented the bombardment of Ceuta by the Republican battleship JAIME I, but this may have been no more than a coincidence.

[74] See also Chapter 4 for a different aspect of the Beira Patrol.

[75] *The Observer*, 30 November 1869. DEDALO was again involved in an expressive confrontation at Gibraltar in 1970. See *The Times* of 3 February.

Chapter Three
THE ALTERED ENVIRONMENT

Historical facts and events are studied not for imitation
and not in a quest for 'prescriptions', but to trace
regularities and to use them as a basis for formulating
the principles of armed struggle best suited to contemporary conditions.

Penzin[1]

I Historical

IT would be surprising if the historical record of any activity so
essentially irregular and *ad hoc* as gunboat diplomacy were to
assume any clearly defined pattern. The conclusions to be drawn from
the analysis of the preceding chapter, or from the more extensive
summary of the Appendix, must accordingly be confined to a few
cautious generalities. First of all, throughout the last fifty years,
albeit with the fluctuations that inevitably result from changes in the
international balance of power, a number of different governments
continued to find various political applications for limited naval
force. Secondly, although the collapse of the Russian and Turkish
Empires, the chaos of China and American policy in the Caribbean
combined to raise gunboat diplomacy during the twenties to sustained
heights of activity not since achieved, the fluctuations of subsequent
decades have not been uniformly downward. The lull of the thirties
prefaced a new peak in the last years of peace; the nadir of 1944 (the
only year without an example) was followed by a fresh outburst as
soon as peace returned and, if the exceptional circumstances of the
Spanish Civil War are excluded, the sixties have seen more use of
limited naval force than the thirties. Thirdly, the varieties of gunboat
diplomacy practised at the beginning of our period may also be distinguished during its later years. Finally, and much more tentatively,
it could be argued that for half a century there has been no clear or
obviously directional trend of change in the principles governing the
use of limited naval force or in the relative incidence of success or
failure in its employment.

It is tempting, but it would be unwise, to seek further lessons in the
record of the past: to argue that more governments use gunboat
diplomacy today than did a century ago; that the rôles of victim and
assailant are now more equally shared between Great Powers and

lesser states; that warships must increasingly be used and not merely moved; that prestige in the sixties had lost the potency it still possessed in the twenties. These, however, are essentially impressions. They could be challenged on a different interpretation of history: they could be destroyed by the events of the coming decade. It is better to content ourselves with the one outstanding regularity that emerges from this survey of fifty lawless years: the continued and frequent use, in one form or another, of limited naval force as a supplement to diplomacy and as an alternative to war.

Nevertheless, this is not the conclusion, but only the indispensable foundation, of our inquiry into the future usefulness of this expedient. The evidence for the repeated and recent use of this type of force had to be deployed to refute the widespread illusion that gunboat diplomacy is already obsolete. It will not suffice to disprove its obsolescence. Similar arguments were used, with a success that was unfortunate, to convince the British Government that the progress of mechanical innovation had not, even in the late thirties, diminished the traditional importance and effectiveness of horsed cavalry. Historical analogies can only constitute the first step towards the crucial question: have technological and political developments so altered – or are they likely, in the near future, so to transform – the environment in which limited naval force must operate, that this ancient instrument of diplomacy must now be regarded as nearing the end of its useful life?

The most practical approach to an answer may be to adopt the standpoint of the victim and to consider how far technological or political changes can be expected to increase his ability to resist or avoid the coercion of gunboat diplomacy. These will constitute the obstacles which future assailants, if this expedient still attracts them, must find new ways to overcome. The existence of potential assailants need not be argued. With their traditional preference for doing what was done last time, governments are certain to seek means of pressure more vigorous than diplomacy, but less violent than war, and for this purpose, at least to consider the use of their navies.[2]

The potential threat is thus taken for granted and we shall initially only be concerned with the means to meet it. These fall into three categories: deterrence – measures to discourage the assailant from even attempting the use of limited naval force; defence – measures to prevent the assailant who actually uses force from achieving his objective; and counter-attack – measures to induce the assailant to disgorge what his use of limited naval force has already swallowed. If a rational assailant is convinced in advance that his victim's defence or counter-attack can be expected to succeed, he will naturally be deterred from attempting the use of limited force, unless he is prepared to proceed to war, so deterrence as such will be examined primarily as the threat of war, other varieties being considered as aspects of defence and counter-attack. All three means of resistance will also be taken to include the help which the victim can expect from third parties and will be discussed in the light first of technological and then of political developments.

II Technological

The first category of developments to be considered might almost equally well be termed military, for they are mainly concerned with the threat or use of armed force. Yet it is neither the existence of exceptions nor mere modishness that dictates a preference for this fashionable adjective. We are, after all, dealing with change and the purely military – or the purely political – principles of resistance to limited naval force were not unknown to the Counts of the Saxon Shore. Deterrence is a case in point. Where this means the threat of war, it has always been impaired by two factors of uncertainty. First of all, the victim – or his allies – might only be bluffing. Secondly, even if the threat were implemented, it might not prove very damaging to the assailant, who could hope to win the war, with or without the assistance of his allies, or at least to terminate it in circumstances no more disadvantageous than those that might have resulted from an initial abstention from the use of limited naval force. Many governments have been more prone to exaggerate than to under-estimate their chances of sinking the enemy's fleet, defeating his army, shooting down his bombers or exhausting his resolution.

Nowadays, however, it is often argued that the development of nuclear weapons has already invested deterrence with a new verisimilitude: that the United States and the Soviet Union each possess an assured capacity for inflicting intolerable damage on anyone else; that Britain, France and China have a good chance of doing more damage than any user of limited force would care to risk; and that the likely further diffusion of these weapons may soon enable other countries, even if defeated in war, to inflict greater injury than most conquerors have previously been prepared to contemplate. Even a country without a sophisticated delivery system may already have the technical ability to construct a small nuclear bomb and smuggle it into the capital of a Super-Power. In principle, at least, these are real changes from the days when a British admiral could guarantee the invulnerability of his country by saying, 'they cannot come by sea', or Bismarck could laughingly proclaim his intention of sending for the police if the British fleet appeared off the coast of Pomerania.

In practice, of course, even the most formidable of nuclear deterrents has its limitations. It did not help the United States to avoid or resist the exercise of limited naval force by North Korea,[3] and it is easy to imagine other situations in which a nuclear power could not expect the threat of nuclear war to constitute a convincing deterrent. Nevertheless, although deterrence is not – and probably never can be – absolute, its dimensions have been significantly altered. There exists today a power to hurt which can be exerted more swiftly, more devastatingly and more certainly than ever before, a power from which neither the strong nor the victorious are immune and a power which is perhaps most dangerous when its controllers are least rational. Even the dying bee may now have a deadly sting to deliver.

The likely influence of this new power on gunboat diplomacy is less easy to discern. So far it has not been employed[4] and, though it has often been threatened, the Cuban crisis of 1962 was perhaps the only occasion of which it can be said with any degree of assurance that one government demonstrated belief in another's threat of nuclear war by a significant change in policy. Most threats tend to be discounted, because most uses of nuclear weapons would expose the user to unavoidable and intolerable retaliation. There has thus been a general assumption that nuclear weapons would only be employed under extreme provocation. Just how extreme no one is sure and, to some extent, the principle of uncertainty acts both ways. There is enough risk that the invasion of West Germany, or North Vietnam, would lead to nuclear war to constitute an effective deterrent in most circumstances. But the further one descends the scale of provocation, the less credible becomes the threat of nuclear war, so that it is now widely accepted that a deliberate process of escalation – as was adopted even in the fairly extreme crisis of 1962 – or an equally elaborate demonstration of prior commitment – as at Checkpoint Charlie – would be required to convince an opponent that the threat was seriously intended.

Escalation and commitment, however, are manœuvres ill-adapted to most of the situations in which limited naval force might be employed. If the credibility of deterrence is to be reinforced by a prior commitment, for instance, it is not enough to issue a verbal warning in general terms. The adversary must be told precisely which of his actions will incur what retaliation and words must be emphasized by visible military preparations, often even by the physical interposition of troops or warships.[5] And the lower the level of the objectionable act that is to be deterred, the more elaborate must be the apparatus of commitment to convince the opponent that even this seemingly trivial move will bring down on him the murderous – and also potentially suicidal – weight of nuclear attack. When the object of deterrence is the use of limited naval force, these considerations have two awkward consequences. First of all, one cannot credibly commit oneself to nuclear retaliation against a specific act unless the nature of this act can be foreseen. This is not always, indeed it is seldom, true of the use of limited naval force. Secondly, even if the act can be foreseen, a nuclear power should be capable of devising deterrents more effective and economical than the ponderous ritual of nuclear commitment. It is hard to imagine any process of prior commitment that could have made nuclear deterrence a more effective safeguard for PUEBLO than a flotilla of escorting destroyers.

Prior commitment, moreover, is necessarily a publicized and provocative process which is more liable to be answered in kind, and thus to usher in a potentially neutralizing escalation, than is the discreet deployment of a conventionally effective defence. In 1958, for instance, a fairly elaborate Soviet escalation failed to frighten the Americans into withdrawal from the Lebanon and, even if this landing had been foreseen in Moscow, an equally ostentatious prior commitment might not have sufficed to deter it as effectively as, eleven years later, the mere presence of the Soviet Mediterranean squadron probably helped to discourage any repetition.[6]

This does not mean that the threat of nuclear war can never have any impact on the use of limited naval force, even in situations where the nuclear armoury of one Super-Power is balanced by that of the other. Without this menace of last resort gunboat diplomacy might be used still more frequently and in less limited forms. But, as long as a convincing threat of nuclear war continues to present greater difficulties and complications than those which, in pre-nuclear days, attended a threat of ordinary war, it seems reasonable to conclude that, in any situation liable to involve both Super-Powers, it will constitute a lesser deterrent. Indeed, it is arguable that their nuclear armoury has actually made both Super-Powers more cautious and more tolerant of affronts, either to themselves or to their clients, than were the Great Powers of the nineteenth century. It is today inconceivable that either the United States or the Soviet Union would contemplate war because the cruiser of one navy turned her guns towards the cruiser of another. Yet, in 1893, 'for some twenty-four hours it was supposed that the French had deliberately challenged us and that war was inevitable. It was reported in the Foreign Office that the telegrams had been shown to the German Emperor, who was then visiting Queen Victoria, on his yacht at Cowes, and that he had expressed with evident satisfaction the opinion that there was no way out of the incident but war.'[7]

This effect of nuclear technology is not necessarily lasting. The nuclear powers have so far been circumspect, because none of them (except the United States during the first decade of the nuclear era) has yet encountered a situation in which they could expect – still less induce others to expect – their use of these weapons to remain unilateral. Even in 1956, when the United States had temporarily turned on their own allies, they were prompt to counter a Soviet nuclear threat to Britain, which consequently exercised less influence than American financial sanctions. But this state of affairs could change. A nuclear power might temporarily acquire a relative invulnerability or nuclear weapons might pass into the control of leaders impervious to any rational fear of retaliation. Circumstances could drive a government to such desperation that a nuclear strike might seem a conceivable response even to an act of limited naval force. Civil war or revolution, for instance, might deprive a Great Power, even a Super-Power, of every other means of organized defence, yet leave potential assailants wondering whether their intervention might provoke a maddened ruler to the discharge of those missiles whose controllers might still be prepared to obey him. These are conceivable contingencies, but so far they are only hypothetical exceptions to the tentative rule that nuclear war is not a credible deterrent to actions which, almost by definition, do not affect the central balance of power. But, suppose nuclear weapons, and the means of their delivery, were acquired by so many states that the central balance ceased to have any significance, that these weapons were regularly employed in the minor wars of lesser states, what use would then remain for gunboat diplomacy? There is no answer to a question involving so many unknown factors, except, perhaps, to recall that the widespread diffusion of firearms in the United States has not yet deterred American citizens from the use of their fists in petty quarrels. We are only concerned with the foreseeable future in which nuclear weapons are more likely to reduce, than to increase, the effectiveness of the threat of war as a deterrent to the use of limited naval force.

Defence is a different matter. Here we are not concerned with nuclear weapons, which are instruments of war, but with new developments which might assist a victim to prevent the achievement of the assailant's objective or else might raise the cost of achieving this to the level of war. This kind of defence demands a local and limited response, although, for reasons to be discussed when we turn to political developments, the victim can often afford a higher degree of violence than the assailant. But a reaction that extends to war is not, for our immediate purpose, one of defence, while any form of retaliation against the assailant, rather than against the forces actually employed in his intervention, will be considered separately as a counter-attack.

The first requisite of successful defence is, as always, detection. Without it even a victim stronger than his assailant may be unable to prevent the latter from establishing a local superiority sufficient to achieve his purpose. Here radar, aerial reconnaisance, even observation from satellites, have impaired the traditional ability of warships to make a surprise appearance over the horizon. Only a submarine – and this is a vessel ill-adapted to gunboat diplomacy – could nowadays count with complete confidence on an unobserved approach and the major warships of the principal naval powers are under more or less constant surveillance by their rivals. As accurate intelligence of the opponent's movements is usually more important to the victim (who may well himself be relying on fixed defences) than to the assailant, this is one way in which technological progress may operate to the detriment of gunboat diplomacy. But the operative word is 'may': no victim was ever better equipped to detect the approach of an assailant, even to deduce his intentions, than the u.s.s. PUEBLO or the u.s.s. LIBERTY.[8]

Nevertheless, even allowing for human error, political surprise and the use of electronic counter-measures by a sophisticated assailant, the average victim's chances of early warning have improved. So have his means of local defence. Cruise missiles, bomber aircraft, radar-controlled guns, coastal submarines, modern mines; all these are formidable, and nowadays not uncommon, impediments to the kind of offshore manœuvre that gunboat diplomacy so frequently entails. Even as long ago as 1958 or 1961 the American and British Navies found it prudent to intervene in formidable strength and at corresponding expense against potential opponents – Syria and Iraq[9] – that might once have been overawed by a single warship (though the Shanghai intervention of 1927 was on an even larger scale than the landings in Kuwait and the Lebanon). Yet, if the cost-effectiveness of these operations is compared with that of others where gunboat diplomacy could not be employed – confrontation against Indonesia, war in Vietnam – the expense of limited naval force is seen to have risen less than the international cost of living. And the Soviet intervention of July 1967, no less than the capture of PUEBLO the following year, demonstrated that even the bargain basement is not yet entirely depleted. Technological progress has

certainly made it more difficult to employ limited naval force successfully – though even the nineteenth century occasionally witnessed the
impotence or repulse of the Royal Navy – but it has not rendered it
impossible in the favourable circumstances it has always required. In
1967 the destruction of the Israeli destroyer EILAT while patrolling
off Port Said made a profound impression on naval opinion, but she
was, after all, acting with an imprudence scarcely rivalled since the
ill-fated patrol of the Broad Fourteens by H.M. ships ABOUKIR,
CRESSY and HOGUE.[10] And both these incidents occurred in war.

Nor have the effects of innovation been entirely one-sided. The
helicopter carrier provides the assailant with a new, and most effective, means of bringing limited naval force to bear on objectives well
inshore. Landing craft enable him to avoid defended harbours and
concentrate tanks on deserted beaches. The hovercraft may prove an
even more flexible instrument, its high speed permitting surprise
landings beneath the victim's radar from a fleet well out to sea. Even
the submarine might come into its own for specialized operations –
landing a small party unperceived by night to kidnap or rescue a
leader – as General Giraud was rescued in 1942.[11]

The difficulty of assessing the impact of technological advance on
the prospects of gunboat diplomacy is, of course, increased by the
very different objectives of the technologists, whose innovations have
often been prompted by the supposed needs of nuclear war, trade
protection or the hazily envisaged contingency of a limited war
fought at sea by the main fleets of important naval powers. The US
Sixth Fleet, for instance, was originally sent to the Mediterranean for
political purposes[12] and it has discharged a variety of diplomatic
functions, but its composition and equipment were long modified by
the different rôle of supporting American capacity to discharge a
nuclear strike against the Soviet Union. Even today, when the main
deterrent burden has been taken over by the Polaris submarines, the
possibility of instant war overshadows the aircraft carriers and their
long-range aircraft. The ever-watchful radar on the screening
destroyers and frigates, the anti-submarine patrols, the disposition
and movements of the fleet, the daily preoccupations of the com-
manding Admiral: all these are influenced by the need for instant
response to the fatal signal from Washington. And, as long as these
American vessels sail that classic sea, particularly in its Eastern
region, their movements are usually noted, and their positions
plotted, by Soviet warships, one of whose tasks may be to anticipate
the launching of bombers by sinking their elaborately guarded
carriers. Both fleets have additional capacities, extra rôles, but at
moments of crisis each may become partially absorbed in the task of

tracking and out-guessing the other.[13] Neither could then afford to relax an instant readiness or to divert their full potential from preoccupation with nuclear Armageddon.

This is not an entirely new phenomenon, nor has the need for ever-increasing sophistication in equipment and training yet deprived the United States Navy of their capacity for simpler forms of intervention, a capacity now being expanded by their Soviet rivals. But it does provide a question-mark for the future. Will the time come when the demands of readiness for nuclear war can only be met by ships, sailors and equipment inherently less suited to the exercise of gun-boat diplomacy than the more moderate navies maintained by nations who have opted out of the nuclear race? There have already been certain pointers in this direction. Not only was the U.S.S. PUEBLO more defenceless than almost any warship that has ever sailed the seas, but the press reported at the time of her capture that some of the American aircraft that might otherwise have intervened were inhibited by their exclusively nuclear armament. Might the Super-Powers be forced to maintain two navies, one a mere floating adjunct to the deterrent, the other equipped for more humdrum, and we may hope, more likely tasks? And, if they could afford such wasteful duplication, could anyone else? Perhaps the day of the general purpose navy, as ready for war as it was adaptable to the more varied exigencies of peace, has already passed.

This is a problem that requires and, when we examine actual navies, particularly those of the middling navies, will receive, further consideration. For the moment we need only note that the peace-time effectiveness of the world's largest navies may sometimes be reduced by their maintenance of instant readiness for war: some ships are too precious, too crammed with fragile and indispensable equipment, to be risked inshore. Others cannot be spared from their picket duties or their ceaseless surveillance of the potential enemy. Between the two world wars, destroyers were released from attendance on the battle-fleet and readily available for other duties – in 1937 Britain and France provided eighty to patrol the Western Mediterranean. But Admiral Jellicoe would as soon have sailed unescorted from Scapa Flow as the Commander of the Sixth Fleet, in today's piping time of peace, would strip his carriers of their screen.

This pre-emption of naval resources by the potential needs of nuclear war is itself a result of technological change that tends to favour the victim, who is more likely to be one of the lesser nations unconcerned by such problems than a Super-Power. But it has also increased the scope for a particular application of limited naval force: inhibiting the operations of a rival fleet. In 1932 Admiral Kelly had to go alarmingly far in making his presence felt by the Japanese,[14] because only a declared intention or an overt act then made one peace-time fleet an immediate menace to another. Today, American and Soviet warships need not even be mutually visible to know that each is the target assiduously plotted by the other.

This reduction in the peace-time availability of navies is not the only way in which technological progress, while distributing its favours impartially between offence and defence in actual war, nevertheless tends to favour the victim rather than the assailant in the very different conditions of gunboat diplomacy. From this judgment, however, we must exempt the definitive use of limited naval force. This is a rare variety, only applicable in specially favourable circumstances, but, when these exist, capable of placing even a Super-Power at a disadvantage. Because it exploits speed and surprise to create a momentary and local superiority, the price of an effective defence is not so much technical sophistication as a perpetually imaginative vigilance – a price even the world's wealthiest nation was evidently unprepared to pay for the protection of PUEBLO; a vigilance that Egypt, after weeks of maximum tension and suspicion, fatally relaxed on the morning of 5 June 1967. No degree or diffusion of technological progress will ever eliminate those intervals of human inattention or negligence that, in war as in peace, must continue to permit the naval bolt from the blue to create an occasional *fait accompli*.

Purposeful and catalytic force (we may safely neglect the expressive mode) are a different matter. These require time to take effect, or for confusion to resolve itself, and time is now more likely to enable the victim to muster his defences than to sap his resolution. The reasons for this are mainly political, and, as such, will be considered in their proper place, but there is also a technical aspect. Modern warships are designed for swift and sudden combat on, or beneath, the open seas, not for lingering offshore. The deliberate approach, the manœuvres for position, the leisurely broadsides of the traditional naval battle: these and the opportunities they afforded for evasion or disengagement have receded into history. Now the ideal is to destroy the enemy before he is in range, the essential to do so before he opens a fire that warships are no longer constructed to withstand.[15] These are tactics ill-adapted to the use of limited naval force. If the defences are smothered at the outset – as at Suez – this may entail an act of war. If they are allowed the initiative, the cost may be far heavier than anything risked by the gunboats of the twenties. It is not technically difficult, or particularly expensive, to threaten a fleet crippled by the dual handicap of confined waters and an initial commitment to minimum violence. At relatively little cost a determined victim can easily equip himself to deny to a far stronger assailant one of the classical gambits of gunboat diplomacy – allowing the looming menace of visible warships time to fray the nerves of those ashore. Admittedly jets can still scream across the roof-tops from a safely distant carrier while helicopters or hovercraft disembark marines to seize key points, capture warships at their moorings and neutralize landward defences. But these manœuvres demand a more elaborate and warlike operation and, above all, a deeper and more uncertain commitment. Technology has provided new resources for amphibious operations, but their employment in acts of limited naval force can carry heavy economic and political penalties, whereas defence, and consequently, deterrence, are now more cost-effective than ever before. In war – or so we are assured – a properly trained and equipped fleet would be immune from anything so simple and inexpensive as a flotilla of Komar boats: in the peculiar conditions of gunboat diplomacy these could be a menace to warships more numerous and far more powerful.[16]

Inshore operations are not, of course, an inevitable feature of the purposeful and catalytic use of limited naval force. The various forms of distant blockade or of interception on the high seas should still leave the advantage with the stronger navy. There are also many nations without effective coastal defence and some whose preparations might be nullified by political disunity. Even today the advantages of the victim are not insuperable. Nevertheless, the sixties produced no convincing example of the employment of limited naval force on a defended coast,[17] and the discernible trends of naval innovation seem unlikely to alleviate the difficulty of such operations during the seventies. Technology, it seems safe to suggest, is not yet ready to extinguish gunboat diplomacy, but is likely to increase its cost and to divert its application towards the open sea or to the coasts of the improvident and irresolute.

The effects of technology in counter-attack are less direct and more intimately intertwined with political factors requiring separate consideration. If we disregard retaliation by acts of war, the new possibilities of counter-attack are all centred on sabotage. The existence of broadcasting stations, the diffusion of domestic receiving sets, improved levels of technical knowledge, the ready availability of firearms and explosives: all these new factors have made it easier for a victim to respond by acts of economic destruction or retorsion that will hurt the assailant more than the victim. Gunboat diplomacy has traditionally been employed to protect economic interests but, if an otherwise successful operation is likely to lead to the cutting of pipelines, the disruption of communications, to strikes and boycotts and the sabotage or hi-jacking of airliners, then this expedient becomes much less attractive. Even if the force employed against Egypt in 1956 had been both limited and successful, the use of the Suez Canal might long have remained dangerous and difficult. Whether or not an otherwise defenceless victim can be expected to react to the exercise of limited naval force by damaging reprisals of this kind is primarily a political question, but technology will probably continue to provide fresh tools for willing hands.

III Political

Political considerations are predominant in all kinds of response to limited naval force, but the military distinctions between deterrence, defence and counter-attack are less relevant than the difference between internal and external factors. It will thus be more convenient, while not losing sight of these three categories, to concentrate on two different kinds of political development: those which affect the victim's own capacity for resistance and those which influence the attitudes and actions of third parties.

Every act or threat – even the possibility of a threat – of limited force confronts the victim government with a range of options. The choice – between spending money on coastal defence or on something else; between resistance and surrender; between retaliation and acquiescence – depends on the general political outlook of the government, on the effectiveness of their administrative authority and on the nature of the popular support they can command. There is also a fourth factor, though this is sometimes difficult to distinguish from external considerations: what experience has conditioned the government to expect. During the twenties and thirties, for instance, suffering the exercise of foreign naval force was such an everyday, such a long-established experience for any Chinese government that mere familiarity must have coloured the choices taken in the light of other considerations. To the bureaucrats of any nation, whatever their ideology and however diverse their real resources, precedent will always be a compelling influence.

For our purposes the general political outlook of the government has little to do with their preference for private enterprise or for socialism, with their authoritarian tendencies or democratic traditions. What matters is the choice they habitually make between maintenance of the authority and independence of the nation–state on the one hand, and such potentially conflicting objectives as peace, prosperity, progress and external ideologies, on the other. A government according a high priority to the preservation of national sovereignty is more likely to divert resources from economic development to coastal defence, to react to infringements (which are a necessary consequence of gunboat diplomacy) by threatening or initiating a war regardless of the likely outcome, by sacrificing the lives of its citizens in even a futile defence, by persisting in reprisals even at great cost to the national economy.

A small, weak state with a government of this kind may seem a much less attractive victim than a stronger nation whose leaders are preoccupied by the material welfare of their people, shrink from violence, take decisions in the light of their immediate advantage and enjoy a reputation for appeasement and compromise. But there is also a third type of government: one divided between loyalty to the interests, however these may be interpreted, of the nation–state and the claims of some wider allegiance: ideological, racial, religious or linguistic. Such a government may react very differently to identical infringements of sovereignty by different assailants: Soviet intervention in Czechoslovakia is not the same as German; interference by an Arab country in the affairs of another is one thing, an American landing in the Lebanon something else.

A prudent assailant will naturally give prior and careful consideration to all these factors in each intervention he contemplates: they vary from one country, one period and one set of circumstances to another. But it would be a rash undertaking, and one subject to an intolerable complexity of qualifications, to postulate a general historical trend towards or away from resistance to external coercion. Too much has been made, for instance, of the defiance which is nowadays so frequent a reaction among Asian and African governments to anything savouring of interference by anyone associated with their former rulers or oppressors. We may admit the fact without making it the basis of a general rule. Certainly warships manned by white sailors can nowadays expect a rougher reception on many of these coasts, but assailants are not always white, nor victims coloured. Any theory which relies on heightened Egyptian resistance to naval intervention must also explain why Japan was a victim in the latter half of the nineteenth century, a conspicuous assailant in the first half of the twentieth and, now that her economic development has outstripped all former records and most of the world, again a victim. It is not enough to point to the defiant chauvinism of Mao Tse-Tung without recalling the even more reckless nationalism of the Dowager Empress. Even the increased diffusion of nationalist sentiment is only partly an obstacle to gunboat diplomacy; it inspires assailants as well as victims and not all modern nationalism finds its expression in the defence of a particular nation–state. We may yet see gunboats achieving easy triumphs in the extension of the Socialist Commonwealth, of Arabism, of *Négritude*.

In looking to the future we may thus find the incidence of change in the capacities and expectations of governments a better pointer than any alteration in their inclinations. Few governments have ever wanted anything more than the maintenance of their own authority or failed to feel resentment and bitter regrets on those occasions when acquiescence in external coercion seemed to offer better prospects of survival than resistance. Important though political attitudes are in determining the choices of individual governments, it may be easier to discern general trends in the means at their disposal rather than in their objectives. Administrative control, for instance, shows an upward tendency that is more obviously widespread than any growth in nationalist intransigence.

This is only partly attributable to technological progress, though telecommunications have naturally been important. The altered structure of most societies, which nowadays demand more centralized control to keep them going at all, the spread of literacy, which provides administrative cadres, the legacies and examples of colonialism: all these have greatly increased the number of states whose governments, as long as they command obedience at all, can nowadays expect it from more of their citizens, and more effectively, than ever before. This is a development almost wholly unfavourable to gunboat diplomacy, traditionally most successful when exerted by a disciplined and co-ordinated navy against a state whose resistance was enfeebled because its inhabitants either received no orders or else disregarded them. During the twenties and thirties, for instance, China was a helpless victim in spite of huge armies, vast quantities of weapons, a substantial number of reasonably modern warships and a widespread and burning popular resentment of foreign interference. Neither nuclear weapons nor the *Thoughts of Chairman Mao* were needed to deny the Yangtse to British warships: a battery of field guns sufficed in 1949 as soon as there emerged an administrative machine capable of harnessing the will and employing the means that had long existed.

Naturally there are now, and will continue to be in the future, instances of states disrupted by civil war, even of states declining into anarchy. There are also states whose administrative structure rests on only the scantiest foundation of national consciousness or political commitment. These are notoriously targets for *coups d'état*, a process much simplified when control of the administration is the only source of authority, but also potential victims of limited naval force whenever this is invited to assist or suppress a *coup*. On the whole, however, the growth of centralized administrative structures can be regarded as a trend that is general, likely to continue and calculated to strengthen the power of governments to resist the exercise of limited naval force.

An even more potent factor, though one which is less general and which has more ambiguous implications, is the growing diffusion of political consciousness. When this takes the form of nationalism it constitutes perhaps the most important single source of strength to a government anxious to resist the purposeful application of limited naval force. Not only does it provide the means of counter-attack – boycotts, strikes, sabotage, passive resistance, terrorism – and hence of deterrence, but it also supplies the incentive. A government expecting popular support for resistance to the foreigner will also see more prospect of continued authority in defiance than in acquiescence. This is the great new strength of such countries as Cuba and Egypt, whose governments can count on popular support not only after outside intervention but also in providing the military means to resist or deter it.

But not all political consciousness finds expression in support for the nation–state or for its government. Pacifism, hedonism, sectarian interests, larger loyalties do not only sap the resolution of potential assailants: they can also make victims of countries not otherwise qualified for that rôle. There could be no greater mistake than to suppose that, because some traditional assailants would now encounter greater difficulty in employing limited naval force against some of their accustomed victims, the general utility of this expedient has therefore declined. The division of the world's nations between assailants and victims is no less subject to change than the relative strength of the world's navies. What one government can no longer do may present fewer problems to another. Gunboat diplomacy is only a tool which anyone can use, not a privilege reserved to a particular class of governments or peoples.

In so far, therefore, as generalizations are possible at all in so complex a field, we may conclude that the predominant trends in international political development have provided, and will continue to provide, governments with new means of deterring, resisting and counter-attacking the application of limited naval force. This is nevertheless a conclusion most applicable to those governments which formerly lacked the confidence to attempt defiance, because they were conscious that orders to this effect would neither be efficiently transmitted nor kindle a popular response. There are

limits even to the predictable diffusion of administrative centraliza-
tion, whereas popular readiness to incur sacrifice to uphold the
integrity of the nation–state is not a reliably directional trend. It is
thus safer to suggest that the political obstacles to gunboat diplomacy
have increased and, in certain countries, are likely to continue increasing, albeit with exceptions and qualifications, than to postulate
any kind of mathematical progression leading ultimately to the ex-
tinction of this expedient. Who, in the aftermath of Suez, would have
predicted success in the Lebanon or in Kuwait? Who, at any time,
would have expected North Korea to get away with the PUEBLO? 'To
every action there is an equal and opposite reaction'[18] and the
heightened toughness of many potential victims will surely be reflected in fresh ingenuities on the part of assailants, who will not
necessarily be the same, or choose identical victims, as in the past.

There exists, it is often argued, a more formidable obstacle to
gunboat diplomacy than the puny efforts of any single state: the force
of international opinion, particularly as this is expressed in the
United Nations. Historically, it is true that there has been a considerable shift in attitudes towards outside intervention. The hierarchy of
nations and the privileged position of Great Powers are less easily
conceded; the fifties and sixties produced fewer examples than the
twenties and thirties of otherwise unfriendly governments combining
to assert a common interest against such a victim as China. The idea
of an international order, a common concern for the rights of property and of the individual, now seem less important than the prerogatives of national sovereignty. When the regular forces – and navies
are almost always that – of one state enter the territory or the territorial waters of another, this is widely regarded as more reprehensible
than any actions which, however significant their international repercussions, do not involve the avowed crossing of frontiers. This is a
widespread sentiment rather than a consistent doctrine. Not all interventions are condemned, nor is every victim encouraged to resist.[19]
The sympathy of third parties usually depends on their ability to
identify with either assailant or victim and the degree of practical
expression given to that sympathy is prompted by interest rather than
ethics. Nevertheless, whereas the use of limited force 'to restore
order' once enjoyed the benefit of some doubt and had to be proved
guilty, there is now an opposite prejudice.

One effect of this change has been in the use of violence. Assailants
and victims have always condemned this in one another but in the
past third parties tended to weigh both sides in scales that, if not
always equal, were seldom biased in the victim's favour. A naval
bombardment would be explained, even excused, by the commission

of atrocities on individual foreign residents. Nowadays there is a widespread feeling that the use of violence by regular forces is less permissible than even worse violence by a mob or popular resistance movement. Terrorism and assassination are accepted as legitimate means of defence or retaliation, a further advantage to the victim. Other results have often been curious. Assailants have not desisted from the use of limited force when opportunities arose or circumstances seemed to require it, but they have justified their action in different terms and have been at pains to associate others in their intervention. The right of one government to protect by force the lives or property of their nationals in the territory of another is nowadays less often advanced as a pretext for intervention (though President Johnson used this argument at the outset of the Dominican affair in 1965). Instead avowedly political motives are proclaimed: to help the victim to overcome externally inspired revolution – or counter-revolution; to overthrow a tyrannous régime; to deter aggression. Whenever possible intervention ostensibly takes place at the invitation of the victim government or of some political group composed of nationals of the victim state. If this cannot be achieved, or as an additional precaution even when it is, efforts are made to give the operation a multilateral cover. The United States make extensive use of the Organization of American States, Britain has tried to enlist the Commonwealth and the Soviet Union went one better by inventing a 'Socialist Commonwealth' for the benefit of Czechoslovakia. Nor are these militarily redundant allies desired only because something done by several seems better than the same thing done by one. Their presence also encourages the notion that the intervention was prompted by 'principles' (preferably embodied in some treaty of convenient ambiguity) rather than by 'selfish vested interests'. None of these devices is entirely new (many British interventions in China extorted treaties by which later interventions could be justified) but they are employed with a frequency and a sophistry that would have startled such candid practitioners as Lord Palmerston or Signor Mussolini.

Prejudice against intervention has another, an equally perverse, but a more practical aspect. Most members of the United Nations have a healthy horror of nuclear war and are particularly anxious to manifest their disapproval of any action that seems liable to provoke one. This tends to enlist sentiment against the use of purposeful or catalytic force, to which nuclear threats or escalation are a possible, though seldom an effective, response, while simultaneously discouraging retaliation against the definitive use of limited force. When US forces landed in the Lebanon, Soviet threats caused more alarm outside the United States than in Washington. When PUEBLO was seized, third parties were less concerned with the morality of this North Korean action than with the risk that the American retaliation might lead to war. In the first case, therefore, the United States were urged to withdraw and in the second to acquiesce. This is naturally a reaction which operates unevenly, because the United States – and other countries with a similar political structure – are rightly assumed to be more amenable to exhortation than governments less exposed to the pressures of public opinion. The resentment aroused by this 'double standard' often impairs the effectiveness of a sentiment that nevertheless has some practical roots; purposeful or catalytic force often poses a greater threat of war simply because it lasts longer and allows more time for tension to build up on both sides. Definitive force is all over when the fuss begins and the only threat of war thus comes from the victim. Although examples of the definitive use of limited naval force are insufficiently frequent to permit firm conclusions, it may be significant that in no instance during the last two decades has the assailant been subjected to significant pressure from international opinion.

These various manifestations of the general sentiment of mankind are perhaps more of a deterrent to sensitive assailants than an encouragement to actual victims, few of whom have recently had much practical assistance from the United Nations. But there have been other, and more important, developments in international relations.

The first of these is bipolarity: the emergence of two mutually antagonistic Super-Powers each with its own magnetic field of attraction for lesser states. This shifting of iron-filings about two fixed and opposite poles is very different from the kaleidoscope of the twenties and thirties, when the relationships of the seven Great Powers were as variable as the estimates of their respective strength. After the comparative stability of the last twenty-five years it requires an effort of the imagination to realize that, as seen from London, France, Germany,[20] Italy, Japan, the Soviet Union and the United States all fluctuated between the rôles of potential ally and principal antagonist. What is even more surprising is that, outside Europe, these shifting patterns actually offered the remaining countries of the world less scope for manœuvre than the more stable divisions of today. The combinations that dissolved and reformed were essentially regional: Japan was only active in Eastern Asia; after the early twenties the United States played no part in Europe, Africa or Western Asia; Britain[21] and France left the Americas alone; Germany's influence was almost exclusively European; Italy made only one significant excursion farther afield and, from 1922 to 1938, the Soviet Union's occasional sallies were made across her Asian borders alone. A handful of lesser states in Europe had a genuine choice of protectors and occasionally exercised it, China had more assailants than one to fear, but the general rule, to which Abyssinia provided a brief and ultimately abortive exception, required the weaker nations outside the European continent to adapt themselves unaided to the exigencies of whichever Great Power happened to dominate that region. Britain alone had any pretensions to being a world power and Britain had no thought of extending an authority she could already scarcely maintain.

From 1945 onwards, however, the United States and the Soviet Union have progressively expanded their respective spheres of influence into a world from which their former competitors have progressively withdrawn. After the early years, when Germany, Eastern Europe and Japan were occupied, they have seldom done so by actual conquest, but by bidding against one another for the allegiance of third states, to whom they have offered protection, arms, economic aid, the blessings of their respective ideologies, and occasional assistance in political change. But the Super-Powers have not achieved a partition of the world between them. Instead their competition has encouraged and stimulated the emergence of more independent states than ever before and has offered to many, both old and new, additional means of asserting and safeguarding a national sovereignty that has sometimes exceeded the expectations, and the desires, of both. China has not been so independent for a century, Cuba for five, Egypt for twenty.

A contemporary victim of limited force ought, therefore, always to have a potential claim to assistance, either as the existing client of a Super-Power or as a state which might turn to one if not aided by the other. In 1956 Egypt was sufficiently adroit to obtain, as had Israel in 1948, the support of both. Unfortunately for the smaller states there are substantial exceptions to this rule. One Super-Power will normally permit the other to discipline its own clients (the Dominican Republic in 1965, Czechoslovakia in 1968) and both are far more reluctant than, for instance, the Great Powers of 1914, to allow the grievances of their clients to involve them in the extremities of mutual war. Egypt, Syria and North Vietnam were left to suffer more than limited force; Laos and South Vietnam have found protection as double-edged as 'liberation'. Nor is it only victims who enjoy, or expect, the qualified support of the Super-Powers. An assailant may sometimes exploit his special relationship to employ limited force with a heightened sense of immunity from retaliation.

More victims can thus hope for assistance than can be entirely confident of receiving it in the desired degree.

Nevertheless these are exceptions that do not disprove the general rule: the existence of bipolarity[22] has increased the ability of weak states to withstand the exercise of limited naval force. They can deter it either by seeking the express protection of a Super-Power or by improving their own defences on the easy terms readily conceded by both the United States and the Soviet Union; they can defend themselves more vigorously in the hope of at least logistic assistance and diplomatic support; they can retaliate with less fear of the consequences. However intemperate their conduct, this will be excused by one Super-Power if it appears to injure the interests of the other. These expectations have not always been satisfied in recent years. They may again be disappointed in the years to come. But they are resources more widely available today than they were even in the fifties.

A less pronounced, but not insignificant, development in international relations is the emergence of associations of states claiming a degree of independence both of the Super-Powers and of the Middle Powers. These groupings vary very considerably in their unity and effectiveness. The so-called Afro–Asian bloc, as the Indian writer Jansen[23] has pointed out, gave India much less support, even verbally, against China than did Britain and the United States. The strongest, in spite of its internecine quarrels, is the Arab League, whose oil resources have been employed with some effect for retaliation. But the poverty of the Africans and Latin-American subservience to the United States still leave them considerable nuisance value, which constitutes an added deterrent to the outside use of limited naval force. It is an irony of history that, after twenty-five years of agitation for European unity, there is today much less likelihood that any such demonstration of solidarity against European intervention would evoke a corresponding response from the divided and increasingly irresolute countries of Western Europe.

Once again, however, we must remember that the existence of a bloc constitutes a stronger disincentive to outside than to internal force. African, Arab, Asian and Latin-American states have shown less reluctance to intervene in one another's affairs, have sometimes obtained external aid for this purpose, and, as their navies develop, may themselves find uses for the gunboat diplomacy that many of them have suffered and only a few have so far practised. Assailant and victim are labels as easily transferable as ally and enemy.

IV Conversely

By now the prospects for gunboat diplomacy may seem gloomy. Technological progress is driving the strongest navies to a pre-occupation with instant war that impairs their peace-time capacity while simultaneously offering victims new means of deterrence, defence and counter-attack. Warships are more vulnerable, less able to employ their visible presence as a sufficient menace, compelled to assemble in greater numbers and to undertake more extensive operations. Only definitive force, the rarest form, may be immune from this bias of change, which is often, though less uniformly, reinforced by the effects of political developments. These give victims added incentives and facilities to acquire and use the weapons now available for their defence. They encourage resistance and, in some circumstances, retaliation and permit a wider licence in violence to the victim than to the assailant. Above all they hold out the hope of assistance. Although new techniques, military and political alike, are also open to assailants, these are not always so uniformly available: the principal naval powers are often politically handicapped, while states with an international licence for assault sometimes lack the warships to carry it out.

So far, however, we have deliberately considered this problem from the standpoint of the victim. As a result the political factors examined have elicited arguments, not so much against the use of limited naval force, as against the use of any force at all. It would be agreeable, but optimistic, to suppose that these arguments – or the more plausible reasoning of writers of greater eminence – would prevail and that diplomacy would no longer be disfigured by a resort to arms. In 1969, another year of conflict in Nigeria, in Vietnam, in the Middle East, a year in which the British Army intervened in strength in Northern Ireland and Eire staged a counter-mobilization, a year when peoples of very different faiths joined in the chorus:

> Now thrive the armourers, and honour's thought
> Reigns solely in the breast of every man:
> They sell the pasture now to buy the horse
> Following the mirror of all Christian kings.[24]

this is unfortunately an illusion requiring no refutation. The question is rather whether limited force is still possible or whether we must resign ourselves to a choice between the equal and opposite horrors of instant nuclear obliteration or indefinitely protracted guerrilla struggle.

This is not a question which can be argued here. Two comments will suffice, not to support, but to illustrate, an optimism essential to the composition of the present work. First of all, the increasing caution of the Super-Powers has confounded the Cassandras of the previous decades. The bombs have *not* gone off and even the rattling of rockets is somewhat on the decline. Secondly, the proliferation and – except in Vietnam – the achievements of guerrillas have fallen short of earlier expectations, whereas limited force, by land if not by sea, has recently had some notable results. Soviet intervention in Czechoslovakia has been much criticized, but the objective was attained with remarkably few casualties. Perhaps the Russians were luckier than some of their critics, but perhaps there is also an inverse ratio between the speed with which adequate force is deployed and the degree of violence this entails. If we assume, therefore, that governments will continue to attempt the coercion of foreigners and that the nuclear revolution will still reinforce the traditional aversion of rational rulers from war, what expedients are available for this purpose? Economic measures need not detain us. Sanctions against Italy, the Arab boycott of traffickers with Israel, the Berlin blockade, the Rhodesian fiasco are only a few of the instances that have rubbed home the lesson learnt by China over a century ago, when even the withholding of the indispensably laxative rhubarb was found inadequate to bring Britain constipated to her knees.[25] There are too many alternative sources of supply and there is too much rivalry among suppliers – a phenomenon much assisted by bipolarity – to make this expedient effective in any but the most unusual circumstances. And then it invites, and has sometimes received, a forcible response. The economic weapon can be a useful supplement: it is not a substitute.

Guerrillas and terrorists, though occasionally effective, even in the territory of an alien victim, require specially favourable political conditions to achieve success. They also constitute a weapon of considerable potential danger to the assailant himself. More governments than one have found these irregulars easier to recruit than to disband. In any case their employment demands the sanctuary of a secure base, either in the victim's territory or in a contiguous state. Not every government, however, enjoys the luxury of an adjacent frontier and guerrillas or an army, its own or a client's, to march across it. And, although Guatemala in 1954, Hungary in 1956 and Czechoslovakia in 1968 are conspicuous exceptions, the movement of armies is hard to confine within the bounds of limited force. This becomes even more difficult if the attempt is made to fly them into some more distant country. Unless airfields have been secured in advance by local sympathizers, this is a hazardous operation and one which confronts the assailant with a choice between initial and perhaps needless violence and the risk of an embarrassing repulse. Parachutists are more easily dropped than withdrawn.

Air forces, on the other hand, cannot be employed on their own without at least the threat of extreme violence. Moreover, bombing, as the experience of Vietnam has so painfully demonstrated, is apt to arouse resentment and outside reprobation before it produces, if it ever does, the compliance intended. Even against the largely defenceless tribesmen of the Yemen and with, so it is widely alleged, the assistance of mustard gas, the Egyptian Air Force were no more successful than their American colleagues against the better equipped people of North Vietnam. It is technically possible to bomb human beings back into the Stone Age, but it has not yet been achieved and it could never be regarded as an act of limited force.

The decisive argument against the use of ground and air forces, however, is often geographical. Unless some contiguous ally offers a base or overflying facilities, a distant victim may only be accessible by sea. Even where these exceptional circumstances exist, naval intervention may seem preferable. The sea still offers a neutral *place d'armes* open to all, where forces may be assembled, ready for intervention, but not yet committed. With greater precautions, perhaps in greater numbers than before, warships can still test the temperature of the water before they venture too far. A ship that has approached the victim's coast, even a fleet that has entered territorial waters, is a lesser involvement than a platoon that has crossed the frontier or an aircraft that has dropped a bomb. And, if intervention takes place but things go wrong, warships are still easier to withdraw.

Naturally it is at the moment of commitment that the assailant must confront and, if he is to achieve success, by-pass or overcome the new obstacles previously noted to the application of limited naval force: the political sanctity of national sovereignty and the military effectiveness of united and organized resistance. These obstacles can, however, be rather less formidable than was suggested in the earlier analysis, which concentrated on the worst case, which is also the rarest case, the purposeful application of limited naval force inshore without any expectation of assistance or acquiescence from the victim until the moment when he finally yields to coercion. Without anticipating the scenarios to be offered in a later chapter, it may be worth while describing some of the easier types of naval intervention that assailants might consider. Being types of operation, this is a military classification according to method which does not coincide with the political classification employed elsewhere: definitive, purposeful, catalytic, expressive.

The first, and most obvious, comprises operations on the high seas: escort, convoy, interception, capture, blockade, surveillance and harassment. Neither the political nor the naval considerations governing such operations have greatly changed since the days of the Spanish Civil War. Provided the assailant enjoys local naval superiority, that he has a colourable pretext for his actions and that he avoids direct confrontation with a stronger naval power, he can still expect to get away with much more at sea than on the land. During the struggle in Algeria, for instance, the French Army were subjected to constant international criticism for their ultimately unsuccessful attempt to restore law and order in French metropolitan territory, whereas the French Navy were not seriously challenged in their probably illegal activities on the high seas. Stopping a merchant ship at sea is just as much an infringement of national sovereignty in international law as crossing a frontier, but it is seldom resented so acutely, either by the victim or by third parties. Indeed, although bipolarity has increased the risk of encountering naval opposition, one earlier disincentive may actually have diminished. There is no longer a predominant navy committed, as the Royal Navy used to be, to the proposition that the seas should be kept open to the ships of all nations not actually hostile to Britain. At sea, there are also more opportunities of employing definitive force, which has fewer political or military snags than the purposeful and catalytic applications.

Even inshore it is also possible to evade or mitigate the obstacles to limited naval force. At the lowest level there is considerable scope for quasi-clandestine, or crypto-diplomatic operations: naval assisted espionage, landing and rescuing agents, perhaps an occasional kidnapping (all operations that are nowadays accorded more international tolerance than formerly), unobtrusive support or opposition to a *coup d'état* or political uprising. One of the crucial factors in many struggles for power, for instance, is the natural concern of leaders for their personal safety or for that of their families. If a friendly warship happens to be in port on a routine visit and is known to be available for a last-minute rescue, leaders may be encouraged to hold out the few extra hours needed for success. Even the rescue of a defeated leader may be useful. The Royal Navy, as will be seen from the earlier pages of the Appendix, once made quite a practice of this, thus providing many foreign politicians with an added incentive to pursue pro-British policies. In the Soviet Union the KGB have recently derived considerable advantage from their own cultivation of a similar tradition which may one day be emulated by the Soviet Navy.

These crypto-diplomatic activities need seldom involve actual violence, as they are conducted clandestinely or with the connivance or acquiescence of those ashore. The point of using a warship is not to overcome opposition by the armed forces of the victim, but to deter and, if things go wrong, to repel interference by the ordinary police, coastguards or mobs. Such methods are naturally only applicable in situations where the involvement of the assailant government can, if necessary, be admitted. If a political upheaval is in progress in a small state, for instance, the outcome may, in any event, decide the possibility of friendly relations with the assailant. If involvement assists the success of the right party in the victim state, their future relations may be even more cordial: if not, they may not be much worse than they would otherwise have been. In such circumstances, particularly if the operation is intrinsically too dangerous for civilians, there could be a strong case for naval participation.

The next level would be overt, but still small-scale operations for the protection of the assailant's embassy, nationals or property in circumstances when organized opposition is unlikely. These have been less common in recent years because of a combination of two political tendencies: a declining interest among some of the naval powers in the safety and prestige of their representatives and nationals abroad; and an increased touchiness in small states about any infringement of their sovereignty. The first factor, however, is one that could easily change, either through altered political attitudes or through an accession of naval strength to governments whose eagerness to protect their citizens has not hitherto been matched by their resources. There are many situations in which a victim government temporarily loses control and only armed intervention from outside can rescue foreigners from the mob. In maritime states, particularly those with capitals on or near the coast, this is a classic case for the use of limited naval force. This type of operation, no less than the crypto-diplomatic, is also well within the capacity of small navies, as it calls for resolution, judgment and good intelligence rather than powerful or numerous warships.

It is at the next level, where significant opposition is likely, that the problem becomes more complex. The obvious method, and one often adopted in recent years, is to arrange for naval intervention to take place at the invitation, or with the acquiescence, of a significant group in the victim state. The government may want assistance against a third state or against an indigenous uprising; a dissident movement may need help to supplant the government. At worst, therefore, opposition to naval intervention will be partially disorganized and hampered by internal conflicts already in progress.

G

At best, the mere show of naval force will be enough to tip the scale and will deter the other side from offering effective opposition. In this type of operation political factors are often predominant and success depends more on the ability to back a winner at the right moment and on the right pretext than on specifically naval skills. Nevertheless, in modern conditions, a full task force will often be needed, both to ensure the protection of the ships and their ability to disengage and also to provide the marines, helicopters, landing craft, etc., necessary for small-scale operations ashore. Such operations, moreover, are particularly vulnerable to harassment by a rival navy. The special problems of the US and Soviet navies in the Mediterranean have already been mentioned, but even an admiral without nuclear preoccupations might find it difficult to concentrate on developments ashore in the presence of an equal or stronger fleet out at sea. Unless the political circumstances are exceptionally favourable (no opposition expected from third parties and nothing very formidable from the victim) this type of operation will demand at least a medium-sized navy and sufficient sympathy from one Super-Power to neutralize any hostility expected from the other.

There is thus a wide range of inshore operations which should still remain feasible in favourable circumstances (which are always required for the exercise of limited force – only war is an ever-open option) for many years to come. Their actual conduct, however, will demand more careful political preparation and more elaborate naval planning than in the past. Governments will seldom be able simply to 'send a gunboat' – or even an amphibious task force – and confide the outcome to the initiative and the improvisation of her commander. Gunboat diplomacy, in common with other contemporary uses of force, even ordinary domestic police work, is going to demand skills more expressly professional than dash and seamanship. Just as amphibious warfare now requires a common training and a single co-ordinated command for soldiers, sailors and airmen, so gunboat diplomacy will need a fusion of political, diplomatic and naval skills. In 1958, the American landing in the Lebanon almost ran into serious trouble at the very outset because of an almost incredible lack of co-ordination among the government in Washington, the Ambassador in Beirut and the marines on the beach. Then luck, the Ambassador's expert improvisation and the prestige of a Super-Power without a naval rival in the Mediterranean enabled the blunder to be surmounted, but even the United States could scarcely afford a repetition and a lesser assailant would have to be far more careful.

Even the utmost skill and care might not, however, overcome the more formidable obstacles to the final category of operations: the inshore coercion of a recalcitrant and undivided victim. There has been no entirely satisfactory example of success in so difficult an undertaking since the Italian seizure of Corfu in 1923. The achievements of the US Seventh Fleet against China were outside the three-mile limit. The German bombardment of Almería was successful, but took place against the background of the Spanish Civil War in which Germany was already deeply, though not avowedly, involved. The similar American retaliation against North Vietnam after the incidents in the Gulf of Tongking in 1964 was a failure: it extracted no concessions and was the prelude to American involvement in virtual war. It may none the less be possible to imagine circumstances in which so difficult a feat might reasonably be attempted. A small state without powerful protectors or unduly formidable coastal defences might have a determined government whose policies attracted strong support from their ruling class and little effective opposition while earning widespread international detestation. In such circumstances an amphibious task force (including an aircraft carrier) might land marines, both on the beaches and by helicopter or hovercraft to seize key points inland, neutralize airfields or other defences by shelling or bombing and, having secured the capital, set up a puppet government to whom generous terms would be offered on condition that the objectionable policies of their predecessors were abandoned or revised. Perhaps Mr Smith had reason to rejoice that Rhodesia has no coast and that Salisbury lies far from the sea, for the military and political obstacles to this imaginary operation might be considerably less than those which have so far deterred the only kinds of intervention which geography would actually permit.

Change, rather than decay, may thus be foreseen for gunboat diplomacy in the altered environment of the seventies and eighties. A reshuffling of identities among assailants and victims, greater sophistication and elaboration in the mounting of operations, a degree of preference for the open sea and new heights of hypocrisy in public justification are all predictable trends. The political applications of limited naval force will be less simple, less straightforward, probably less romantic than hitherto, but they may be even more effective. Instead of providing a welcome break in the tedious peace-time routine for dashing young naval officers, they may become the regular preoccupations – and offer the subject of serious study – to the political specialists of future navies. *Qui vivra verra.*

NOTES

[1] Captain First Rank K. Penzin, 'The Changing Methods and Forms of Warfare at Sea', article in *Soviet Military Review*, March 1967.

[2] Even the Koreans, though newcomers to gunboat diplomacy in the twentieth century, have a naval tradition almost as ancient as the British and much older than the Americans.

[3] See Chapter 2.

[4] When the bombs were dropped on Hiroshima and Nagasaki, it is arguable that neither side realized what was at stake.

[5] Even in the extreme Cuban case, enormous effort and expenditure were incurred to demonstrate the serious intent of President Kennedy's words, 'it shall be the policy of this nation to regard any nuclear missile launched from Cuba against any nation in the Western Hemisphere as an attack by the Soviet Union on the United States, requiring a full retaliatory response upon the Soviet Union', Broadcast of 22 October 1962, Robert Kennedy, *13 Days*, Macmillan 1969.

[6] See Chapter 2.

[7] This remarkable occurrence took place off the mouth of the Siamese river Menam and was aggravated by a mistaken report that the French Admiral blockading Bangkok had ordered H.M.S. LINNET to leave that port. It all came to nothing, thanks to the good sense of the French Admiral, who 'without waiting for any demand from us, had sent the Captain of the French cruiser to apologize to the British Captain for the unprovoked breach of naval conduct'. Grey of Fallodon (he was Parliamentary Under-Secretary for Foreign Affairs at the time), *Twenty Five Years*, Chapter 2, Hodder & Stoughton 1925.

[8] See Appendix, 1967 and 1968.

[9] To whom the Soviet Union had supplied not only aircraft, but also a dozen motor-torpedo-boats, then at Basra.

[10] They were all three sunk in succession on 21 September 1914 by the same German submarine.

[11] See Appendix.

[12] See Appendix, 1946.

[13] 'They keep an eye on us – and we do the same to them. . . . I consider it a fundamental part of my job to know where the Soviet forces are in the Med.', Vice Admiral Richardson, Commander US Sixth Fleet reported in *US News & World Report*, 21 July 1969.

[14] See Appendix.

[15] In 1941 an hour's steady shelling by two battleships at close range failed to sink the already crippled BISMARCK, which had to be finished off with torpedoes. One hit could destroy the mightiest of American carriers.

[16] A greater menace than shore batteries, which failed to deter or prevent regular bombardment of land targets by US cruisers during the war in Vietnam, see 'The Eight-Inch Gun Cruiser', article by Commander Richard F. Rockwell in *USNIP*, January 1970.

[17] The Bizerta operation of 1961 (see Appendix) was the nearest approach, but the main defensive positions were not in Tunisian hands.

[18] Isaac Newton op. cit.

[19] Efforts to condemn the seizure of Goa and American intervention at the Bay of Pigs failed to secure the requisite majorities in the United Nations.

[20] This is an over-statement where Germany is concerned, but it was the implication of the Locarno Agreement.

[21] See Appendix, 1924, for an interesting exception to this rule.

[22] If China eventually provides a third magnetic pole, this seems more likely to give victims an extra option than to transform the system.

[23] Jansen, G. H., *Afro-Asia and Non-Alignment*, Faber and Faber 1966.

[24] *Henry V*, Act II, Chorus I.

[25] Arthur Waley, *The Opium War Through Chinese Eyes*, p. 33, George Allen & Unwin 1958.

Chapter Four

NAVAL CAPACITIES AND DOCTRINES

> An American child crying on the banks of the Yangtse
> a thousand miles from the coast can summon the ships
> of the American Navy up that river to protect it from
> unjust assault.
>
> *Wilbur*[1]

THE purpose of this chapter is to examine the resources available to various governments for the political application of limited naval force and to consider how far their previous words or actions indicate their readiness to employ this expedient. Obviously this cannot be a comprehensive survey. *Jane's Fighting Ships* lists over a hundred navies and, even if all those with good reasons for not venturing beyond their own territorial waters are excluded, too many remain for even cursory treatment in a single chapter. It may thus be better merely to attempt the definition, and the illustration by examples, of zones of probability for the exercise of limited naval force. The object would be to establish the minimum naval resources required before a government could reasonably contemplate resort to this expedient at different levels. These are naturally purely naval calculations and necessarily subject to wide margins of error. A government may have enough ships, but lack the will to employ them; another may attempt operations beyond the true capacity of the naval resources available; a third may rightly believe that the personal qualities and professional skills of their sailors will outweigh the deficiencies of their ships. In principle, however, it should be possible to deduce from the state of a navy the kind of operational ceiling that was expressly proclaimed for Britain in 1966:

> It is only realistic to recognize that we, unaided by our allies, could not expect to undertake operations of this character (the landing or withdrawal of troops against sophisticated opposition outside the range of land-based air cover).[2]

Admittedly, this was as much a political as a military decision and few other governments have set such explicit bounds to their ambitions. But it was supported by the argument that operations of the excluded type required the use of aircraft carriers, which Britain did not propose to retain. If, therefore, we find that certain levels of operation demand particular types of warship, or the possession of a minimum number of warships, we may legitimately regard such operations as being above the normal ceiling of navies which do not meet these requirements.

Unfortunately this attempt to circumscribe zones of probability entails the infliction on the reader of yet another set of categories. When we were concerned with the political objectives of limited naval force and asked *why* this was employed, we spoke of definitive, purposeful, catalytic and expressive force.[3] In answering the question *how* this force was employed, distinctions were drawn between one type of operation and another, on the high seas and inshore, for instance.[4] Now the problem is *what* resources are needed for different levels of operation and the following seems the most useful classification, in ascending order of resources required:

SIMPLE SHIP	(use of individual warships where significant resistance is not expected)
SUPERIOR SHIP	(use of individual warships able to overcome expected resistance)
SIMPLE FLEET	(unopposed tasks beyond the capacity of single ships, e.g. blockade)
SUPERIOR FLEET	(tasks demanding numerous ships able to overcome expected opposition)
SIMPLE AMPHIBIOUS	(unopposed landings from ships unlikely themselves to be attacked)
OPPOSED AMPHIBIOUS	(landings where significant opposition is expected)

Simple ship operations are within the capacity of at least fifty navies, all of whom have warships with enough speed, endurance, armament and seaworthiness to intercept merchant vessels on the high seas or to reach and enter the territorial waters of another state. Thirty-seven of these navies, by undertaking actual operations outside territorial waters since 1939, have provided a recent demonstration that they possess the necessary minimum of seamanship and twenty-four have used limited naval force, as defined in the present work, on at least one occasion during this period. And these statistics of experience exclude some very efficient navies (that of Sweden, for instance) which undoubtedly possess the capacity for gunboat diplomacy, but which have been prevented by circumstances or the policy of their government from exercising this art. At this very elementary level, therefore, further argument or illustration would be superfluous. Proved capacity for simple ship operations is widespread and probable capacity even greater. And, as so many of these operations are regarded by the initiating government as self-evidently legitimate (arresting a ship in an area of the high seas over which the assailant claims special rights not recognized by the victim, for instance), domestic political inhibitions are often minimal. This is a game which almost anyone can, and, in favourable circumstances, quite probably will play.

Simple ship operations are not, of course, necessarily so innocuous. The 'unknown' submarines of the Spanish Civil War or the anonymous warships which mined the Corfu Straits in 1946 expected no resistance and, in the latter case, encountered none. Such drastic applications of limited naval force have latterly been infrequent, but, if altered political circumstances were again to make them appear expedient, a modern assailant might profit by two contemporary developments. Submarines and minelayers are now so widespread as to permit a more genuine uncertainty regarding the national origin of their depredations and nuclear submarines, in particular, are admirably suited for sinking merchant ships without revealing their identity.

The field for *superior ship* operations is slightly more restricted, even though the principle of superiority relates only to the particular operation, or class of operations, envisaged. A superior ship does not have to be a supreme ship. Indeed, there is no warship afloat which cannot be sunk by something. On the other hand, a warship which might expect to emerge victorious from a desperate battle with a given rival is not a sufficiently superior ship for gunboat diplomacy, which aims at achieving results without extremes of violence liable to lead to war. Ideally, a superior ship is one to which no more than token resistance will be offered, because even the victim recognizes that any attempt would entail certain defeat. This is not an outcome which can safely be predicted without considering a specific operation against a known victim, because national attitudes differ so widely in these matters. Some governments issue standing instructions that superior force is not to be resisted; others expect heroic sacrifices; many would probably attach as much importance to the identity of the assailant as to his strength. A Peruvian naval officer, for instance, might be excused for yielding to the demands of an American warship, but would risk the firing-squad if his assailant, however superior, had been Ecuadorean.

Nevertheless, however much circumstances can alter cases, serious resistance is inherently less likely if the assailant is manifestly superior, whereas, whatever the political conditions, officers of any nationality will always at least be tempted to open fire when challenged by a warship of inferior or even equal strength. And, for this purpose, the appearance of superiority may be more important than its reality. The hierarchy of warships is today more misleading than ever. The strongest battleship afloat, the U.S.S. NEW JERSEY, could be out-ranged as well as out-manœuvred, if anything so improbable as a single-ship duel were to take place, by the Soviet destroyer ADMIRAL GOLOVKO,[5] but an uninstructed public opinion might make it embarrassing for NEW JERSEY's commander to behave with the circumspection demanded by the facts but seemingly inconsistent with naval nomenclature. A superior ship must obviously and generally be recognizable as such, which usually means that there must be more than one. It is highly improbable that, in 1963, either the French or the Brazilians ever contemplated anything so extreme as a naval battle resulting from their dispute over lobster catching,[6] but contemporary press reports suggest a remarkable Brazilian naval concentration (involving the cruiser BARROSO, five destroyers and two corvettes) in response to the dispatch of the single French destroyer TARTU. Admittedly the Brazilian press reported (and the French denied) that TARTU would be reinforced by a naval squadron (including the small aircraft carrier ARROMANCHES) then off the West African coast. Nevertheless, just as the dispatch of TARTU was prompted by the desire to *marquer le coup*,[7] so the Brazilian concentration may reasonably be regarded as the gathering of a force sufficiently superior to invest the withdrawal of TARTU (she was temporarily replaced by a warship so small as to be entirely symbolic) with the character of prudence rather than pusillanimity. The encounters of gunboat diplomacy often resemble those of the Condottieri of Renaissance Italy, which were not decided by fighting but by manœuvre, one side withdrawing or yielding once the other had assembled superior forces in an advantageous position.

A particularly good example of the definitive use of this superior ship technique occurred on 6 May 1937, when the British battleship ROYAL OAK and her two escorting destroyers interposed themselves between the Spanish nationalist cruiser ALMIRANTE CERVERA and some Spanish merchant vessels carrying 2,500 Republican refugees (mainly children) away from Bilbao. The intentions of both sides were made explicit in an exchange of signals, ALMIRANTE CERVERA protesting:

> I got orders from my government to stop any Spanish ship leaving Bilbao. I protest if you stop me in the exercise of my rights.

and ROYAL OAK replying:

I have orders from my government to protect them on the high seas.[8]

ALMIRANTE CERVERA gave way gracefully and it is interesting to note how relatively amicable most of these encounters were, though a signal from one of ROYAL OAK's escorting destroyers (*not* to the Spaniards) during this incident records that ALMIRANTE CERVERA's starboard torpedo tubes were not loaded, thus showing that the British at least were alert to the possibility that this could be more than a contest in resolve.

The value of employing a superior ship was, of course, realized at the time. After an earlier encounter between British destroyers and ALMIRANTE CERVERA, British destroyers off the northern coast of Spain were reinforced first by a cruiser and then by the battle cruiser HOOD, the latter flying the flag of the Vice-Admiral Battle Cruiser Squadron. Soon afterwards, on 27 April 1937, Vice-Admiral Geoffrey Blake made this significant recommendation, which the Commander-in-Chief Home Fleet endorsed when he forwarded it to the Admiralty:

> to avoid 'incidents', i.e. the Spanish warship opening fire on a British merchant ship, or warship, the British warship present must be unquestionably more powerful than the largest Insurgent ship.[9]

In modern conditions, of course, it might be more difficult to establish superiority so clearly: in 1937 a battleship, with or without accompanying destroyers, was manifestly stronger than a cruiser, but the capital ships of today – aircraft carriers and ballistic missile submarines – are scarcely suitable for single-ship operations. Submarines, for instance, lose much of their potency as soon as they reveal themselves and would thus seem ill-suited to the superior ship rôle, though admirably adapted to defence or deterrence, particularly in their own territorial waters, where it is politically easier for them to launch a surprise attack on the assailant's ships. Nevertheless, it is conceivable that one submarine might surface to announce that others remained hidden below and that this implied threat might seem compelling to a single warship ill-equipped for sophisticated anti-submarine warfare. In many of these contests in resolve, moreover, the decisive factor will not be the certainty of victory in naval battle, but the extent to which the victim can plausibly plead *force majeure* to his own government and public opinion.

Therefore, although success can only be predicted, if at all, after considering the particular circumstances of a specific operation, failure is likely to await any assailant unable to employ a force that is at least plausibly superior. This immediately allows us to exclude some otherwise efficient navies whose resources or whose geographical situation make it inherently unlikely that they could ever employ convincingly superior force in any operation to which resistance was expected. The Belgian Navy, for instance, makes an important contribution to the minesweeping resources of NATO, but has no vessels capable of outfacing another warship or overawing a foreign port. The Finnish Navy is as efficient as the martial valour of the Finns is unsurpassed, but the Baltic contains no potential victim whose resistance could be overcome by two Finnish frigates.[10] To qualify for the superior ship category a navy must be capable of deploying a demonstrably stronger force against an armed victim within its operational radius. This does not mean an ability to defeat the entire armed forces, even the whole navy, of the victim, but only to cope with the opposition likely in some plausible contingency. Suppose, for instance, that defectors seized a Swedish ship in Lübeck and set out across the Baltic in quest of political asylum in Sweden and that they were pursued by an East German warship. Whichever vessel the East Germans chose for this purpose, the two Swedish missile destroyers could, with complete naval confidence, interpose themselves to prevent interception.

Superior ship operations, however, demand more than the ability to produce two ships in circumstances where the victim has only one. The best of navies does not have all its ships available all the time; the most reckless would usually be reluctant to commit all it had to a single operation in which, however limited the intentions of the assailant and the expected response of the victim, there would always be some risk of loss or damage. If two ships are sent, for instance, one would normally expect that more would be available to reinforce or rescue them and that the combined total would still be substantially less than national naval resources. Unfortunately these ideas are desperately hard to quantify. A reckless assailant undertaking a brief operation against a weak victim within a couple of hours steaming needs so much less than a prudent admiral would demand in different circumstances. The sixties alone produced half a dozen instances of relatively small navies using or threatening limited force in conditions where resistance was possible. The most one can say is that, whereas inadequate resources only constitute a major obstacle to superior ship operations for a relatively small number of seaworthy navies, many more are likely to regard these as too difficult in most circumstances. But any kind of list would be futile because it would be riddled with qualifications and exceptions. In purely naval terms and bearing in mind that favourable circumstances are always required for the exercise of gunboat diplomacy, the minimum resources demanded by superior ship operations are too low to constitute a useful ceiling.

Politically the case is different. Although no country which goes to the expense of maintaining a dozen seaworthy warships is likely to exclude the possibility of their employment against an inferior force outside territorial waters, the possibility of encountering resistance does introduce a psychological barrier which did not exist at the simple-ship level. Mere declarations that navies are maintained for defensive purposes alone are worthless – governments seldom regard their own use of armed force in any other light – but there are many countries whose policies, whose traditions or whose national characteristics would inhibit them from naval initiatives involving an element of risk. Unfortunately these inhibitions are neither reliable (governmental attitudes can change and risks be under-estimated) nor directly related to the size and naval resources of states. In Israel, for instance, the word 'impossible' appears to be imperfectly understood and, if the methods employed in augmenting the strength of the Israeli Navy were wrongly described by the press as 'gunboat diplomacy' (there was no use or threat of naval force in the departure from Cherbourg of five gunboats on 25 December 1969) they nevertheless illustrate the futility of setting purely quantitative bounds to possible Israeli use of this expedient in future. Some countries (and not only those important powers who have traditionally enjoyed this advantage) only need to hoist their flag to invest almost any warship with the appearance of a superior ship.

This prestige of the flag is a factor equally applicable to a class of superior ship operations not so far considered: the landing of a small party of marines or sailors capable of overcoming local opposition ashore. This is something much smaller than the opposed amphibious operations to be discussed later. The local resistance might not amount to more than a single battery or a small detachment of troops. Surprise and speed would probably be more important to the assailant than fire-power and such operations would not involve the use of landing craft or any resources not normally available to an ordinary warship, which would be discharging the classical gunboat rôle of the twenties. The prevalence of limited war makes it difficult to quote a really satisfactory recent example – the Cuban raid on the Bahamas in 1963 encountered only minimal resistance[11] – but Israeli exploits against Egypt leave little doubt of their ability to employ this expedient against far stronger opposition. And, if the Israeli raid against Beirut Airport in December 1968 is any guide, a nominal state of peace would not necessarily constitute any political impediment. This was not, of course, a naval exploit, but it was an act of carefully limited and purposeful force intended, by the infliction of damage, to deter the Lebanese Government from allowing their territory to be used as a base for guerrilla operations against Israeli aircraft on foreign territory.

Its political conception and results may not altogether have matched the flawless efficiency of its military execution, but it was not an act of war and, for this very reason, could become a precedent for future naval emulation. There are many lightly guarded coasts open to raids by a single warship and, if the incentive happened to coincide with the prospect of impunity, at least some nations with more ships than scruples. Indeed, if there is a ceiling for this type of operation, it is qualitative rather than quantitative, political not naval.

The real naval boundary is that dividing ship operations from fleet operations. A *simple fleet operation* is more than an operation involving several warships. It is usually some kind of blockade or patrol system intended to bar access to a particular coast, port or sea area. The blockade may be total or intended only to identify and intercept vessels flying certain flags or carrying certain cargoes. The operation may be part of a war or civil conflict and constitute an exercise of limited force only in so far as it is applied to neutrals, or it may have a more pacific and innocent purpose: preventing incursions into the danger zone around a nuclear test or satellite splash-down. During the late sixties, for instance, as much as 40 per cent (by tonnage) of the French Navy was thus employed in the Pacific and the warships dispatched to the area *'pour des besoins de surveillance'*[12] included one aircraft carrier, one cruiser, three destroyers and five frigates.[13] The distinguishing features of this type of operation are that it takes place on the high seas (or in foreign territorial waters), that either the area covered or the number of potential targets demands the co-ordinated use of several warships and that armed resistance is not expected.

Such operations are liable to make heavy demands on naval resources. The newspaper *Figaro* pointed out on 30 November 1966 that the naval concentration required by French nuclear tests in the Pacific had seriously impaired the French Navy's capacity for amphibious intervention during the same period. The Beira Patrol,[14] which began in December 1965, though it was not fully effective before the Security Council Resolution of 9 April 1966, is another case in point. Admittedly this operation took place thousands of miles from British bases and, at the time of writing, has already lasted over four years. Distance and duration so greatly increase the demands on naval resources that it would be unfair to regard the employment of forty-six different warships over a period of two years[15] as typical. In other ways, however, the Beira Patrol was a relatively undemanding operation. As Mr Healey told the House of Commons, it was 'not a blockade, it has the limited object of preventing the arrival at Beira of vessels believed to be carrying oil for Rhodesia'.[16] These were tankers – conspicuous and easily identifiable ships taking many days to reach the Mozambique Channel from their distant loading-points. By the time they arrived in the patrol area, their identity, movements and cargoes had usually been ascertained from other sources and reported to the waiting warships, who were only required to make twenty-eight actual interceptions in over two years.[17] Tactically, therefore, fewer ships were needed for this task than for other simple fleet operations which have been carried out in the past and could be needed again. If the purpose, for instance, is to patrol an entire coast-line in order to intercept motor-boats capable of a high-speed dash within the hours of darkness (carrying arms or infiltrators from nearby ports), then the number of warships required at any one time will be far greater, even if the operation only lasts a few weeks and takes place within easy reach of the assailant's base.

If, therefore, we try to eliminate the time factor by looking only at the resources employed during a period of a few weeks, the additional burden imposed by distance may be regarded as in some measure counter-balanced by the advantages of tactical simplicity, thus permitting us to take the demands of the Beira Patrol as a rough guide to the minimum needs of simple fleet operations. The first point to note is that, for political reasons, naval deployment had to precede arrangements for the use of land-based reconnaissance aircraft. The press reported British warships in the Mozambique Channel during December 1965,[18] but the first Shackleton aircraft only reached the Malagasy Republic on 16 March 1966. Some weeks more elapsed before land-based reconnaissance was fully effective and until then an aircraft carrier was the only alternative to the deployment of the much larger number of warships needed to maintain a purely surface watch. Admittedly, as no armed opposition was expected, a strike carrier was something of a luxury,[19] but only eleven navies have as much as a single helicopter carrier. Nor would one carrier have sufficed. H.M. ships EAGLE and ARK ROYAL took turn and turn about from December 1965 to April 1966. Admittedly *The Times* was unduly pessimistic in arguing on 11 March 1966 that:

for continuous surveillance to be maintained over a period of more than three weeks, two carriers are required.

H.M.S. EAGLE once kept the sea for seventy-two days at a stretch and even longer periods might be possible with a full fleet train. More frequent reliefs, however, are clearly desirable in time of peace. Moreover, as British readers will be well aware, carriers are particularly susceptible to the demands of modernization and tend to spend long periods in dock. A total strength of three carriers is thus needed by an assailant wishing to be sure that he can, at short notice, keep one carrier on continuous surveillance of uncertain duration. Only the British, French and United States Navies have so many and no other country could long sustain a simple fleet operation beyond the reach of shore-based aircraft.

Even when land-based air reconnaissance was available (as it could be in many cases), maintenance of the tactically undemanding Beira Patrol still required a minimum at any one time of two frigates and two Royal Fleet Auxiliaries. According to Rear-Admiral Morgan Giles[20] (who was not contradicted by Mr Foley from the Ministry of Defence) the regular replacement and refitting of two frigates meant monopolizing the services of six, though a total of four auxiliaries would probably suffice to keep two on station. A smaller number might have sufficed for a shorter period, but an assailant could seldom be confident that such a selective patrol (as opposed to a total blockade demanding many more ships) would achieve its objective any sooner. And the longer such a simple fleet operation was expected to last, the greater would be the likelihood that other demands for warships would arise meanwhile. In September 1967 it was even rumoured,[21] though incorrectly, that the Beira Patrol would have to be abandoned because the assembly of a task force for Aden[22] would make it impossible for the British Navy to keep even two frigates (and smaller warships could scarcely have maintained a continuous patrol 'in all weathers')[23] on station. This may seem an absurd rumour, but the multiplication of demands on naval resources does not end when we have calculated that two frigates on patrol means another two on passage and a further two refitting; a total of six. These six are all committed to a single operation of uncertain length. A prudent admiral would want six more in readiness to provide reinforcements or to undertake separate but simultaneous tasks. But no navy ever has all its ships fit for service at once (even counting as fit those undergoing routine maintenance). To mobilize twelve frigates (four of them in port) may demand a total of eighteen to allow for one that ran heavily aground, two being re-equipped with a new weapons system, another utilized for trials and two employed as training ships. These are only some of the ways in which ships can cease to be available. It thus seems reasonable to hazard a guess that eighteen frigates together with half a dozen auxiliaries is about the minimum strength required for simple fleet operations within the range of shore-based air support but at a distance from the naval base. If we assume that navies without enough regular auxiliary vessels could requisition tankers and improvise repair ships in emergency, there are perhaps a dozen navies that meet these criteria and which are accordingly capable of a small and relatively simple fleet operation.

Politically, however, the Beira Patrol was an exceptionally easy operation. Before it even began the General Assembly of the United Nations had voted by 107 to 2 against Rhodesia and there was never the least likelihood of Rhodesia's two supporters (Portugal and South Africa) attempting any forcible resistance. The prospect of such resistance is admittedly excluded by definition from all simple fleet operations, but there has probably never been a case in which the assailant could feel such confidence on this point. This must have influenced the British assessment of the naval resources required. In most simple fleet operations initial calculations of political reactions, whether from the victim or from third parties, are liable to be eroded by the mere passage of time. A blockade, for instance, may be correctly assessed at its outset as tolerable, but, if it goes on too long, the absence of success and the cumulative inconvenience may cause third parties to revise their views; or the victim, though initially defenceless, may acquire or devise means of retaliation. During the Spanish Civil War the Non-Intervention Patrol began as a simple fleet operation supported by all the principal naval powers, but soon ran into political difficulties which eventually compelled Britain and France to deploy eighty destroyers (and other warships as well) as a superior fleet. In most other circumstances, therefore, a prudent Ministry of Defence would have had to envisage the possibility of eventual opposition to the Beira Patrol and a consequential increase in naval requirements that might altogether be disproportionate to the two frigates needed to stop consenting tankers. Instead, the naval resources allocated have actually been reduced as one uneventful year has succeeded another.

Looked at in this light it would appear that, even for simple fleet operations within easy reach of home bases, the earlier estimate of eighteen frigates as the minimum naval strength required is more likely to be too low than too high. There is a further consideration. One of the attractions of the Beira Patrol to members of the United

Nations was undoubtedly the thought that the effort, the expense and the risks, minimal though these were, would all fall on Britain. It is not too difficult to imagine a similar case arising again: a small state vulnerable to maritime pressure becomes so unpopular internationally that some naval power is urged to undertake a simple fleet operation as an expression of the general sentiment of mankind. Next time, however, opinion might be less unanimous and the victim might possess a greater incentive and ability to undertake armed resistance. The first flush of international enthusiasm begins to evaporate as the blockade drags on without achieving the swift success originally predicted. Then one or more of the patrolling warships are sunk by mines, by unknown submarines or by unidentified aircraft. The assailant realizes that a superior fleet is needed, may even conclude that an opposed amphibious operation is the only sure means of stifling this unexpected resistance. He turns to the General Assembly for help and discovers, to his surprise and dismay, that votes are not always equivalent to warships, nor applause to the provision of marines. A prudent assailant, therefore, will not regard international approval as an adequate reinforcement of his own resources, though he may nevertheless be encouraged to embark on an otherwise hazardous operation by the comforting thought that, if the worst comes to the worst, he can always withdraw his ships as easily as he deployed them.

This imaginary instance also illustrates the sharp rise, which takes place at the level of simple fleet operations, in the inherent defensive advantage of the victim. More precisely, it is much harder for an assailant to be sure that a fleet operation will be unopposed than to predict that a single warship will encounter no resistance that cannot easily be overcome. There are three reasons for this. Firstly, a fleet necessarily operates over a much larger area of sea than a single warship, thus presenting a more extended and accessible target. Secondly, fleet operations usually last longer and, if their character is that of a blockade or patrol, the time needed to achieve the objective may not depend on the assailant alone. Finally, unless a fleet is actually deployed in readiness for an expected attack (which may impair its ability to discharge its original task) some of its component vessels are often more vulnerable than a single warship, specifically chosen as a superior ship. Such a warship can dash into a harbour known to be inadequately defended, rescue a detained ship and be out of reach before the victim can assemble his forces. Few victims can always guard every point on their coast or each of their ships at sea: even the United States have twice been the victim of superior ship operations. But, when a fleet must patrol an entire coast-line for days or weeks, when it must be attended by lightly armed auxiliaries, when warships must oil at sea or stop to investigate a merchantman, then the victim needs only the scantiest resources to raise the ante and deny the assailant the economies of a simple fleet operation. If he has a couple of submarines, some mines and a converted trawler to lay them, a few Komar boats or a handful of bombers, then either the assailant must be completely convinced that the political will to resist is absent or else he must employ a superior fleet. In practice, therefore, the potential victims of simple fleet operations may well be as few in number as the potential assailants.

There is, however, one rôle in which the simple fleet would be immune from such vexatious impediments. Recent years have seen the revival of one variant of the expressive use of limited naval force for which this type of operation is particularly well suited. As well as manifesting power in the form of an implied threat, warning or promise, warships can also veil impotence by a parting gesture of defiance. If troops must be withdrawn, colonies given up, allies abandoned or injuries shrugged off, a naval demonstration may alleviate bitterness at home even if it does not always efface triumph or indignation abroad. But, whereas a single warship can symbolize an otherwise convincing power and resolve, a fleet may be necessary to cock a fugitive snook. Some governments, indeed, have employed more than a simple fleet for this purpose: an American task force including the battleship NEW JERSEY as well as aircraft carriers glossed over the destruction of one of their reconnaissance aircraft in April 1969; the British squadron that excused the evacuation of Aden in 1967 counted a strike carrier and a commando carrier among its eight warships and nine auxiliaries.

The 1967 episode, incidentally, was a good example of the flexibility of naval force in its political applications. The British squadron was originally conceived in the hope that its presence offshore might be welcome to a friendly post-independence régime in Southern Arabia. Just what it – or the bomber force to be stationed on Masirah Island – might actually do was left conveniently vague. The one plausible military function was expressly excluded: 'there are, of course, to be some combat troops in the carrier-borne force. But there is no intention that these troops should be deployed on the shore.'[24] The purpose to be served by keeping this squadron offshore for six months after independence was thus essentially political and, in so far as it was intended to reassure conservative Arabs and deter revolutionaries, had evaporated before British troops completed their withdrawal on 29 November. Yet the squadron still assembled; it covered the evacuation; it stayed another two months in case

British subjects still ashore needed rescue; and, when it finally dispersed, it may perhaps have alleviated some of the smarts and stings inflicted upon British public opinion.

In principle, however, this was a simple fleet operation, because landings were excluded (in the original concept of the fleet as a comfort for conservative sheikhs, though perhaps not in the later rôle as a potential rescue force for British subjects) and there was no potential naval antagonist. If the need were to arise again, whether for Britain or for some other retreating nation, cost-effectiveness might demand a fleet that was simple in its composition as well as its purpose. This would be particularly true of protracted operations. In 1967, for instance, the original conception envisaged keeping this fleet on station for over six months, thus entailing constant reliefs for its component ships – a much more awkward and expensive process with carriers than with the lesser vessels that would surely have been symbolically adequate. Indeed, the political upheaval that produced the People's Republic of South Yemen may have disconcerted the British Foreign Office, but it must have had considerable compensations for the British naval staff. Moreover, even if these political developments further impaired the credibility of the entire project, as this was originally conceived, the fact that there was no one left ashore in a position to call on the fleet to do anything may well suggest future uses for this gambit. Other governments bent on disengagement from embarrassing involvements may reflect that the presence of a fleet initially softens the shock of abandoning a commitment, because these cruising warships suggest that, in circumstances and by methods left conveniently vague, the withdrawing government might still return. If political changes then take place ashore, these can at first be represented as insufficient to justify the intervention of the fleet and, when they subsequently go further, as having so altered the situation that the presence of the fleet no longer serves any useful purpose. The reader will have little difficulty in devising scenarios adaptable to several governments and more than one contingency that can already be foreseen for the years ahead.

The attractions of employing the simple fleet in the expressive rôle are naturally increased by the extent to which the movements of warships can be improvised at short notice. If the fleet is not really intended to do anything except to exercise a 'kind of vague menace',[25] its composition and readiness for war are relatively unimportant: any warships that are available might as well float in one sea as in another. They are easily dispatched and still more easily withdrawn. And, although the symbolic rearguard seems the most likely purpose, it is not necessarily the only one. Major naval powers, admittedly, would probably have to employ more than a simple fleet as a presage of action, whereas minor naval powers would, in any case, experience great difficulty in investing such manœuvres with any conviction. But there could be exceptions. Japan, for instance, already has twenty-eight destroyers and sixteen frigates, more than enough to provide a simple fleet of respectable size, and the present building programme will further increase her resources.[26] The self-denying provisions of her constitution[27] have proved so insignificant an obstacle to the creation of this navy that they can scarcely be regarded as a serious impediment to its employment. In the event of a further shift in Japanese attitudes – away from passive reliance on the American nuclear umbrella and an exclusive preoccupation with economic development and commercial expansion – the formidable dynamism of the Japanese people, their outstanding naval tradition and their great industrial resources, particularly in shipbuilding, would enhance the impact of any demonstrative manœuvre executed off an Asian coast by even a simple Japanese fleet. Naval analysts might sceptically inquire what such a fleet could actually do and reinforce their doubts by arguing that, for many years to come, the maritime defence of the Japanese Islands will depend more on the US Pacific Fleet than on anything the Japanese Navy could achieve, unaided, against the Soviet Far Eastern Fleet. To an Asian politician, however, the economic statistics of the sixties and the naval memories of earlier decades might combine to invest the appearance of a Japanese fleet with far greater significance: to make it seem the first wave of an advancing tide rather than the last breaker of the ebb.

This is not an immediately plausible scenario and the political changes required to make it so are potential rather than inevitable or imminent. But it is a reminder that the present state of international relations is no more immutable in its naval than in its political balance. It is easier to foresee the scope for simple fleet operations than to predict when, in what circumstances and by whom they might be conducted.

Potential assailants are more easily identified when we enter the high-priced area of gunboat diplomacy: superior fleet, simple amphibious and opposed amphibious operations. Although each of these categories differs from the other two and itself covers a wide range of magnitude, they have certain features in common which constitute a new threshold in the use of limited naval force. Politically there is a sharp rise in the level of risk and commitment. Even a *simple amphibious operation* – the disembarkation of marines or

troops on a defenceless coast or one controlled by the inviting government – usually represents a deeper and more uncertain involvement than the average superior ship operation. When H.M.S. CENTAUR
landed marines in Tanganyika, for instance, the carrier was in no
danger and her helicopters reached their objective unopposed.[28]
But, once they had arrived, there was no certainty that the mutinous
Tanganyikan soldiers would be subdued without serious casualties,
without widespread racial resentment, without snowballing popular
and international resistance to this neo-colonialist intervention. The
smoothness of the actual operation, and its early conclusion, should
not blind us to the extent of the political risks run by the British
Government in responding to this Tanganyikan request. When one
government invites the armed intervention of another, this usually
implies the existence of a serious threat, whether external or internal,
to the authority of the first government, a threat which the intervention is intended to neutralize but which, failing swift success, it may
actually exacerbate.

The risks of involving soldiers in someone else's country are
naturally even greater when opposition is expected to the actual
landing, but even a *superior fleet operation* at sea implies a possibility of resistance politically much more significant than anything to
be feared from an inferior ship. When two fleets are in contact, the
possibilities of mistakes, of violence intended by neither government,
are multiplied: even an inferior fleet is less easily, less gracefully
withdrawn than a single ship. And, if a superior fleet has been
assembled to enforce a blockade to which resistance is expected,
the victim may only have to sink a single warship to expose
the assailant government to demands for the use of less limited
force. In all these types of operation the assailant is placing a stake
on the board which he may have to increase before he can even
retire it.

It follows, therefore, that these operations cannot prudently be
undertaken by any assailant incapable of reinforcing his initial commitment or of withstanding the repercussions this may provoke. In
extreme cases – the American landing in the Lebanon, which was
conceived and mounted as an opposed amphibious operation – the
assailant may have to be prepared to face a threat of war; in other
instances it may be only swelling international censure, growing
domestic opposition or the expenses and casualties of an operation
that lasts longer and encounters more resistance than had originally
been foreseen. Political stability at home, economic and military
reserves, a capacity for defence of one's own country (or a strong
and reliable protector), a readiness to run risks and some disposition

to the exercise of power: most of these conditions ought to be met before naval resources are even considered.

In some ways they are even more important than naval resources. When Britain attempted a superior fleet operation against Italy in 1935[29] or an opposed amphibious operation against Egypt in 1956 (though the preliminary aerial bombardment deprived the latter of any claim to the character of an act of limited force), the naval resources available were more adequate than the political resolve behind them. Shortage of ammunition in 1935 or the inadequate speed of landing craft in 1956 were excuses rather than insuperable deficiencies. Nevertheless, they both suggested awkward answers to the prudent question: what to do if the bluff is called or the initial attack repulsed? So did a host of other factors: the vulnerability in 1935 of the fleet's Mediterranean bases, the fragility in 1956 of the pound sterling, the divisions and uncertainties in both years of British public opinion. Militarily either operation might have succeeded, but only at the risk of a price Britain was not prepared to pay.

For the reasons discussed in the preceding chapter the potential cost of such operations is likely to be even higher today. It may thus be sensible, rather than attempting a detailed analysis of the naval requirements for each of these categories of operation, to lump them together as ventures probably beyond the capacity of anyone except a major power and to consider how far Britain, France, the Soviet Union and the United States are equipped to tackle each type. These are not necessarily the only potential assailants at this level. Exceptional circumstances might create opportunities for a lesser navy, particularly one able to count on the backing of a Super-Power. A Soviet writer has recently suggested, for instance, that West Germany and Italy ought to be considered,[30] though it is difficult to see how the external preoccupations of the former, or the domestic problems of the latter, would permit such ventures in the foreseeable future. Argentina[31] and Brazil, if naval expansion were accompanied by major political changes, might one day be conceivable contenders. Japan, as already suggested, is an obvious possibility for the future. China, on the other hand, is surely not. Her large navy would have to be radically reorganized before its capacities for coastal defence and minor forays could be supplemented by the ability to intervene at the higher level we are now considering. And, as long as she must anxiously watch the Seventh Fleet off her coast and the Soviet Army on her landward frontiers, it is difficult to see how her resources could permit her to emulate and avenge the 'tail-twisting' and the 'beat-ups' that enlivened the routine of the Yangtse Flotilla in the vanished and now almost incredible twenties of this century.[32] The remaining permanent members of the Security Council may not always be the only potential assailants at this higher level; they may none of them attempt such an operation in the seventies or eighties; but they are at present the most plausible contenders and an examination of their actual resources and doctrines may be of more assistance in circumscribing zones of probability than any more abstract and theoretical analysis.

The remainder of this chapter will accordingly concentrate on the naval ability and the political readiness of Britain, France and the United States to undertake operations in the highest price range of limited naval force, the Soviet Union being reserved for separate and fuller consideration in the following chapter. The motive of this discrimination is not political, but arises naturally from the present state of our knowledge. The British, French and United States Navies each have a long tradition of gunboat diplomacy; their capacities and their doctrines are established subjects for public debate; enough is known or can be taken for granted to curtail the evidence and argument needed to support even tentative predictions. None of these factors is true of the Soviet Navy, whose future rôle is the subject of hot controversy among Western commentators and ambiguous generalization from Soviet writers. The uncertainties that enshroud this issue, no less than its potential importance, demand separate treatment.

At first sight the French Navy presents a simpler problem. Its capital ships (aircraft carriers and nuclear powered missile submarines), the numbers, modernity and sophistication of its warships of other classes, its amphibious and logistic support capability, all combine to justify its claim to fourth place among the navies of the world. Its ocean-going abilities have been demonstrated in the simple fleet operations required for the supervision of nuclear tests, when the absence of local bases compelled the French fleet to depend on its own resources for six months.[33] In technical innovation the French Navy has occasionally surpassed even the American Navy, notably in the development of surface to surface missiles and of fast missile-firing patrol boats said to be better than the famous Osa and Komar craft of the Soviet Navy.[34] Above all, the French admirals have repeatedly and publicly proclaimed French readiness to employ limited naval force in time of peace. When Admiral Cabanier, for instance, was Chief of the Naval Staff, he included in his article on the evolution of the French Navy,[35] a classical definition of '*Les Missions du Temps de Paix*' of his force:

Pour appuyer sa politique éxterieure, le governement a besoin d'un appui souple. La Marine est en mesure, de par sa nature même, de remplir ce rôle . . . les bâtiments de guerre constituent le seul moyen de rendre notre présence tangible à nos amis comme à ceux qui le sont moins. Ils ont l'avantage d'être visibles, ou au contraire discrets, suivant la signification qu'on veut donner à leur présence . . . les porte-avions constitueront encore pendant long-temps l'ossature indispensable des forces d'intervention . . .

His words were subsequently echoed by other naval writers[36] and were amplified in 1967 by the claim that the French Navy was capable, at any point of the globe, of destroying the fleet of a minor power or of denying full freedom of action to a major power.[37]

These doctrines, amply supported by the record and traditions of the French Navy, were modified, but not repudiated, in 1969, when the Amphibious Intervention Force was disbanded and replaced by a modest Centre Amphibie for study and training, on the grounds that the French Navy was no longer capable of carrying out an opposed landing on its own.[38] Although the highest category of limited naval operations was thus excluded from the capacities of the French Navy, their ability to undertake *simple amphibious operations* still remains. Even without calling on the French Army, there are some 600 Marines, to whose careful training for limited emergencies an American writer has paid recent tribute,[39] as well as adequate numbers of fairly modern assault ships and landing craft together with three aircraft carriers[40] and a helicopter carrier. The French Navy are thus fully capable of emulating CENTAUR's Tanganyikan intervention or of landing and supporting an even larger force at the invitation, say, of some West African government. Nor is this the only part of the world in which France's somewhat independent international posture might make the assistance of her marines or her warships politically more acceptable than those of other naval powers to some harassed government. The possibility of soliciting French help was publicly discussed in the Lebanon during 1968 and 1969, when Lebanese ports remained open to visiting French warships, though closed to those of Britain, the Soviet Union and the United States.

This capacity for solicited intervention would also extend to other landings in circumstances where significant opposition was not expected: the rescue of French nationals during a local conflict between third parties, for instance. And, even if the advocates of prudence and cost-effectiveness find a readier hearing from a French Government no longer dominated by the panache and self-assurance of de Gaulle, there has hitherto been no reason to regard his successors as less anxious to maintain, to the extent that their resources permit, the international prestige and authority of France, particularly in those countries where history has given France a special degree of influence. In terms of resources, too, the French Navy of 1969 was well equipped to provide the small, self-contained fleet often desirable for simple amphibious operations. Although these take place, by definition, in political circumstances that make organized resistance unlikely, it is important for the assailant to possess sufficient capacity to operate flexibly, thus enabling him to avoid courses of action liable to excite opposition and, if this should nevertheless develop, to cope with it economically. For instance, if the victim government invites outside intervention to assist in the suppression of local disorders, it might seem sufficient to land troops from merchant vessels or commercial aircraft and this appears at present to be the preferred French doctrine, particularly for those African states where small French garrisons could still be relied upon to secure the airport in advance. Yet harbours and airports are easily occupied or obstructed even by unarmed rioters or strikers, who might not be able to prevent a landing altogether, but who could make it necessary to employ violence at the outset, thus producing casualties and a degree of resentment capable of prejudicing the future course of the operation. These hazards can often be avoided by bringing landing craft to a deserted beach or helicopters to some trouble-free area inland. If the intervening troops can complete their concentration ashore in imposing strength before any contact is necessary with dissident elements of the population, violence may be averted, not only at the outset, but altogether. Similarly, if the intention is to restore order, or to assemble the assailant's nationals for evacuation, gradually and gently, it is a great advantage if the intervening forces can supply and support themselves without any need for premature strike-breaking or over-hasty measures of pacification. Finally, if anything goes wrong and resistance unexpectedly assumes serious proportions, it may be of great importance to be able to reinforce or safely withdraw the contingent already landed. However confident politicians may be that resistance need not be expected, a prudent commander would prefer to have a helicopter carrier, an assault ship, a few landing craft, supply vessels and enough other warships to provide his landing force with radar cover and a minimum of protection against attack by the odd aircraft, submarine or boatload of terrorists with explosives. A sufficient concentration of force, which the French Navy should be able to provide for such purposes, is often the best method of avoiding violence, the presence of warships the best insurance against the need to use them. Simple amphibious landings may now rank low among French naval priorities, but, if the political requirements were to arise, the capacity still exists to meet it, provided, of course, that when the crisis breaks a nuclear test in the Pacific does not happen to be tying up 40 per cent of the Navy and most of its amphibious vessels.

It is this last factor – and all that it implies – which demands considerable qualification of the assessment so far attempted. The French Navy lacks the numerical strength to undertake more than one operation at a time. Some emergencies might thus find too many warships already committed to other tasks; some interventions might have to be ruled out because, though initially feasible with the resources available to them at the time, they threatened to tie up ships for longer than these could be spared. France has the resolution and the resources for some simple amphibious operations, but these would have to be brief and conveniently timed.

Superior fleet operations are another matter. Technically the French Navy is still capable, in favourable circumstances, of a convincing threat to the fleet of a minor power; the Brazilian press had good naval reason to be apprehensive in 1963 at the prospect of French reinforcements for TARTU. And, if the political circumstances in which the French Government might wish to overawe another fleet or to impose a blockade against opposition are less obvious, this is no less true of stronger naval powers. Operations at this level are necessarily rare and are only feasible in exceptional situations. Nevertheless, the French Navy must contend with two special handicaps. It has only half the number of ocean-going surface warships possessed by the British Navy, whose difficulties in sustaining prolonged simple fleet operations have already been noted. Fifty-odd warships, even allowing for those unavailable at the moment of crisis, are more than enough to assemble a fleet superior to most navies, but they leave very little margin for maintaining one for any length of time in distant waters: even if this margin could be increased by a really sophisticated fleet train of the American type. A superior fleet, after all, is not simply a larger number of warships than those locally available to the victim. It must be capable of withstanding possible resistance, particularly from such characteristic weapons of the victim as aircraft, submarines, mines or even fast patrol craft armed with torpedoes or missiles. If the Beira Patrol ratios are any guide, this might require a total strength of three ships for every one of each class actually engaged. It is thus difficult to envisage a superior fleet operation which would not mean earmarking most of the French Navy. Against some victims and in certain circumstances this could be done, provided the French Government were sufficiently sure that surface warships would not be required for any other purpose meanwhile. This would demand a higher degree of political assurance than sending a simple fleet to the Pacific to supervise a small nuclear test. Even though that operation tied up 40 per cent of the French Navy for six months, it was at least terminable at the sole discretion of the French Government, whereas many superior fleet operations, particularly those involving a blockade or patrol, are somewhat unpredictable in the extent of their commitment or its duration. Although the French Navy is technically capable of prolonged confrontation in distant waters, it is hard to imagine that this would be politically feasible. Present French capacity for superior fleet operations might thus be more plausibly confined to brief encounters in the Mediterranean (if the US and Soviet fleets were neutral or neutralizing one another) or off the Iberian peninsula or in the Eastern Atlantic. Only in war or in purely peaceful manœuvres is it a practical proposition to commit the whole of one's naval strength: in the first case because the threat is already total, in the second because none exists. The use of limited naval force, being an attempt to resolve a dispute without recourse to war, necessarily involves, at least in the higher range of operations now under consideration, some risk that the threat will increase. This risk demands the maintenance of reserves not committed to the actual operation, which must be limited in its employment of total resources as well as in its objectives and scope. It follows, therefore, that French ability to defeat another navy in war is an inadequate measure of their capacity to mount a superior fleet operation against that same navy as an alternative to war. The latter task demands a greater total strength, though a lesser commitment. Even allowing for the long shadow cast by the French tricolour, the substance of French naval resources would scarcely permit superior fleet operations in any but the most favourable circumstances.

But how long would even this be possible? The second handicap of the French Navy – and this is one which also confronts the larger navy of Britain – is the increasing difficulty of maintaining a general purpose navy as suitable for peace-time employment as for nuclear war. The expense, actual and prospective, of the naval contribution to the *Force de Frappe* has already compelled France to abandon her *Force Amphibie d'Intervention* as similar considerations persuaded the British Government in 1966 to plan the eventual renunciation of strike carriers. Strategic missile submarines are not only expensive in themselves, in their double crews of highly trained specialists, in their ever-mounting costs of modifying delivery systems to keep up with the increasing sophistication of anti-missile defence: they also demand an extravagant degree of naval support if they are to discharge their deterrent mission effectively. A nuclear submarine may be undetectable while secretly patrolling the ocean depths, but it is acutely vulnerable to the killer submarine lurking outside its inevitably known base. At times of crisis, it seems likely that an efficient and sophisticated anti-submarine force would be needed to sweep the approach channels and to ensure that the missile-firing submarine cannot be followed to its secret launching-area. The ships and aircraft and personnel required for this purpose are no less expensive, a consideration which reinforces Vice-Admiral Pollock's view that:

> The effort and money required to develop and sustain a force of nuclear-powered submarines could have a detrimental effect upon the balance of forces in smaller navies.[41]

More specifically, the expansion of France's naval contribution to her *Force de Frappe* seems likely to take place at the expense of her *Force d'Intervention*. By 1980, unless successive French governments have meanwhile significantly increased their total naval expenditure, we may see a French Navy with ships that are more powerful, of more recent construction, of greater technical sophistication, but also fewer in number, more inextricably committed to maintenance of the nuclear deterrent, less available for the minor emergencies of peace-time. In the ability to fight, or to threaten, nuclear war, the French Navy will probably conserve its present position in the international hierarchy: for the modest operations of peace-time it may well be outclassed by half a dozen navies with no nuclear capability. There may simply not be enough ships to spare to support the smallest superior fleet operation beyond easy reach of Brest. Indeed, if each new warship continues to cost more, to be more specialized in its rôle, to require a larger and more highly trained crew than its predecessor, there will have to be a marked change in present political and economic trends if France is to avoid an eventual division of her Navy between deterrence and coastal defence. Both tasks might be efficiently performed by warships of high quality (the recent introduction of fast, missile-firing patrol craft may be a significant pointer) but there might be no surplus capacity remaining for more than a minimal employment of limited naval force.

This is not an inevitable, perhaps not even an imminent prospect. As long as France can retain – as at present she intends – her aircraft carriers and their escorts, she will have a *force d'intervention*, albeit small and ageing, superior to many of her rivals. The attrition of time will be only gradual, but each successive year will sharpen the choice between greatly increased expenditure and growing obsolescence. Unless by 1975 or 1976 a big new building programme has been approved, it will be hard to avoid the conclusion that, in the long run, the maintenance of a general purpose navy will probably prove more than her economic resources and her political purpose will support.

Indeed, it is arguable that such a navy will soon be beyond the capacity of anyone except the Super-Powers, or, given the necessary changes, of Japan or a Federal Europe. In 1970 the British Navy still meets this criterion. It is stronger than the French, has many more ships, a greater range of capacities and a wider deployment. It is still just capable of an opposed amphibious operation in favourable circumstances; it could produce a superior fleet in most situations in which the United States were friendly, and the Soviet Union neutral or neutralized; its capacity for simple amphibious operations is more than adequate. As long as only one operation is contemplated at any one time, the resolution of the British Government will probably impose severer limitations than the resources of the Navy – for the next few years.

But, if the aircraft carriers disappear, the picture will change. British naval capacity for the higher price range of gunboat diplomacy is heavily dependent on these powerful, expensively modernized ships. It is not, with all respect to the 1966 Defence Review, only the opposed amphibious operation that will then have to be removed from the range of British naval capacities. The possibility of superior fleet operations will also be reduced. At present an aircraft carrier enjoys the prestige and the potency that once surrounded the battleship. It is a capital ship and, properly screened and escorted, will often be regarded as a superior fleet by the commander of a larger number of lesser warships. Without such vessels, and given the decline of the British reputation for reckless persistence, a British naval commander will less often be able to overawe a foreign victim without actual numerical superiority. And the advantage of numbers is already being lost by the British Navy. Leaving the Super-Powers altogether aside, there are very few seas in which no other navy could assemble more ships than Britain would be likely to produce. 'Numerical strength,' in the congent words of those admirable historians of an earlier era, 'is essential if any type of gunboat diplomacy is to work.'[42]

The following table has no political significance. The countries included have not been selected as either potential victims or prospective assailants. They are merely middling countries with navies and the intention is to illustrate relative strengths in the vessels most useful for the exercise of limited naval force in time of peace. The figures have been taken from those for all types of surface warship, from corvettes upwards, listed in the respective editions of *Jane's Fighting Ships*.

OCEAN GOING[43] SURFACE WARSHIPS

	1963	*1969*	*Change %*
Argentina	20	18	− 10%
Brazil	34	29	− 14%
Britain	110	96	− 13%
France	64	54	− 16%
Germany (West)	33	39	+ 18%
India	20	22	+ 10%
Italy	55	49	− 11%
Japan	47	39	− 16%
Spain	45	33	− 27%
Sweden	23	16	− 30%

There are two ways of interpreting these figures. The first is to argue that there are special reasons why India[44] and West Germany constitute exceptions (soon, probably, to be joined by Japan) to the general rule that the rising cost of new ships results in a declining numerical strength and that, with these exceptions, the British Navy still retains its relative preponderance even if its important gains in submarine strength are ignored. The second is to remember that the rest of these dwindling navies (with the temporary exception of the French) are each concerned with a single sea area and that their primary function is defensive. Britain still has certain world-wide interests, a deeply-rooted tradition of naval initiatives in peace-time and a declared readiness, however discreet its contemporary phrasing, to use warships to promote political objectives. The 1966 Defence Review stated the policy in general terms:

On more than one occasion in the recent past, we have seen how local conflict in a faraway country has threatened to embroil the major powers in a direct confrontation, directly endangering world peace.
Britain's forces outside Europe can help to reduce this danger. Recent experience in Africa and elsewhere has shown that our ability to give rapid help to friendly governments, with even small British forces, can prevent large-scale catastrophes. In some parts

of the world, the visible presence of British forces by itself is a deterrent to local conflict. No country with a sense of international responsibility would surrender this position without good reason, unless it was satisfied that others could, and would, assume a similar rôle.[45]

The four years that followed saw Britain threatening or using limited naval force on five occasions.[46] Four out of five entailed the use of a superior fleet. Only one of these – the 1967 concentration to open the Straits of Tiran – was a complete failure and that for political and not naval reasons. This is a better record than the much larger navies of the Soviet Union and the United States could show during the same period. One is almost tempted to take at its face value that unexpected Soviet tribute:

The Royal Navy . . . provides an ideal police force turned to by British imperialism in what remains after the collapse of the Empire and in areas where British monopolies are still clinging to their economic and political positions.[47]

Of these five operations, however, four entailed, at least initially, the use of carriers and the only one that failed was also the only one in which opposition could seriously be expected.

In 1970, the *Defence Review*[48] again envisaged, though less explicitly, a far-ranging rôle for the Royal Navy. During the preceding twelve months, it explained, there had been operational patrols off Beira, in the Persian Gulf and in the West Indies and, on 1 January 1970, one-third of the Royal Navy afloat was outside United Kingdom waters. For the coming year the following deployment was envisaged:

Mediterranean and Near East – an aircraft carrier *or* a commando ship *or* an assault ship with Royal Marines embarked, support ships, a destroyer and two frigates.

Persian Gulf – frigates and minesweepers.

Far East – amphibious ships, destroyers, frigates, submarines, minesweepers and support ships.

Caribbean and South Atlantic – two frigates, Royal Marines and a hovercraft unit.

In other words, whatever the area, reinforcements would have been needed for any operation in the higher-priced category. At present, given adequate notice and the essential condition of only one operation at any one time, these could just be provided. But what will be the position, 'with the rate of new construction not nearly keeping pace with the rate of scrapping older ships',[49] once the carriers are gone? Could the Royal Navy then concentrate a superior fleet off the Falkland Islands while still providing Gibraltar with the necessary minimum of maritime protection?

This may seem an unfairly loaded question, but what is at issue here is not the ability of the Royal Navy to fight a war – in which its new fleet submarines could be employed – or to deter one with its missile-firing submarines, or to join its allies in assembling a fleet for the peace-time confrontation of an agreed opponent, but its capacity to serve a British policy that seeks simultaneously to avoid war and to maintain, without any expectation of allied assistance, certain overseas positions of exclusively national importance. This is the most crucial, and not perhaps the least plausible, motive for employing a superior fleet in the coming years: to demonstrate to a potential assailant that a *coup de main* is unlikely to succeed and to ensure that he, and not Britain, must choose between acquiescence and war. In certain circumstances this could require the Royal Navy to deploy, at a considerable distance, a superior fleet against an adversary able to use his entire navy within easy reach of his bases. For such a purpose a three to one superiority in total numerical strength must now be regarded, for all the residual prestige of the White Ensign, as a bare minimum. And, in the future, even triple strength may not be enough. If present trends continue, and however lightly future British governments may regard their naval commitments to NATO, the increasing specialization of surface warships will make it harder to divert radar pickets or anti-submarine frigates to other jobs. Their absolutely declining numbers and their reduced availability seem likely, in the long run, perhaps a little later than in the case of France, but no less inexorably, to exclude Britain from the higher-priced range of limited naval force. The preservation of peace, if this is to be combined with maintenance of anything approaching the *status quo*, is unfortunately a much more expensive and demanding policy than mere preparation for war.

Just how expensive may be seen – and some of the reasons for this gloomy prognosis appreciated – by anyone who cares to consult the 161 pages devoted by the 1969–70 Edition of *Jane's Fighting Ships* to the United States Navy. There are 725 ocean-going surface warships in this Navy, nearly twice as many as the combined strengths of the ten countries listed earlier; there are more American carriers than there are ocean-going French surface warships; if every ship in the Royal Navy down to the last tug is counted, the total is precisely equal to the number of American destroyers and frigates. Against any likely peace-time opposition and without reinforcement two of the four American fleets are superior fleets (while the other two could cope with most situations) and American capacity for opposed amphibious landings was defined with a staggering concision by Mr McNamara:

> We should have enough assault ships to lift and land the assault echelons of one Marine Expeditionary Force (division/wing team) in the Atlantic and one in the Pacific.[50]

After so much anxious analysis of what the British and French Navies might just still be capable of doing, these statistics inspire the same awe as the opening notes of the late Kirsten Flagstad: one wonders how anyone else could have the impertinence to sing on the same stage.

Of course, the United States Navy have problems concealed by these statistics, of which the most serious is block obsolescence: 58 per cent of US warships, including most of the carriers, cruisers, destroyers and frigates, are more than twenty years old. As a result nearly half the Navy's ships are in the Reserve Fleet and *The Military Balance*[51] for 1969–70 reduces the total of ocean-going surface warships in commission to 452. This is still larger than the combined strengths of our ten countries and more than adequate for any possible requirement of limited naval force, which seldom demands modern ships as long as these are sufficiently numerous and versatile. Nevertheless, construction is proceeding slowly and the numbers of new surface warships expected are only a fraction of those which will soon have to be scrapped or laid up. Neither the absolute numerical strength of the United States Navy nor the present overwhelming degree of relative ascendancy is likely to be maintained much longer.

There are also other problems. The United States are heavily committed to the expensive and demanding task of maintaining the seaborne nuclear deterrent in the face of a smaller, but more modern and, in some respects, technically more sophisticated Soviet Navy. They are deeply involved in military operations in Vietnam (which have created certain difficulties in the training and manning of other fleets) and they have more obligations in a wider area of the oceans than any other navy. At any given moment only a fraction of the vast

I

total of American ocean-going surface warships could readily be diverted to meet some new requirement for the use of limited naval force.

Nevertheless, even if the United States have a navy that is ageing and shrinking, even if the cries of woe emanating from American admirals are taken at their face value, even if Secretary of the Navy Chafee fails to get all the $3.5 billion a year he wants for the next decade just to maintain 'the continued effectiveness of our Navy',[52] it is difficult to envisage a time when lack of resources will inhibit American use of limited naval force at any level. Their only significant rival is the Soviet Navy and, if there is one factor which seems certain to produce most of the money which Mr Chafee wants, it is the continued growth of the Red Fleet. At least as long as this book is in print, it may safely be predicted that Americans will be able to chant:

'We've got the ships, we've got the men, we've got the money too.'[53]

But will they continue their long tradition of employing these ships in peace-time? Here prediction is more hazardous, for so much depends on American national resolve, on political developments within the United States, on the international balance of power. But at least there is no doctrinal objection. On the contrary, US Navy Regulations are unusually explicit. Section 0614 on the *'Use of Force Against Friendly States'* covers most situations:

The right of self-preservation . . . is a right which belongs to states . . . it includes the protection of the state, its honor, and its possessions, and the lives and property of its citizens.[54]

And the last two Secretaries of the Navy have made it clear that American ships must be as ready for peace as they are for war. 'Our objective,' Mr Ignatius declared, 'is to maintain a modern balanced fleet capable of performing assigned tasks on a world-wide basis in time of peace, limited war or war.'[55] He was a Democrat, but his Republican successor reiterated this emphasis on the peace-time rôle of the US Navy by predicting that an eventual withdrawal of American forces from Vietnam would merely mean that:

The Seventh Fleet, operating as it does in international waters, will be moved, as appropriate, to support US national policy and objectives.[56]

Indeed, it is even arguable that the present American mood of disenchantment with the troubles of the outside world is more likely to lead to military than to naval withdrawals. As foreign garrisons are reduced, overseas bases abandoned, allies urged to cultivate the virtues of self-reliance, the diplomatic and political functions of the US Navy may actually expand: those grey, restless, innumerable ships will console Americans and reassure their friends; they will constitute the universal, the flexible, the removable reminder of American power and concern.

As might be expected, international capacity for the exercise of limited naval force thus resembles a pyramid, the number of potential assailants dwindling as we rise from one category to another, until the United States are left in solitary occupation of the summit: the only navy with the sheer number of ships, with enough aircraft carriers, ocean-going surface warships, amphibious craft and supply vessels, to undertake every class of operation, in any part of the oceans and for as much of the future as can yet be foreseen. These are the tests of capacity – the ability to spare enough ships at short notice, to provide air cover without land bases, to show strength before it need be used, to land where opposition is least, to stay long enough at sea to achieve results – that must be met before a navy can claim *'un caractère polyvalent ... pour toute mission'*.[57] Other navies can occasionally hope, in special circumstances, or in particular seas, to attempt even the highest class of operation, but, of those so far considered, only the American can confidently expect to furnish sufficient resources for most contingencies. For a few more years Britain and France will still be capable of a rare visit to the upper floors; the Soviet Union is still to be examined; but even the larger navies of the rest of the world must expect to buy their gunboat diplomacy in the bargain basement – a repository of not always inconsiderable trifles which luck and good judgment may sometimes render accessible to the thirty navies probably capable of superior ship operations. Where the will exists, the world still holds enough warships for some of them to find a way.

NOTES

[1] The then US Secretary of the Navy in a speech of 7 May 1925 to the Connecticut Chamber of Commerce, quoted in Lamar T. Beman, *Intervention in Latin America*, H. W. Wilson Co., N.Y., 1928.

[2] *The Defence Review*, H.M.S.O. London, 1966, Command 2901.

[3] Chapter 2.

[4] Chapter 3.

[5] This warship would in earlier days have been called a light cruiser and is armed with Shaddock cruise missiles, to which *The Military Balance* (I.S.S.

London 1969) attributes a range of 250 miles compared with the 23 of NEW JERSEY'S guns.

[6] See Appendix

[7] *Le Monde*, 23 February 1963. In the context this ambivalent phrase may be rendered as 'to express resentment'.

[8] The particulars are to be found in an interesting scrap-book, entitled H.M.S. ROYAL OAK, *1936–1938 Commission: Executive Officer's Log*, in the National Maritime Museum at Greenwich. Quoted by kind permission of the Trustees.

[9] *File ADM 116 3679* in Public Record Office, London.

[10] Though the Finnish Navy played a political rôle in 1948, when a warship anchored off the Presidential Palace as one of the precautions taken to deter a supposedly imminent Communist *coup d'état*. See Max Jakobson, *Finnish Neutrality*, Hugh Evelyn 1968.

[11] See Appendix.

[12] *Le Monde*, 18 and 22 April 1967.

[13] Admiral Cabanier 'Evolution de la Marine Française', article in *Revue de Défense Nationale*, July 1965.

[14] See F. C. Gregory, 'The Beira Patrol', article in the *Journal of the Royal United Services Institution*, December 1969, for an interesting analysis.

[15] Answer by Secretary of State for Defence to a Parliamentary Question on 1 May 1968.

[16] *Hansard*, Vol. 789, Col. 299.

[17] Written answer to Parliamentary Question 12 June 1968, *Hansard*, Vol. 766, Col. 39.

[18] *The Times*, 7 January 1966.

[19] H.M.S. EAGLE may have been selected because she had already been sent to East African waters for a task that did need a strike carrier, Appendix, 1965.

[20] *Hansard*, 13 December 1967, Vol. 756, Col. 415.

[21] *Sunday Telegraph*, 3 September 1967.

[22] See below.

[23] *Statement on the Defence Estimates*, February 1969, Command 3927.

[24] Mr Thomson, Minister of State, Foreign Office, in the House of Commons, 19 June 1967, *Hansard*, Cols. 1256–7.

[25] This was the objective assigned by Sir Winston Churchill to H.M.S. PRINCE OF WALES and H.M.S. REPULSE on their brief excursion into Far Eastern waters in 1941, but the disastrous outcome of that venture in a war situation does not mean that it could not be attempted in peace-time. See W. S. Churchill, *The Grand Alliance*, Chapter 32, Cassell & Co. 1950.

[26] *Jane's Fighting Ships 1969–70* Edition.

[27] Article 9 'Aspiring sincerely to an international peace based on justice and order, the Japanese people forever renounce war as a sovereign right of the nation and the threat or use of force as a means of settling international disputes.

'In order to accomplish the aim of the preceding paragraph, land, sea and air forces, as well as other war potential, will never be maintained. The right of belligerency of the state will not be recognized.'

[28] But see Lt.-Col. T. M. P. Stevens 'A Joint Operation in Tanganyika', *RUSI Journal*, February 1965, for an interesting analysis of the military problems that *might* have arisen.

[29] See Appendix.

[30] K. Timofeev, 'The Rôle of Navies in Imperialist Policy', article in the Soviet weekly *New Times* of 28 November 1969.

[31] Who, as long ago as 1948, sent a simple fleet of two cruisers, six destroyers and five Admirals to assert her claims to dependencies in the Antarctic. Fortunately the simultaneous expeditions of the President of Chile (on board a frigate) and of the Governor of the Falkland Islands (on board H.M.S. NIGERIA) were equally expressive in character and all concerned contrived to remain cool. See *Survey of International Affairs*, 1947–48, O.U.P.

[32] For these phrases see an interesting manuscript diary by Commander Louis Hamilton in the Library of the National Maritime Museum at Greenwich. Quoted by kind permission of the Trustees.

[33] *Figaro*, 30 November 1966.

[34] *Military Review*, April 1969.

[35] 'L'Evolution de la Marine Française', *Revue de Défense Nationale*, July 1965.

[36] See, for instance, Contre-Admiral Lepotier, 'La Marine Française En 1970', article in *Revue de Défense Nationale*, March 1966.

[37] Admiral Cabanier, 'L'Avenir de la Marine', *Revue de Défense Nationale*, April 1967.

[38] 'Chronique Maritime', *Revue de Défense Nationale*, February 1969.

[39] Lt.-Com. Thibault, 'The French Marines', *USNIP*, March 1968.

[40] One is normally employed only for training, but might be available in emergency.

[41] 'The Progression in Submarine Warfare', article in *Jane's Fighting Ships*, 1969–70.

[42] Preston and Major op. cit., p. 185.

[43] The term ocean-going has two possible meanings: that the ship is big enough to be used on the oceans or that it does actually sail the oceans frequently. In this chapter only the first sense is intended.

[44] Admiral Chatterji, Chief of the Indian Naval Staff, has had little verbal support from his government for his statement that the Indian Navy will be in complete charge of the Indian Ocean with the withdrawal of the British fleet in 1971, *The Times*, 4 March 1968, but he is getting new Indian-built frigates.

[45] Command 2901 of February 1966, H.M.S.O. London.

[46] See Appendix, this does not include such essentially domestic incidents as Anguilla.

[47] K. Timofeev op. cit.

[48] Command 4290 of February 1970, H.M.S.O. London.

[49] *Jane's Fighting Ships 1969–70* Edition.

[50] Statement by Secretary of Defense, Robert S. McNamara on the 1969–73 *Defense Program*, Department of Defense, U.S.A. 1968.

[51] Institute for Strategic Studies, London.

[52] Quoted in Grover Heimar, 'The Ageing Fleet: US Seapower at the Crossroads', article in *The Armed Forces*, May 1969.

[53] G. W. Hunt, music hall song 1878.

[54] Lt.-Com. Bruce Harlow, U.S.N., 'The Legal Use of Force – Short of War', *USNIP*, November 1966.

[55] Reported in *Armed Forces Management*, October 1968.

[56] Quoted in *The Armed Forces*, October 1969.

[57] 'La Défense: la Politique Militaire Française et Ses Réalisations', *Notes et Études Documentaires*, No. 3343 of 6 December 1966, Secretariat Général de Gouvernement, Paris.

Chapter Five

THE SOVIET NAVAL ENIGMA

En cas de troubles ou de conflits limités intéréssant des
pays satellites ou amis une intervention de la Marine
soviétique est non seulement possible, mais probable
et cela avec efficacité.

Cabanier[1]

FOR years admirals and naval commentators from half a dozen
Western countries have been warning the world of the dangers
of the steadily reddening sea. For years they have been answered,
not in the cautious ambiguities of Russian professional writing, but
by Western exponents of the thesis that the capacities of the Soviet
Navy have been exaggerated; that this is the inadequate and
essentially defensive instrument of a circumspect régime determined
to avoid any adventure or initiative capable of provoking a confrontation with the superior Navy and the devastating nuclear
capability of the United States. The experts being in such disagreement, the intelligent layman has tended to conclude that no opinion
is certain and to dismiss the whole controversy as of secondary
importance. The SS-9 inter-continental missile is such an appalling
threat, the presence – and the recent use – of the Red Army in
central Europe is so evident, that the conjectural and only potential
dangers of Soviet warships tend to be dismissed as bogeys yet to be
substantiated.

This scepticism is often reinforced by exaggerated, and trans-
parently interested, efforts at alarmism. Crude statistics are quoted –
the number of Soviet submarines, for instance – with little attention
to qualitative evaluation or to the likelihood of the contingencies to
which they are applied. As a result the debate tends to be polarized
between extremists: believers in the sinister omnicompetence of the
Soviet Navy so exasperate their critics, that the latter are sometimes
driven to discount a threat of which they have correctly perceived the
distortion. Most of these arguments are naturally concerned with
issues beyond the scope of the present work: what could, or would,
the Soviet Navy do in war, nuclear or conventional, general or
limited? They are mentioned here, so that the reader should be aware
that all opinions, not least those that follow, on the Soviet Navy are
acutely controversial. There is also a further aspect of relevance.

130

Because the Soviet régime has made little use of its naval resources, there are few precedents on which to base prediction; because Soviet statements have often been belied by subsequent performance, these are usually analysed with considerable scepticism. There has accordingly been a tendency to prefer the evidence that seems sufficiently concrete to be indisputable: the record of Soviet naval construction. The ships actually built are listed, the dates when they were laid down are noted, the modifications of announced programmes are analysed and compared with the apparent international situation existing at the start, in the middle and at the end of building. These data are then employed as the basic bricks of theories which assume that each ship was planned for a specific purpose which now determines the scope of its future employment.

The argument of the present chapter, however, adopts a different assumption, namely, that the motives for which warships are built seldom foreshadow the actual nature of their employment, even in war, and are almost irrelevant to their utility in time of peace. When a keel is laid, this is necessarily part of a wider plan: it is a contribution to the distant contingency of naval war or deterrence in circumstances that may have been transformed long before the completed ship reaches the end of its useful life. H.M.S. ROYAL OAK[2] was conceived as one unit in a battle-fleet that discharged, somewhat inconclusively, its appointed rôle at Jutland. No one intended her to enable Spanish children to reach safety in France;[3] no one could have foreseen this as a British objective. Yet, whereas her presence at Jutland made little difference one way or the other, her availability during the Spanish Civil War met a political requirement which every naval expert responsible for her construction would have dismissed as trivial, implausible and inherently unsuited to the characteristics and functions of battleships. What mattered in 1937 was her existence: not the rôle for which she was built in 1914 or which she might have played in 1939.

In assessing the peace-time capabilities of Soviet warships, therefore, it may be more useful to disregard the intentions of their designers and to ask only the negative questions: is there a peace-time rôle of which they are technically incapable or from which they are manifestly debarred by the need to maintain instant readiness for nuclear war? If this analysis reveals the existence of useful warships not irretrievably committed in time of peace, it will then be necessary to consider whether there are Soviet doctrines that might encourage or prevent their diplomatic employment and, without trespassing too far on the subject of the following chapter, to examine the kind of contingencies in which the use of limited naval force might seem politically feasible to the Soviet Government.

Soviet submarines need not detain us long, even though the Soviet Navy have more of these vessels than any other Navy. Admittedly, such writers as Herrick and MccGwire[4] have argued plausibly that the obsolescence, particularly its concomitants of inadequate range and endurance, of so many Soviet submarines, together with the obstacles imposed by Russia's geographical situation and consequent need to divide her resources among four separate fleets, severely restrict Soviet ability to employ their submarines in offensive war. Nevertheless, if resources were the only issue, the Soviet Union would have more than enough modern submarines for peace-time use. Even the conservative Herrick, for instance, credits the Soviet Union with the ability to deploy twenty to twenty-five submarines against Atlantic shipping during the first few weeks of a war.[5] It is hard to envisage any peace-time operation for which a much smaller number would not suffice.

It is harder, however, to construct a convincing scenario in which submarines might be the preferred instruments of limited naval force, otherwise than in clandestine missions of the crypto-diplomatic kind. The advantages of submarines – their ability while undetected to sink even a superior ship and to do so anonymously – are inconsistent with the usual motives of assailants, who wish to avoid warlike acts, to threaten force rather than use violence, and to reap benefits that can seldom be anonymously enjoyed. The 'unknown submarines' of the Spanish Civil War admittedly offer a contrary precedent, in which a relatively weak naval power incapable of mounting a surface blockade attempted to discourage seaborne assistance to the Spanish Republicans by sinking ships which could not be stopped or seized in sufficient numbers by the Spanish Nationalists. This expedient failed, because the submarines, being 'unknown' and operating in the no-man's-land of the high seas, could be counter-attacked with just as much political impunity as was claimed for their own operations. Anonymity is thus a double-edged weapon, which tends to favour the stronger naval power in a prolonged conflict, whereas more overt forms of intervention may only demand stronger nerves. Spanish Nationalist warships and allegedly Spanish bombers operating from bases in Nationalist Spain never attracted French or British retaliation by their interference with shipping. If no British or French warship was at hand to provide immediate, local defence, then merchant vessels were stopped, seized or sunk with relative impunity.

In a similar situation today, therefore, the Soviet Union might well prefer to provide bombers or Komar craft able to operate under the colours of the client state (or faction). These could hope to execute tip-and-run raids on merchant vessels and to be back inside the national territory before counter-attack, which would then involve a higher degree of political commitment, was possible. Only in the most exceptional circumstances and if no other expedient was available, does it seem plausible that Soviet submarines would be used covertly. If the sinking of a few ships in a one-shot operation would make a decisive difference – the destruction of an invasion convoy in a local war, for instance – it is just conceivable that Soviet submarines would come to the aid of a client state whose own submarines were unseaworthy or whose crews could not be depended upon. Such an operation might be deniable and thus escape the American reaction that would presumably be the obstacle to overt Soviet intervention.

This choice of scenario – one in which responsibility for sinking ships can not only be attributed to another state, but also to a state which is actually a belligerent – illustrates the difficulty of adapting this particular application of naval force to a peace-time environment. The violent and inherently warlike act of sinking a ship at sea might be tolerable to other maritime nations if it was a belligerent state which suffered and that ostensibly at the hands of another belligerent. Similar arguments might even hold if a warship engaged in the application of limited naval force – a blockade, for instance – were sunk by a submarine that could conceivably belong to the victim state. A weak and irresolute assailant might thereby be compelled to realize that his objective could not be attained by the use of force as limited as he originally had hoped. In each case the objective, if it could be achieved at all, would only require a single blow, thus enabling the submarine or submarines to withdraw before naval resources could be gathered to counter-attack them and perhaps to establish their national identity. There would thus be no essential difference between this scenario and the sinking of the Israeli destroyer EILATH on 21 October 1967, when no outside observer could be certain that the STYX missiles had actually been fired by Egyptians.

The obstacles to a more protracted operation, however, would be far greater. If warships, for instance, do not withdraw as soon as they are first attacked, they will be reinforced and will adopt active anti-submarine measures likely to expose the true identity of the assailant and perhaps to cause him substantial losses. Escalation and even a Super-Power confrontation would then be probable and the use of naval force would rapidly cease to be limited. Similarly, if submarines attempt a blockade by sinking merchant vessels, their depredations can scarcely be confined to the ships of a belligerent or otherwise friendless victim. Ships of other nationalities must also be deterred and, in any case, a submerged submarine experiences great difficulty in identifying the nationality of its targets. Yet, if vessels flying the American flag, or even the flag of some country allied to the United States, were to be sunk by 'unknown submarines', the minimum reaction to be expected would be the concentration of a superior naval force in the area concerned, as has several times happened in response to lesser threats in the Gulf of Akaba. Any extended use of Soviet submarines in this way would thus surely be rejected in Moscow, both as liable to defeat even by limited naval force and as calculated to increase the risk of a warlike confrontation with the United States and their Allies.

Even in the improbable event of it proving possible to confine attacks to the ships of a single victim unlikely to attract Western support, this expedient might still appear undesirable to the Soviet Government. With a large and growing merchant marine now sailing the oceans of the world, they can scarcely afford to allow the thirty-one other navies with submarines to suppose that merchant vessels can be torpedoed with impunity in peace-time. The 'unknown submarine' is the weapon of a government with nothing to lose and sinking ships an act of such violence that its consequences can seldom be expected to remain limited.

Yet, if submarines do not actually sink ships, their mere menace is likely to prove ineffective. A submarine cannot communicate a threat without making its presence known. Indeed, unless the victim is a fairly sophisticated and consequently dangerous, warship, the submarine will actually have to surface, when it ceases to be a superior ship and becomes acutely vulnerable to almost any warship. Even a merchant vessel with a bold captain might treat a summons to 'heave to or be sunk' as constituting a threat too violent to be credible. Perhaps the greatest weakness of the modern submarine – for Soviet submarines do not mount guns – is that it has no equivalent to the graduated ladder of violence enjoyed by surface warships.[6] If the initial summons is disregarded and the fire of small arms ignored, the submarine must sink its victim or submit to the calling of its bluff. Nor is the silent menace presented by a flotilla of submerged submarines to a surface fleet which has detected their presence likely to cow a resolute victim, who will calculate that, irrespective of the probable outcome of a local naval battle, the submarines will only take action if war is intended. The six Soviet submarines that entered the Caribbean during the Cuban missile crisis would have been the least of American worries even if they had not been continuously tracked by the US Navy[7] and even if their numbers had been many times greater.

The size of the Soviet submarine fleet thus offers no argument for departing from the view previously expressed in relation to other navies that, except in very special circumstances, the submarine in time of peace is the weapon of the victim rather than of the assailant and is inherently ill-suited to the exercise of limited naval force. Indeed, although the variegated and ingenious uses to which warships have been put during the last fifty years make one chary of altogether excluding any possibility from the future range of gunboat diplomacy, it is at least probable that the main peace-time rôle of Soviet submarines will be to preoccupy, and thereby neutralize, surface warships of the United States and, to a lesser extent, of their allies. Although an American admiral on a peace-time mission need not fear attack from Soviet submarines, he may have to consider the safety of his own strike carriers or missile-firing submarines. Any American ship committed to instant readiness for nuclear war must be protected against Soviet submarines in its vicinity. It is thus conceivable that a strong concentration of Soviet submarines in the Mediterranean would further reduce the number of surface warships which the Commander of the Sixth Fleet could spare for the exercise of limited naval force. But the credibility of even this threat would be dependent on the general level of tension between the United States and the Soviet Union and, unless the imminence of a general war seemed plausible, might not be independently and intrinsically effective. On the whole, therefore, we are probably safe in discarding from our calculations the 385 miscellaneous Soviet submarines listed in the 1969–70 edition of *Jane's Fighting Ships* and in focusing our attention exclusively on ocean-going surface warships.

The concept of an ocean-going warship, however, now involves a difficulty which scarcely arose when other navies were under consideration. Ships large enough to go anywhere, to keep the seas in all weathers and, when attended by appropriate auxiliaries, to remain on station for an appreciable time were obviously best suited to the exercise of limited naval force and, if all lesser craft were excluded, the resulting total figure provided a rough and ready yardstick for assessing the numerical capacity of a navy for diplomatic tasks and for comparing the strength of one navy with another. No significant distortions were introduced, because warships of doubtfully ocean-going capability made only a minor contribution to the total strength of most of the navies considered likely to intervene at any distance from their own shores. The Soviet Union, however, has 275 coastal escort vessels, 125 missile patrol boats and 350 motor-torpedo-boats, almost as many, in each class, as the rest of the world's navies put together (if China's 290 motor-torpedo-boats are excluded). These are such formidable numbers – and the Osa and Komar boats are such formidable craft – that their potential contribution to the resources of naval diplomacy has to be rather more carefully weighed. It scarcely needs saying that they could obviously be used in the vicinity of their own bases: the PUEBLO and EILATH incidents demonstrated that and one can imagine various situations in which the Soviet Union might wish to employ limited naval force in what they call the pre-coastal zone – up to 150 miles offshore[8] – and would find this type of vessel suitable. It is their employment farther afield – and one of the strongest arguments for gunboat diplomacy has always been the length of its arm – that seems less likely. The voyage need not be an obstacle – smaller craft have sailed from Europe to the Pacific – though they would need more refuelling and assistance than larger warships. But, once they had arrived, their greater dependence on bases, lower operational endurance, reduced fighting ability in bad weather and less impressive appearance would probably more than outweigh the speed of the missile and torpedo boats and the armament of the former. And the coastal escorts lack even these advantages.

Moreover, these vessels may not be so readily available as their numbers would suggest. The Soviet Union has a total coast-line of 66,090 miles, the largest of any state and thirteen times greater than that of the United Kingdom. Although parts of this coast are, for many months of the year, economically protected by ice, this natural ally has the drawback of the human variety: it separates one sector from another and greatly complicates the tasks of deployment and reinforcement. Even a conventional coastal defence would thus demand a far greater commitment from the Soviet Navy than from any other. But the obsessive anxiety manifested by the Soviet régime for the impenetrability of its landward frontiers is also extended to its territorial waters. In the eyes of the Kremlin it is not enough to guard against the approach of invasion fleets, missile-firing submarines, carrier task forces or scouting warships: fishermen, straying freighters, explorers, seaborne spies and agents of subversion are omnipresent dangers. Nor can the guardians of the Soviet shores be content with a merely outward vigilance: they must be equally alert in preventing the unauthorized departure of Soviet nationals.[9]

This kind of coastguard obviously demands formidable resources. If it were entrusted to the minor warships previously mentioned and if, as seems plausible, the usual ratio of a total establishment of three ships for every one on station applied to these exacting, if short-range, conditions, then even 750 minor warships would furnish only one patrol craft for every 264 miles of coast-line. Although evidence of their precise deployment is lacking, their preoccupation with coastal defence seems plausible and might help to account for their non-appearance in more distant seas. This, in its turn, militates against their prospective employment in gunboat diplomacy. A ship which never sails the oceans does not exercise its crew in the seamanship this demands: it is not, therefore, in the fullest sense an ocean-going ship. It thus seems unlikely that the Soviet Navy would ever wish to face the problems – of withdrawal from priority tasks, of training, of the organization of logistic support, of overcoming the inherent disadvantages of small size – that would be entailed by the deploying of a flotilla of Osa boats, even to the Mediterranean, let alone to more distant oceans. And less than a flotilla would surely be markedly less cost-effective than one or two larger warships.

Thus far – indeed, even farther – there is relatively little difficulty in accepting the doctrine of the conservative school that the tasks of the Soviet Navy, even in peace-time, probably exceed its imposing capacities, which cannot be regarded as constituting a new Armada able to pose an offensive threat to the superior maritime might of a united Western Alliance. Doubts creep in only when one attempts to assess the availability of the ocean-going surface warships of the Soviet Navy:

   2 helicopter carriers
   9 surface-to-surface missile cruisers
 11 gun cruisers (one with surface-to-air missiles)
   4 other cruisers
 10 surface-to-surface missile destroyers
 19 surface-to-air missile destroyers
 70 other destroyers
100 other ocean-going escorts
___
Total 225 ocean-going surface warships (excluding fleet mine-sweepers)[10]

Naturally, most of these ships have a rôle to play in deterrence or readiness for war: Western missile-firing submarines and strike carriers must, so far as this is possible, be detected and shadowed; Soviet missile-firing submarines must be screened and protected; Western naval manœuvres and exercises must be followed and observed by at least some of the ships that would be employed against Western fleets in war. Moreover, because of the inconvenient facts of Russian geography, these vessels must be distributed among four separate fleets, where they are not always quickly or conveniently inter-changeable. It would clearly be wrong, even allowing for the extent to which the new Soviet nuclear submarines will presumably take over the main burden of counter-deterrent defence, to suppose that all or most of these warships would be readily available for merely diplomatic duties. Yet it seems implausible to go to the other extreme, as sometimes happens, and to argue that the inadequacy of Soviet resources for major naval warfare is reflected in a corresponding lack of warships available for peace-time employment.

A relatively simple argument against this extreme thesis may be deduced from the fluctuations of Soviet naval strength in the Mediterranean. This has always been provided by the detachment of ships, sometimes for three months or more, sometimes just on passage, from one of the four standing Soviet fleets: the Baltic, Black Sea, Far Eastern and Northern. Until 1963 there were frequent visits, but also long intervals with no Soviet surface warship in the Mediterranean. From 1963 to 1967 there were nearly always four or five. Since the summer of 1967 the number has seldom fallen so low, has averaged from eight to twelve and has sometimes risen as high as eighteen. As one of these peaks coincided with a prolonged cruise in the Indian Ocean by three other Soviet warships, it seems that the four main Soviet fleets can spare as many as twenty-one major warships.

It can, of course, be contended that the eighteen ships in the Mediterranean had only been redeployed from one warlike task to another, that their location, rather than their rôle, had altered. Some of these ships do undoubtedly appear to have spent part of their time shadowing the US Sixth Fleet, particularly the American aircraft carriers, and one of the functions of the Soviet naval presence must be to hamper an American nuclear strike. But it is questionable whether this is the only function or even the most important function or an altogether indispensable function.

The growth of the Soviet Mediterranean squadron happens to coincide with the declining significance to the United States of that sea as a nuclear launching area. In the late fifties, when Soviet surface warships were only occasional visitors, carriers sustained the entire naval contribution to the American deterrent and the Eastern Mediterranean was their most advantageous location. Today Polaris submarines provide most of the seaborne strike potential of the United States and 90 per cent of these submarines are, it seems, normally outside the Mediterranean. It is uncertain whether a strategic strike is still included among the tasks of the Sixth Fleet's carriers, but even if it is, the destruction of all American surface forces in the Mediterranean would only fractionally reduce American ability to devastate the territory of the Soviet Union.[11]

If the purpose of the Soviet Mediterranean squadron is strategic defence, then the last few years have seen the Russians pursuing a shrinking prize with ever larger forces.

And even these are inadequate and ineffective. Herrick is explicit:

> Except by a wholly unexpected attack, the USSR could not realistically entertain much hope of their missile destroyers or submarines successfully attacking the Sixth Fleet aircraft carriers, let alone the Polaris submarines, and, in any event, not before the latter were able to launch their initial retaliatory strike against the Soviet Union.[12]

The British Minister of Defence insisted that Soviet warships in the Mediterranean would be sunk in a matter of minutes,[13] a claim later described by Admiral of the Fleet Gorshkov as 'unpardonable bragging',[14] but Admiral Rivero, the NATO Commander-in-Chief, Southern Europe, is only one of the American admirals who have always denied that the Soviet Mediterranean squadron constitutes a serious threat to the US Sixth Fleet.[15]

These gloomy predictions, even if they are shared by Russian admirals (traditionally inclined to pessimism), need not prevent the presence of Soviet warships from imposing an added strain on American naval resources and even on American nerves. Shadowing American carriers and trying to detect American submarines makes the task of the United States Navy more difficult and more expensive; it provides admirable training for Soviet sailors; in the eyes of Soviet planners it may even prevent the United States from locating in the Mediterranean a still greater nuclear menace. As long as there are Soviet warships in the Mediterranean, strategic defence is obviously one task which they might appropriately attempt. But, if they are unlikely to succeed, would it make much difference if there happened to be no Soviet surface ship in the Mediterranean when war broke out? Is there much reason to regard this task as indispensable or ships as more irretrievably committed to this rôle than to another? If the nuclear strike capacity of the Soviet Union, which is mainly provided by land-based inter-continental missiles, fails to deter the United States, it is hard to see how the relatively minor damage-limiting potential of Soviet surface warships could exert a decisive influence on American calculations.

Indeed, history suggests that inadequate naval resources are more likely to impose a policy of cautious conservation on the stronger, rather than the weaker, of two rival naval powers. When confronted by an inferior German Navy, the British hoarded their battleships, whereas the Germans gambled their entire fleet on the conquest of Norway and won. If the primary objective of naval victory is impossible, it is worth while to run considerable risks in pursuit of secondary goals. Jellicoe, in Churchill's famous phrase, was the only man on either side who could have lost the war in an afternoon,[16] but, in both World Wars, Germany could have afforded much greater naval disasters than she actually suffered.

This argument should not be pushed too far. There are obviously many considerations – political, professional, temperamental – which would prevent Soviet admirals from subscribing to the full implications of the idea that, if their Navy cannot significantly limit the destructive impact of an American nuclear strike against the Soviet Union, then the strategic rôle of the Navy is – as Churchill once said of the German High Seas Fleet – a luxury rather than a necessity.[17] All that is here contended is that commitment to strategic defence need not be absolute because, unlike the different task of coastal defence, the chances of success are too small even if maximum strength is available, to prevent the Soviet Navy from deploying ocean-going warships for other purposes in time of peace.

Just how many might be thus available is impossible to estimate. Soviet naval movements in the Mediterranean cannot be concealed and have gone on long enough to establish a pattern of deployment which at least permits some guessing at functions and purposes. Published information is inadequate to support similar deductions about the four main Soviet fleets, but it would be surprising if at least the Black Sea Fleet did not have considerable capacity to spare.[18] Their rôle at the outset of general nuclear war seems unlikely to be crucial or to demand extensive resources. And, even if we make the rather large assumption that the other three fleets have already diverted to the Mediterranean and to ocean-going cruising as many ships as they could possibly spare from their war-time rôle, it does not necessarily follow that the Soviet Government will always regard every peace-time use of warships as automatically entailing the risk of general war. This theory, to be considered further when political factors are examined, would run counter to the entire argument of this book on the scope for the political application of limited naval force.

So far as resources are concerned, therefore, it seems safer to assume that the Soviet Navy could already spare at least a dozen ocean-going surface warships, that this minimum might well be increased by drawing on the Black Sea Fleet, that the demands on surface warships of instant readiness for nuclear war are likely to diminish as the number of modern submarines rises and that, unless the next few years see a substantial decline in the total number of Soviet ocean-going warships, the proportion of these available for peace-time missions will steadily increase. Indeed, if resources are to provide a serious obstacle to Soviet employment of limited naval force, this must be sought in the characteristics of individual ships rather than in the total strength of the surface fleet.

One obvious weakness, for instance, is the absence of aircraft carriers. This must exclude most *opposed amphibious operations* beyond the reach of shore-based air cover, though it is conceivable that a squadron of ships with surface-to-air missiles might be capable of adequate defence against a small, unsophisticated and disorganized air force. If a small force of naval infantry, for instance, had to be landed to support one side in a civil conflict, there might be nothing worse to fear than sporadic and unco-ordinated attacks from the handful of aircraft available to the other side. And, if air attack need not be expected, there seems no reason to dissent from the view that 'Soviet capacity for amphibious operations must be considered significant, particularly in the Mediterranean',[19] where six Alligator-class landing ships (each capable of lifting a naval infantry battalion) were deployed in March 1970[20] and where a helicopter carrier is a frequent visitor.

Simple amphibious operations, given favourable political circumstances, must accordingly be regarded as well within the capacity of the Soviet Navy, which has frequently undertaken large-scale landing exercises in the Baltic and Black Sea. Admittedly these seem to have been in the context of flank support to military operations envisaged as taking place in war-time conditions, but the training and experience they provided would be no less useful in peace-time. Moreover, as Western military commanders have often discovered to their cost, undue realism in the political scenario of military or naval manœuvres can be a serious source of embarrassment and one which Soviet leaders, whose every move is exposed to hostile scrutiny and liable to be accorded the worst possible interpretation, would be particularly careful to avoid. Nevertheless, even manœuvres ostensibly conceived as training for war can also have a political application in time of peace and the major amphibious operation of May 1969, which involved the landing of naval infantry at a point on the Soviet coast immediately adjacent to the Norwegian frontier,[21]

K

can scarcely be considered in isolation from the continuing Soviet propaganda campaign against Norwegian membership of NATO.

The obstacle to *superior fleet operations*, on the other hand, is primarily political. These are scarcely conceivable in any circumstances in which American hostility might be expected, for the strength and world-wide deployment of the US Navy would make it difficult for the Soviet Union to assemble a strong enough force anywhere outside the Baltic and Black Seas in which a superior fleet could plausibly exercise a peace-time rôle. To admit this as a possibility, one would have to postulate some rather unlikely political situations: perhaps a Soviet naval blockade of South Africa in response to a United Nations resolution which the Western Powers were prepared neither to implement nor to oppose.

Lesser operations are still more feasible in terms of resources. Indeed, the Soviet Navy actually executed a *simple fleet operation* of the expressive variety in January 1968, when sixteen warships, including cruisers and missile-armed ships, were deployed in the Sea of Japan and apparently manoeuvred between the North Korean coast and the American naval task force which threatened that country after the seizure of PUEBLO.[22] Such a small Soviet force (some of the sixteen ships were tankers and intelligence trawlers) offered no serious threat to the American carriers ENTERPRISE, RANGER and YORKTOWN with the three cruisers and twenty-six destroyers that accompanied them;[23] the Soviet ships could neither have prevented a nuclear strike against North Korea nor even have defended themselves. But it was a discreet, yet unmistakable indication of Soviet interest and concern in American reactions to what Mr Rusk had described as being 'in the category of actions that are to be construed as acts of war'.[24] Indeed, in so far as it was intended to symbolize Soviet commitment to the defence of North Korea, it may even have been a more effective threat than that posed by the greatly superior American fleet. It was also a striking instance of the occasional willingness of the Soviet Government to divert their ships to tasks which are both intrinsically risky and are likely to increase tension with the United States even at a moment of crisis.

It thus seems reasonable to reject the argument that Soviet surface forces are irretrievably committed to instant readiness for nuclear war and to conclude that, bearing in mind the modernity of Soviet warships (less than 1 per cent are as much as twenty years old),[25] their technical sophistication and their powerful armament, Soviet capacity for the exercise of limited naval force will be comparable with that of Britain and France as long as these two countries retain their carriers, and, once those are relinquished, will probably be second only to that of the United States. This is naturally a calculation from resources alone: as long as Britain and France can depend on full American backing, they may be able to run proportionately greater peace-time risks than the Soviet Union. In terms of naval capacity, however, Soviet readiness for distant deployment may be expected to rise and that of Britain and France to fall.

Soviet readiness to use this capacity for the political application of limited force in peace-time is nevertheless hard to support with convincing precedents or explicit doctrine. To make a case for this at all one must start with the proposition that an ocean-going Soviet Navy – one whose ships regularly sailed distant seas as well as possessing the theoretical capacity to do so – first emerged during the sixties,[26] so that Soviet admirals have not had much time either to establish a record of forceful activity in peace-time or to reveal any ideas they may have formulated on this subject. Needless to say, this argument does not imply that the new Soviet Navy was created, or its forward deployment decided, for the express purpose of peace-time use. On the contrary, all the evidence suggests that Soviet planners, wished to provide themselves with the naval means to deter, or to wage, general nuclear war.

It is thus scarcely surprising to discover that official Soviet pronouncements are as predominantly warlike as they are often unrealistic. The 1966 programme of the Communist Party of the Soviet Union on the Defence of the Socialist Fatherland defined the task of the Navy as:

destroying the enemy's fleet, disrupting his sea and ocean communications, carrying nuclear rocket strikes on shore and interior communications and, also, co-operating with its own ground troops and assuring the protection of its own sea communication.

The History of Military Art published in the same year was even more explicit:

The Soviet Navy can perform any strategic task in distant ocean regions, it can battle with the enemy's fleet on the sea and in bases, destroy his strike aircraft carriers and rocket-carrying submarines.

Such claims are too exaggerated to be taken seriously, but there is one theme that runs through all the bombast and of which the results are already apparent:

We must be prepared . . . on the whole territory of the world ocean (Admiral of the Fleet Gorshkov, 1963).[27]

Our fleet has become an ocean fleet and has acquired ocean-going qualities closing the era of undivided rule of the oceans by the American and English Navies, *History of Military Art,* 1966.

The Soviet Navy has now become an ocean-going navy (Admiral Grishanov, 1967).[28]

The modern fleet is capable not only of frustrating the attack of any aggressor from the sea but also of striking crushing blows at his fleet in the most remote areas of the ocean (Admiral of the Fleet Gorshkov, 1969).[29]

The Russians may still be exaggerating the ocean-going character- istics of a navy which does not yet maintain a permanent presence in any distant sea, but the extensive and increasingly frequent, cruises of their warships in the Atlantic, in the Caribbean, in the Indian Ocean, in the Persian Gulf, suggest that this has become a genuine naval doctrine rather than a mere propaganda declaration. There is also a variation on this theme, which is less frequently heard, but which may acquire increased significance if general nuclear war – and the part to be played in it by Soviet surface warships – begin to seem rather less probable. It was first enunciated in 1962, soon after the humiliating American demonstration of sea-power in the Cuban missile crisis, by Admiral of the Fleet Gorshkov, then, as now, the Commander-in-Chief:

the Soviet Navy . . . is obliged to be prepared at any moment and at any point of the globe to secure the protection of the interests of our state.[30]

This interesting, if ambiguous, phrase 'the interests of our state', with its suggestion that the Soviet Navy might have a rôle not con- fined to general nuclear war, was occasionally echoed in subsequent years, but does not seem to have received any significant interpre- tation or specific application until 1967, when, in one of the spate of articles elicited by the Fiftieth Anniversary Celebrations, Admiral of the Fleet Gorshkov paid tribute to:

the crews of ships sailing in the Mediterranean Sea, who are ful- filling the responsible task of safeguarding the state interests of the Soviet Union in this region.[31]

The Commander-in-Chief used almost identical words in February 1968[32] but it was left to his First Deputy, Admiral of the Fleet Kasatonov, to provide further elucidation on 3 January, 1969:

Soviet warships entered the Mediterranean to consolidate international peace and security . . . in conformity with the interests of the Arab states who are victims of Israeli aggression.[33]

As 'Israeli aggression' took place only in June 1967, Admiral of the Fleet Kasatonov's words invite speculation concerning the nature of the 'state interests' to which Admiral of the Fleet Gorshkov referred in February of that year, but all doubts should have been stilled on 17 May 1969, when Rear-Admiral Navoitsev achieved an unctuous rectitude worthy of any of his Western colleagues:

the presence of the Soviet Navy in the Mediterranean is a most important factor for stabilization in that troubled area of the globe.[34]

These were, admittedly, rather lonely notes amid the crashing brass of an orchestra otherwise devoted to the rôle of the Soviet Navy as an instrument for the deterrence, or the waging, of general nuclear war. Were they merely an effort to extract propaganda advantage from the presence of Soviet warships in the Mediterranean or did they perhaps represent the tentative emergence of a new doctrine originally foreshadowed by Admiral of the Fleet Gorshkov seven years earlier?

The evidence is insufficient to permit firm conclusions either way, but it is worth examining the opposing arguments, which rest on different analyses of the significance of Soviet naval activities in the Mediterranean from 1967 onwards. The contention that Soviet warships had an exclusively strategic purpose has already been discussed and found less than fully convincing, but it is sometimes bolstered by the observation that no diplomatic use was made of these ships before or during the Six-Day War. But what could they have done? The threat of naval intervention by Britain and the United States,[35] whose available forces were greatly superior, was originally intended to prevent the closure of the Straits of Tiran and thereby to remove one motive for war between Israel and Egypt. Whether this project would have succeeded will never be known: there was a failure of political nerve and it was abandoned. But, when the Six-Day War did break out, the Arabs remembered the earlier threat and, linking this with the presence of British and American aircraft carriers, believed the lie that these had participated in the Israeli attack on Egypt. It was thus this ambitious and abortive attempt to employ limited naval force that was largely responsible for the June explosion of wrecked Embassies, broken relations, oil boycotts and injury to the economies, the interests, the influence and the Middle

Eastern residents of Britain and the United States. Measured against this lamentable record, Soviet naval inactivity in a crisis that offered no scope for the diplomatic employment of their ships needs neither explanation nor excuse: it reflected an elementary prudence and a proper understanding of the restricted role of limited naval force.

Once the dust of war had settled, however, Soviet warships intervened in a manner that was appropriate and that reaped a modest diplomatic reward. It was a little risky to send eight ships (including a cruiser and two destroyers, one with missiles) into Port Said – the Israeli forces across the Canal were still flushed with victory and only a month had passed since the attack on LIBERTY – but Admiral Molochov's bold declaration on 10 July 'we are ready to co-operate with Egyptian armed forces to repel any aggression'[36] achieved its objective. Whether or not the Israelis had ever intended a further advance, none was made, and some of the credit earlier lost by the Soviet Union in Arab eyes was regained. Indeed, this seemingly trivial intervention probably had more immediate impact than the intrinsically more important deliveries of arms, because the Soviet Union was seen by the Arabs as at last having actually displayed some resolution.[37]

This success may also have contributed to Soviet acquisition of a base for their ships at Alexandria, to their continuing welcome in other Arab ports closed to the warships of their rivals, to the eager and gleeful attention still devoted by the Arab press to Soviet naval movements in the Mediterranean. As a clear-cut case of the purposeful threat of limited naval force, it offers some support both to the claims of Admirals Kasatonov and Navoitsev and to the theory that:

> the aim of the new Soviet naval development in the Mediterranean is not war-time combat with the US Sixth Fleet, but the furtherance of Soviet policy objectives at a much lower level of risk and in an environment considerably less drastic than one of total US–Soviet hostility.[38]

It was not, however, the only occasion on which the Soviet Union may have sought, or derived, political advantage from the presence of their warships in this sea. When tension again flared up on the Suez Canal, for instance, Soviet warships returned to Port Said on 25 October 1967, and their propagandists claimed, and some Egyptians seem to have believed, that this prevented a renewed Israeli attack on Egypt.[39] Some ships, at least, seem to have remained at Port Said until November 1968.[40] Then, on 4 September 1969,

Tripoli radio announced that the presence of Soviet warships had deterred British intervention against the Libyan *coup d'état*.[41] Although it is most unlikely that British intervention was ever contemplated, there were in fact Soviet warships in the vicinity and this was known in London as well as in Libya. What mattered, however, both in Libya and in the Lebanon, was what people believed. The United States probably never considered a repetition of their 1958 landing in the Lebanon, but one of the reasons given by the US News and World Report on 3 November was:

> the US Navy's Sixth Fleet is less visible in the Eastern Mediterranean than it once was. There is *a new presence* in those waters – *the Soviet Mediterranean Fleet*.[42]

All this is fairly flimsy stuff. It does not prove that the Soviet Government have decided to emulate the United States and to use their Navy to support Soviet policy and diplomacy in the Mediterranean area. It does suggest the possibility of something besides propaganda behind the words of Admirals Kasatonov and Navoitsev, but it also makes it worth while to consider whether there are any further obstacles to the future diplomatic employment of the Soviet Navy. If the resources exist, if the initial emergence of a doctrine can be tentatively discerned, if one or two gingerly experiments have been attempted, is there anything to prevent this process from continuing and developing?

There is naturally no need to recapitulate the general arguments of Chapter Three to support the proposition that, if naval resources are available, political situations could arise in which warships might be employed without the risk of a dangerous confrontation with the United States. The objection that limited naval force is impossible in a bipolar world has been dealt with already: what remains to be considered here is an obstacle peculiar to the Soviet Union and supposedly to be deduced from the history of Soviet foreign policy and the ideological principles of Soviet Communism. The Soviet Union, so it is argued, is essentially a continental power, which has employed military force only to defend, to consolidate and occasionally to enlarge its landward frontiers, together with the glacis of political influence and ascendancy which surrounds them. The use of military force, even on a considerable scale, during and after the Civil War, against China in 1929, against Japan in 1937, 1938 and 1939, against Poland and Finland in 1939, against the Baltic States in 1940, to a lesser degree in Iran in 1945 and 1946, against Hungary in 1956 and against Czechoslovakia in 1968 thus finds no parallel in the extra-peripheral activities of the Soviet Union, where the methods employed have exclusively been those of diplomacy, propaganda, subsidy (economic aid, technical assistance and the supply of arms) and subversion. This pattern, it is further argued, is not merely a historical coincidence arising from a combination of past naval weakness with more urgent preoccupations on the European and Asian frontiers of the Soviet Union, but also reflects an ideological aversion from anything smacking of imperialism or adventurism, and a realistic appreciation of the long-term interests both of Russia and of the Communist movement. The doctrine of the war of national liberation,[43] for instance, enables the Soviet Government to encourage and assist the use of force against Western interests or influence in third countries, yet themselves to avoid the intervention for which they denounce others. As a result, limited war, let alone limited force, finds no place in Soviet political or military doctrine. 'Wars can be started only by imperialists',[44] unless they are national liberation wars, which can be fought by someone else. It would thus be unprecedented, ideologically inconsistent and against the best interests of the Soviet Union, to employ limited naval force in quest of advantages more easily secured by traditional Soviet methods. Indeed, even if some opportunity should present itself which only warships could seize, the Soviet Union would still be deterred by the fear of ruining their sedulously cultivated image of 'respect for the rights and national independence of all peoples, big and small'[45] and of jeopardizing the gains already made in Africa, Asia and the Middle East.

This is a persuasive thesis, not least because all governments do prefer to go on doing what they have done before. But two major qualifications are necessary. First of all, the objective position of the Soviet Union in the international firmament has undergone a transformation so profound that significant changes are conceivable in the foreign policy of the Soviet Union. This is a proposition which demands some amplification. It does *not* necessarily imply any fundamental change in Soviet ideology or subjective Soviet attitudes. In 1937, for instance, the Soviet Ambassador in London anxiously inquired of the British Foreign Secretary whether a British ship, if chartered by the Soviet Government to evacuate from Gijón the children of Spanish Communists, could still count on the only protection which experience had demonstrated to be efficacious against Spanish Nationalist cruisers – that of the Royal Navy.[46] The request and the condescension with which it was granted would be inconceivable today, but not because of any ideological upheaval. The attitudes of Mr Brezhnev are not so different from those of Marshal Stalin; Sir Alec Douglas-Home has much the same outlook as Mr

Eden. It is the objective capacities of their countries that have altered beyond the recognition of either.

And different capacities, whether those concerned care to admit it or not, do ultimately result in different policies. So do different interests. These are not the same as aspirations.[47] When Mr Churchill became the Prime Minister, in 1951, of a British Government which no longer ruled India, his aspirations – and those of his countrymen – had not appreciably altered since 1945: their interests and capacities had, though several years and some painful lessons were needed before policies were adapted accordingly. It is only in the last few years that the Soviet Government have had a major stake – in men, money and prestige – across the seas. This transformation of Soviet interests has so far been slow to reflect itself in perceived Soviet ideology, aspirations or even policies. The American people took still longer to absorb the implications of interests and capacities that were already global as early as 1919.

The extent of objective change is naturally most blatant if one chooses as the starting point some year before the Second World War. But even the last quarter of a century has been revolutionary. It has witnessed a fundamental change in the international posture of the Soviet Union. For most of the two decades after the Second World War the Soviet Union swam with an advancing tide that was steadily demolishing the sand-castles of privilege, of feudalism, of alien capitalism and of European imperialism. In Eastern Europe, in China, in the Middle East, in South-East Asia and in Africa the old order was already under attack and only limited Soviet assistance was needed to complete its destruction. National liberation, whether from native oligarchies or from foreign domination, was an objective which was widely, sincerely and independently pursued. It suited both the interests and the ideology of the Soviet Union and, as long as the struggle continued, involved no major conflict of purpose between Soviet state interests and those of the subject peoples.

But this phase has largely come to an end: not because the Soviet Union has changed, but because the world is a different place. The weakest bastions of the old order have all crumbled and some of those still under siege are either better defended or assailed by forces less compatible with Soviet purposes. What is more is that, in the otherwise advantageous process of expelling or eroding hostile influences, the Soviet Union has acquired responsibilities and commitments of its own. These may be different in conception, even in their objective nature, from the relationships they replaced, but they confront the Soviet Union with problems that were familiar to the former Great Powers and that still perplex the United States. It is in

Eastern Europe that the liabilities of the Soviet Union's new posture are most obvious, because it is there that time has completed the transformation of revolutionary Russia into the jealous guardian of the *status quo* and the anxious upholder of painfully acquired influence and authority. Even outside Europe, however, there are now countries where a radical change in existing régimes or policies would be embarrassing, even humiliating, to the Soviet Union. This is not because the Soviet Union derives much concrete benefit from the present state of affairs or would necessarily sustain material loss by its transformation, but simply because, in the eyes of the world, these governments are Soviet clients and their overthrow, even by their own people, would thus constitute a defeat for the Soviet Union and entail a consequential loss of prestige. In some cases – Egypt is an example – the danger threatening these governments does not derive from their compliance with Soviet policies but, as this is probably seen from the Kremlin, from their pursuit of irrelevant adventures, from their faulty ideology, their disregard of Soviet advice and their misuse of Soviet aid. There is thus a new need for the Soviet Union to exercise a more effective influence over foreign governments – to prevent their follies from jeopardizing their own survival and the prestige of the Soviet Union. The latitude that could be permitted to governments and movements revolting against Western ascendancy[48] may no longer be tolerable in those whose primary function, as seen from the Kremlin, is now to preserve the position since acquired by the Soviet Union.[49]

These international considerations may also be reinforced, though here we are trespassing on more speculative ground, by domestic political factors. There is some evidence of a growing impatience among the Soviet ruling class at the seemingly inadequate rewards of the foreign aid which has been provided at such cost to the Soviet consumer. If this feeling that he who pays the piper should call the tune does exist, it may strengthen other factors that seem to be working in favour of tightening centralized control over the Soviet sphere of influence. The Yugoslavs, for instance, have already expressed alarm at an East German suggestion that the scope of the Brezhnev doctrine of limited sovereignty may not be confined to members of the Warsaw Pact.[50] Although it would be premature to conclude that the Soviet Union regards its position in the Middle East, for instance, as requiring the same kind of consolidation as its ascendancy in Eastern Europe, there can be little doubt that Soviet foreign policy has entered a new and more defensive phase. In the seventies the Soviet Government are more likely to be concerned with holding on to what they already have than with undermining the position of others, with resisting revolutionary forces rather than with fanning their flames. This new posture – and this is the second qualification needed to the traditional view of Soviet policy – is liable to restrict the utility of the techniques they have previously employed. Communism, at least as this is understood in Moscow, no longer commands the same enthusiasm from the masses or the same obedience from the initiated. There are newer and more exciting faiths, rival and more charismatic Popes. There are even heretics who claim the protestant right to make their own interpretation of the sacred dogmas. Above all, the ideological arguments that served so well in subversion are less efficacious when the lessons to be inculcated are those of prudence, restraint, conformity and the paramount importance of avoiding excessive demands on Soviet resources. A revolutionary ideology is an imperfect instrument for a conservative policy.

It goes without saying that the Soviet Government will still remain reluctant to contemplate the risky alternative of coercion, particularly if this must be exerted overseas, without the overwhelming strength of the Red Army and in an area less generally regarded as exclusively within their own sphere of influence. If political arguments could be effectively supplemented by economic pressures, for instance, this would doubtless be the preferred course. Withholding aid or suspending imports are often suggested as possible weapons, but they will not necessarily prove more efficacious in Soviet hands than on the many occasions when they have been wielded in vain by Western governments. And the comparison is appropriate, because the very success of the Soviet Government in eroding Western positions is gradually forcing it into postures more and more analogous to those of the Powers it has displaced. As a state with an overseas influence and prestige to defend, the Soviet Union is now more likely than hitherto to face similar problems and to be compelled at least to consider similar solutions.

The undoubtedly new capacities of the Soviet Navy and the conjecturally nascent doctrines of Soviet admirals are thus matched by a novel political situation, to which the methods employed even in the recent past may no longer be applicable. The late twentieth-century world is changing so rapidly that patterns of behaviour are necessarily variable. A mere fifteen years ago the Soviet Union had no stake beyond the seas. Communism seemed a continental monolith and China, North Korea and North Vietnam merely Asian extensions of the land-mass that began at the Elbe. When, in 1955, arms were first supplied to the Middle East and economic aid to a non-Communist country (India), these were new departures as surprising as the arrival at Spithead, two years earlier, of the cruiser SVERDLOV for the Coronation Naval Review. It would be rash to assume that the next fifteen years have no comparable surprises in store or that an altered challenge will elicit only a recently traditional response. Algeria, Cuba, Egypt, Libya, North Korea, Syria, North Vietnam, Southern Yemen, Yemen – these are only some of the countries across the seas in which the Soviet Union has invested scarce resources, acquired influence, staked prestige. Perhaps none of them will ever provide an occasion for the exercise of Soviet limited naval force, but each new outpost increases the chances as much as each new warship augments the possibilities.

For those who still find it impossible seriously to entertain the idea of a coercive application of limited Soviet naval force, there is one last argument, which may be easier to reconcile with the lessons of the past and with the public pronouncements of Soviet leaders. Though a novice in the rôle of assailant, the Soviet Union has had considerable experience as a victim. From 1919 to 1921 the shores of Russia were constantly assailed by the 'interventionist' warships of Japan, of the European Powers and of the United States. During the Spanish Civil War her merchant vessels were stopped, seized and sunk with impunity on the high seas and these injuries were compounded by the insult of a Non-Intervention Patrol she lacked the warships to join. In 1948 Stalin was compelled to declare: 'We have no navy. The uprisings in Greece must be stopped and as quickly as possible.'[51] Even when the possession of thermo-nuclear weapons had given the Soviet Union immunity from direct attack, Soviet leaders still had to watch in impotent fury the use of warships against others and to admit their auxiliary effectiveness in the confrontation of 1962 with the United States.

No doubt these bitter experiences reinforced their sympathy with other victims and their denunciation of gunboat diplomacy as an essentially immoral instrument of policy. But these were not the only lessons they learned. It was of the Spanish Civil War that a former Soviet Commander-in-Chief, Admiral Kuznetsov, remarked:

At that time it became particularly apparent how important the sea is for us and how we need a strong navy.[52]

Since then 'our navy has been turned completely into an offensive type of long-range defence force'[53] and the Soviet Union has new means of promoting the avowedly defensive and pacific purposes of Soviet foreign policy. It has earlier been argued that there is little objective difference between the offensive and defensive application of limited naval force, but that is not how governments habitually represent, perhaps even see, these problems. If the Soviet Mediterranean Squadron had existed in 1956 and had interposed its ships between Port Said and the advancing Anglo-French convoy, daring the latter to shoot its way through, would not this have been regarded, even in the West, as a course of action more defensive in its nature, even less reprehensible, than the actual threat of using 'rocket technique' 'to crush the aggressors and restore peace in the East'?[54] It might also have been more effective.

Even on the most generous interpretation of Soviet sincerity in rejecting the use of limited force as an instrument of policy, it would be hard to rule out the possibility of such defensive applications. And defence, it must be repeated, is everywhere a flexible and adaptable concept. In the Lebanese crisis of 1958 both the Soviet Union and the United States could sincerely and plausibly argue that they were supporting their friends against external aggression, but only the United States then possessed the means to do so effectively. And no one has ever accused Soviet leaders of lacking the political sophistication to adapt their doctrines to the exigencies of the moment.

In considering the possible use of limited naval force by the Soviet Union in the years to come, it may accordingly be better to disregard those patterns of behaviour which Western Sovietologists have invented and in which they have sought to confine the fluidity of Soviet foreign policy and instead to remember what Chairman Khruschev told the Hungarians:

> The Soviet people have always complied with their international obligations and will go on doing so.[55]

NOTES

[1] Admiral G. Cabanier, then Chief of the French Naval Staff, 'L'Évolution de la Marine Française'. Article in *Revue de Défense Nationale*, July 1965.

[2] H.M.S. ROYAL OAK was laid down in 1914 and sunk in Scapa Flow by a German submarine on 14 October 1939.

[3] See Chapter Four for one incident in this battleship's eventful peace-time service.

[4] See Robert Waring Herrick 'Soviet Naval Strategy', *USNI* 1968 and M.K. MccGwire 'The Background to Russian Naval Policy', *Brassey's Annual* 1968.

[5] Herrick op. cit., p. 133.

[6] A ladder that broke down when the French tanker ARTOIS ignored a summons from H.M.S. MINERVA in December 1967. Even a single shell might have produced an explosion capable of destroying the tanker. Indeed, the use

of limited naval force against a super-tanker – so much larger and sometimes faster, than most warships – still awaits an entirely satisfactory solution. See Gregory op. cit.

[7] *USNIP* of May 1963 published a photograph of one of them that was forced to surface. See also Mitchell, Donald W. 'The Soviet Naval Challenge' article in *Orbis* Vol. XIV No. 1 of 1970.

[8] See Herrick op. cit., pp. 137–9.

[9] 'The following shall be deemed violators of the state boundary of the USSR ... persons who are discovered on means of navigation, or swimming, in territorial and internal sea waters of the USSR ... if they ... are illegally attempting to leave their limits.' Extract from Article 26 of *Statute on the Protection of the State Boundary of the Union of Soviet Socialist Republics*, see William E. Butler *The Law of Soviet Territorial Waters*, New York, Praeger 1967.

[10] *The Military Balance 1970–71*, Institute for Strategic Studies, London.

[11] 'If the Sixth Fleet were not here, the Polaris submarines would still operate successfully in the Mediterranean,' Vice-Admiral Richardson, Commander US Sixth Fleet, quoted in *US News and World Report*, 21 July 1969.

[12] Herrick op. cit.

[13] Interview with *Der Spiegel* on 10 February 1969.

[14] *The Times*, 5 April 1969.

[15] *The Times*, 18 December 1968.

[16] Winston S. Churchill, *The World Crisis*, Chapter 41, Four Square Books 1960.

[17] Winston S. Churchill op. cit., Chapter 4.

[18] *Special Report on Soviet Sea Power*, Center for Strategic and International Studies, Georgetown, Washington, June 1969. Estimated the strength of the Black Sea Fleet at 'about seven cruisers, at least fifty destroyers, frigates and escorts plus two helicopter carriers (700 ships total).'

[19] *Special Report on Soviet Sea Power*, The Center for Strategic and International Studies, Georgetown University, Washington D.C., June 1969.

[20] *The Times*, March 1970.

[21] Article 'The Northern Flank of the Atlantic Alliance' in *NATO letter* of 1969.

[22] *Time* Magazine 23 February 1968, see Appendix for another Soviet operation in 1968.

[23] *Baltimore Sun*, 4 February 1968.

[24] *Keesing's Contemporary Archives*.

[25] *Special Report on Soviet Sea Power*, Center for Strategic and International Studies, Georgetown, Washington, June 1969.

[26] Although Soviet claims to present strength must be treated with reserve, admissions of past weakness may be accorded more credence: 'For the first time in our history our Fleet has been fully transformed into an offensive type of long-range armed force. Never before has it possessed such striking force ... our Fleet in recent years has acquired the capability for a qualitatively new sort of military training – exercises in remote regions of the world ocean.' Admiral Kasatonov in *Red Star*, 30 July 1967.

[27] *Red Star*, 5 February 1963.

[28] *Izvestia*, 29 July 1967.

[29] *Pravda*, 28 July 1969.

[30] Quoted in 'Sea Power and Soviet Foreign Policy', article by David R. Cox in *USNIP*, June 1969.

[31] *Krasnaya Zvezda*, 11 February 1967.

[32] See *Joint Publications Research Service Bulletin* of 6 May 1968.

[33] Quoted in *International Herald Tribune*, 4 January 1969.

[34] *Moscow News*, 17 May 1969.

[35] See Appendix.

[36] *International Herald Tribune*, 11 July 1967.

[37] President Eisenhower's words of 1958 (see Chapter 2) – 'Sentiment had developed in the Middle East, especially in Egypt, that we were afraid of Soviet reaction if we attempted military action', could have been applied in 1967 by a Soviet diplomat to his own country.

[38] 'The Kremlin Builds a Cold War Fleet', article by George Fielding Eliot in *Marine Corps Gazette*, June 1969.

[39] *Daily Telegraph*, 27 October and 13 November 1967; *The Times* 27 October.

[40] *Jewish Observer and Middle East Review*, 29 November 1968.

[41] *International Herald Tribune*, 5 September 1969.

[42] Italics in original.

[43] 'The national liberation war of a dependent people against a colonial power will always be a just defensive war', *Soviet State and Law*, No. 10 of October 1956.

[44] Khruschev in *Pravda*, 11 October 1957.

[45] President Voroshilov, *Pravda*, 4 November 1956.

[46] Mr Eden's account of this conversation on 27 August 1937 will be found in File FO 425 414 in the Public Record Office in London.

[47] For an exposition of the difference, see Grant Hugo, *Britain in Tomorrow's World*, Chapters 2 and 3, Chatto & Windus 1969.

[48] 'The proletariat must support bourgeois liberation movements in colonial countries when these movements are really revolutionary', Professor E. M. Zhukov in *International Life* No. 9 of September 1957.

[49] 'The conspiracy of the counter-revolutionary forces, supported by imperialist reaction from without, created a direct threat to socialism in the Czechoslovak Socialist Republic, the threat of its being torn away from the socialist community.

In this situation, the Soviet Union and the other socialist countries, true to their internationalist duty and allied commitments, to the principles embodied in the Bratislava Meeting Statement, were forced to take extreme measures, including that of bringing armed forces into the Republic,' *On Events in Czechoslovakia*, Press Group of Soviet Journalists, Moscow 1968.

[50] Although the term 'Brezhnev doctrine' has been repudiated by Soviet writers and seems to have been invented by Western journalists as an eye-catching pendant to the better known Doctrines of President Truman and Eisenhower, the principle that sovereignty is meaningless if divorced from its class content has been argued by the Soviet press on a number of occasions since it was allegedly endorsed by Mr Brezhnev at the congress of the Polish Communist Party in November 1968. A recent instance was an article by O. Pavlov in *Sovetskaya Rossia* of 29 January 1970, but what prompted the protest from the Yugoslav daily *Borba* in November 1969 was the use, in the October issue of the East German monthly *Horizont* of the phrase 'community of Socialist States' to describe those bound by common obligations transcending national sovereignty. The Yugoslavs, of course, are not entirely disinterested commentators, but their expertise does offer some guidance to the significance of these theological obscurities.

[51] Quoted in Herrick op. cit.
[52] Quoted in Herrick op. cit.
[53] Admiral of the Fleet Kasatonov, *Red Star*, 30 July 1967.
[54] Marshal Bulganin to Sir A. Eden, quoted in Anthony Eden *Full Circle*, p. 554, Cassell & Co. 1960.
[55] Budapest Radio, 4 April 1958.

Chapter Six

APPLICATIONS

Diseases desperate grown
By desperate appliance are relieved
Or not at all
Shakespeare[1]

THIS book has had to explore a subject of which even the existence is controversial. The reader has been dragged through
thickets of objections merely to establish that the concept of limited
naval force is capable of definition, that its employment can be discerned and analysed in recent history, that the likely pattern of
future developments need not exclude an expedient for which the
resources and, in a lesser degree, even the doctrines are available. A
vast array of conditional and dependent clauses, all in the subjunctive
mood, has been piled up and now awaits, as if it were the nightmare
sentence of some German pedant, significant release in the final verb.
Having explained what has been done, having argued at length what
might be done, it would be agreeable to reach a conclusion, whether
by venturing a prediction or by hazarding some recommendation.
At the very least some indication is needed of the potential utility of
these ideas.

One might, for instance, offer some scenarios of the future.

Scenarios – the description of imaginary events – are familiar and
often helpful devices for illustrating the potential applications of
theoretical arguments. Their narrative form is occasionally refresh-
ing to readers desiccated by abstractions. The opportunities they
offer of testing principles and propositions can be illuminating. But
scenarios have their pitfalls. They necessarily involve assumptions
about the future, which events may disprove. The scenario that was
plausible when written may have become absurd before it is read. An
unlucky illustration may thus destroy an otherwise plausible argument. Some theories, of course, are predictions and must run this
risk, because they propound a definite sequence between cause and
effect. But the application of limited naval force demands a peculiarly
elaborate set of initial causes: the characteristics and resources of
both assailant and victim, the geographical setting, the political circumstances, the international situation must all combine in a manner
which, for a quarter of a century, has seldom happened more than
half a dozen times a year. Any scenario must thus begin by postulating

a statistically improbable contingency and, to make this plausible, must not merely portray the actors, but sketch in those significant details of the background which determine and explain their conduct. In the field of gunboat diplomacy a safely blurred scenario is as useless as an anonymous case history. Without its identifying particulars the story of PUEBLO would be as meaningless as some dreary anecdote of an Englishman, an Irishman and a Scotsman. 'To point a moral, or adorn a tale'[2] it is not enough to describe a sequence of actions: something done by one government does not have the same results as the identical deed of another; what is possible today in the Caribbean may be inconceivable in the Baltic tomorrow. To add anything to argument one must accordingly run the risk of an elaboration that may ultimately diminish the impact of reasoning. The fuller and richer the picture, the more easily will the decoration be confused with the structure.[3]

Some writers, admittedly, prefer to evade this dilemma by plumping for unabashed fiction and discussing Ruritanian descents on the sea-coast of Bohemia. This avoids the strain on credulity – or academic objectivity – which sometimes occurs when reprehensible actions are attributed to actual governments. Others employ symbols and describe the conflicts of state A, aided by its allies B and C, with states X, Y and Z. The latter method has the added attraction of facilitating the use of graphs, matrices and, supreme bliss, equations incorporating the letters of the Greek alphabet. But the very ease with which such devices may be adopted to any argument whatsoever should caution the reader against their acceptance.

There is also a practical aspect. The ultimate test of this book must be its utility, even if only at second hand, to politicians, diplomats and naval officers. If there is any truth in its theories, any lesson to be distilled from its argumentation, it is they who must apply it. But the needs of practitioners have altered. In the twenties China and the Caribbean were established theatres for gunboat diplomacy: an occasional incident might, by its scale or its bizarre circumstances, depart from the familiar pattern, but a tradition, almost a routine, had grown up. It would not have been unfair to include in an examination for promotion a question beginning: 'while cruising off Shanghai (or Florida) you receive a telegram from the Consul at Hankow (or Tampico) . . .' There would have been a conventional, an indicated answer. And, for practical purposes, a scenario is a staff college question that includes the preferred solution.

This is possible whenever there is an established pattern of challenge and response. It is valuable whenever the decision is likely to be left to the man on the spot, who then needs a doctrine to determine the range of his options and to guide his choice within that range. In the second and third decades of this century that choice, particularly in China and the Caribbean, but to a lesser extent elsewhere as well, tended to be taken jointly by the Consul and by the commander of the warship he had summoned. London and Washington assessed the general situation, laid down a policy and provided the resources, but seldom attempted to decide whether a particular dispute required the use of limited naval force or precisely how this should be employed.

Flipping through the record, as this is set out in the Appendix, of US naval activities during the sixties leaves a different impression. Each intervention reflected a decision – often a Presidential decision – determined by the specific characteristics of a particular problem. It was no longer a question of implementing, but of devising, policy. WASP's uneventful cruise off the West African coast was no routine response to the familiar perils of American nationals abroad, but an important element of American participation in the crisis of the Congo. In the early thirties, when attitudes were already beginning to change, Mr Stimson, the Secretary of State, complained that even the Navy Department did not know what initiatives had already been taken by the commanders of American warships in Nicaraguan waters.[4] In 1958 instructions from Washington specified in such minute detail the precise timing of the landing at Beirut that no argument from the American Ambassador could arrest the onrush of the Marines. Today and, in all probability, tomorrow, the use of limited naval force is really, as well as legally, an act of state, the result of an express governmental decision.

These decisions are not readily predictable, because they are taken afresh on each occasion and, in all probability, on the basis of a new and independent assessment. Except for zones of coastal defence or actual hostilities (such as the Gulf of Tonkin) it is hard to think of sea areas where any government would automatically contemplate the peace-time use of limited naval force in response to a preconceived doctrine. Even if one tries to imagine the reaction in Washington to some Caribbean *coup d'état*, the first question asked would scarcely be 'which ships shall we send?' A preliminary decision would be needed that American intervention was desirable and that limited naval force was appropriate. Even on such an issue as the installation of Soviet missiles in Cuba, when there was an obvious initial assumption that American interests had been threatened and that action was required to protect them, five days of intensive discussion were needed to reach the decision that limited naval force would be an appropriate element in the American response.[5]

The manner in which this limited naval force was applied then depended on the precise nature of the contingency which demanded it. Different measures would obviously have been needed if the cargo vessels carrying missiles to Cuba had all arrived already or if they had been escorted by Soviet warships. Even if the imaginary crisis depicted in a scenario finds a useful reflection in the clouded mirror of the future, the theorist cannot hope that this will provide guidance on the conduct of operations unless his foresight has been accurate in every one of a myriad essential particulars. The peace-time use of naval force does not benefit from any of the simplifying and standardizing prior assumptions of war. On the contrary, because the purpose is to reinforce diplomacy, yet to avoid actual hostilities, it calls for a succession of complex choices, each involving both political and naval factors peculiar to the actual – and unforeseeable – situation. Any contribution which theory can offer towards the making of these choices must thus come not from the construction of models – which are unlikely ever to be realized in practice – but from devising questions which might usefully be asked before each choice is made.

How, for instance, do governments decide even to consider the use of limited naval force? Obviously this does not happen unless one government has become involved in a dispute by identifying as objectionable the conduct of another. Equally obviously the question does not arise if the dispute is trivial, if the government concerned rejects the very idea of using force, if other expedients are likely to succeed, if no warships are available or if they could not conceivably be relevant. Yet, in the small minority of cases where the use of naval force is not clearly excluded, it sometimes seems as if the mere absence of contra-indications has been accepted as sufficient grounds for precipitate action. In 1967, 1968 and 1969 appearances suggest the following sequence of reactions to the perception as objectionable of the threatened closure of the Straits of Tiran, of the seizure of PUEBLO, of the destruction of an American aircraft engaged in electronic surveillance: ordering a threatening movement of warships; considering what those warships might do; deciding there was nothing useful they could do; being dismayed at the unfortunate repercussions of this empty gesture. Perhaps the wrong questions were asked – or in the wrong order.

The first step, as has been argued elsewhere, should surely be to decide on the preferred terminal situation.[6] A dispute exists when one government regards the conduct of another as likely to produce a state of affairs disadvantageous to the first government. But it is only worth doing something about the dispute if action is likely to produce a final result less disadvantageous than anything to be expected from inaction. This result then becomes the preferred terminal situation, which necessarily represents a compromise between what is desirable and what is possible. To define it demands a dialogue between those who want something, whom we may call the politicians, and those who might help to achieve it, who, for the purposes of this argument, may be taken as including the naval staff. The former must decide the least they can accept, the latter, the most they can achieve.

Unfortunately, it is not as simple as that, because what warships can achieve is more than a merely naval question. In the PUEBLO affair, for instance, there was no doubt of the ability of the US Navy to blockade North Korea, to seize North Korean shipping, to dispatch bombers against North Korean territory from American aircraft carriers. But would any or all of these actions have produced the minimum American political requirement: a terminal situation in which the crew of PUEBLO returned alive to the United States? Evidently and understandably the American answer to this question was in the negative. But then why send the fleet to the Sea of Japan in the first place, why incur the odium of seeming willing to wound yet afraid to strike?

Human nature and the exigencies of domestic politics being what they are, not all the possible explanations are necessarily discreditable, but, in terms of the ideal application of limited naval force, this does seem to be a case in which the wrong initial choice was made. Warships were set in motion even though there was no task they could usefully perform, a conclusion which might have been reached at the outset if the problem had been subjected to methodical analysis on the basis of arguments expounded in earlier chapters in this book.

In any such analysis the first questions would naturally concern the possibility of employing definitive force. Can the preferred terminal situation be achieved without the co-operation, indeed even against the resistance of the victim? Is there an accessible objective – a person, place or ship, that can be seized, rescued, protected or destroyed? If so, are the available naval resources adequate to complete this task before the problem can be transformed by any measures open to the victim or his potential supporters? If success is probable, what are the likely repercussions and would these be acceptable?

These questions do not come first merely because of the order

adopted in Chapter Two. The definitive mode deserves consideration before any other, because this is the use of force most likely to
succeed and most likely to be limited both in its application and in
its repercussions. It is also a type of force which may have to be
used at once or not at all. This is admittedly a poor recommendation
to the prudent leader who prefers time to reflect and consult, to
explore alternatives, to enlist public opinion, but, once force is contemplated, then the longer it is delayed, while emotion is generated,
positions harden, prestige is staked and defences are strengthened,
the greater may be the extent of force ultimately required and the
more unpredictable its consequences. In many disputes an initial
rejection of force should imply its renunciation at later stages as
well, because a decision to employ force 'in the last resort' may be a
decision for what is truly the last resort of rational men – war, or at
the very least, the use of force in circumstances, to an extent and
with repercussions that can neither be predicted nor controlled.
Finally, and this is a point often overlooked, force is not necessarily
the exclusive prerogative of the government mulling over its employment: definitive force may have to be guarded against as well as
considered.

What distinguishes definitive force from other applications is the
predicted inability of the victim to prevent the creation of a *fait
accompli* which, in the eyes of the assailant, satisfactorily terminates
the dispute. For complete success, however, this *fait accompli* must
be accepted. It is accordingly necessary to consider whether subsequent retaliation is possible and, if this could be damaging, how it
might best be averted. One method might be to invoke the 'ALTMARK
principles',[7] so as to demonstrate to the victim that the actual operation cannot be prevented from achieving an objective which is both
limited and intolerable. This process may well involve crucial decisions about the nature and timing either of communications to the
victim or of publicity about the operation. The need to assure the
victim that an act of war is not intended may sometimes be difficult
to reconcile with the avoidance of premature threats, whether express
or implied, that could forfeit the advantage of surprise or arouse
unwanted public emotion. Ideally, the plan should be completed and
the decision taken before publicity is permitted. At the very least any
publicity should be considered as an integral part of the plan, bearing
in mind that taciturnity has imperilled fewer operations than saying
too much, too soon.

If a true *fait accompli* cannot be expected, then the use of force
by the assailant, if this is still contemplated, will not of itself achieve
anything: it can only induce someone else – usually, though not

always, a government – to do something, to stop doing something or
to refrain from doing something. Whereas the victim of definitive
force may retaliate after success has been achieved, the victim of
purposeful force must actually co-operate in some degree if the
objective is to be attained at all. The first question to be considered
by such an assailant is thus how force can be employed to narrow the
range of options open to the victim, so that the course of action the
assailant wishes him to follow actually become the easiest for him to
adopt. In other words, the closer that purposeful force comes to
definitive force, in the sense of confronting the victim with the need
for acquiescence in the inevitable, the more likely this force is to
succeed and to remain limited. When ROYAL OAK, for instance, interposed herself between ALMIRANTE CERVERA and the Spanish refugee
ships, the options remaining to the Nationalists were confined to
acquiescence or a desperate and probably futile act of war: it might
not even have been possible to summon bombers to sink the battleship and her escorting destroyers before the refugee ships reached
safety in France. If the purpose is to induce the victim to refrain from
doing something, the ideal method is to make it physically impossible
for him to do so, thus placing on him the onus of firing the first shot
or otherwise extending the dispute. This kind of blocking action can
sometimes also be used to persuade the victim to stop doing something and is well suited to the ability of warships, if time and circumstances permit, to put themselves in the way or to close a particular
sea area by laying a declared minefield or announcing a prolonged
firing practice.

Opportunities seldom occur for employing purposeful force so
simply and effectively, but the classical example of ROYAL OAK was
not the only one to emphasize the importance of such simple questions as: who has to fire the first shot; who has to make the next
move: on whose side is the passage of time? In April 1969 all these
answers favoured Iranian action in her dispute with Iraq, but were
against the United States in their quarrel with North Korea.[8]

It would over-tax the patience of the reader to specify and illustrate all the questions which ought to be asked in different types of
dispute or at various stages of the same dispute. But these examples
of testing the simpler problems demonstrate the need for a similar
process when tackling the more difficult and complex issues of
coercing the victim into positive action, of damage-infliction, of the
catalytic use of force. In every instance and at each level of choice
there is an obvious need to reach decisions only after their results
have been predicted and to move ships, not on impulse or as an
automatic reaction, but with the deliberate purpose of thereby

reaching a terminal situation which is both probable and preferable to the expected result of other courses. If this book's analysis of gunboat diplomacy has any practical application, this must reside in its capacity to suggest such questions.

These should not, of course, be exclusively political, though the record of the past suggests that the major errors have more often been political than naval. Nevertheless, lack of foresight or knowledge has occasionally, and very embarrassingly, resulted in warships running aground beneath the victim's fire. Pirates have sometimes proved faster than the men-of-war sent to intercept them and more than one warship has actually been sunk by a merchant vessel. Perhaps the most catastrophic instance of the kind was a pure accident: the destruction of H.M.S. CURAÇAO by the liner QUEEN MARY on 2 October 1942.[9] Nevertheless, the fact that this cruiser could be sliced in two by a merchant ship which herself remained seaworthy illustrates one of the many technical hazards of gunboat diplomacy. Broadly speaking, there is a tendency for merchant ships to become larger, stronger and faster, whereas warships, as more and more of their cost goes into electronics, are growing smaller and more fragile. Just as politicians may sometimes be too concerned with their own motives, their 'image' and the electoral impact of their actions to provide a clear and concrete definition of the precise political objective they have in mind, so naval officers, their ideas centred on major naval warfare and the prestige of their service, may occasionally overlook certain practical limitations on the peace-time employment of their ships. In the dialogue suggested as necessary to reach agreement on the preferred terminal situation, each might benefit from being subjected to a vigorous cross-examination on his own subject.

This dialogue, however, will not take place at all unless the government concerned actually possess a navy capable of peace-time use. Navies are expensive, the relevance to nuclear conflict of most of the world's warships is problematic, and, where this does exist, is liable to restrict their adaptability in time of peace. The peace-time navies of the Super-Powers, admittedly, have hitherto been supplied, automatically, by the accelerating technological obsolescence of the ships they have built for war, but Britain and France may not long be able to afford dual-purpose navies, while other governments may grudge their own expenditure on ships incapable of nuclear combat. This book should thus prompt further, and more fundamental questions: does the possible exercise of limited naval force justify the maintenance of navies and, if so, how far should this factor be allowed to determine their size and composition?

One answer is obvious. There are already more navies than there are rational governments. Some of these navies may only be intended to provide remunerative and respectable employment for the officer class, but many could actually be used and some probably will be, whether or not the results commend themselves to reasonable men. The existence of such navies is a sufficient cause for maritime states to equip themselves for coastal defence. In Chapters Three and Four, for instance, possibilities for the peace-time application of limited naval force were examined on the assumptions that the assailant expected material advantage and that he would, to some extent at least, be constrained by the influence of nuclear duopoly and of international opinion. These assumptions could, however, be too optimistic. Recent years have seen a growing tendency towards the use of violence without too nice a concern for its practical results. When Ambassadors are murdered, politicians kidnapped, aircraft hi-jacked, bombs set off in crowded places, these methods are explained and justified by a new political casuistry, in which violence, far from being a regrettable last resort, has become an intrinsically valuable expedient. It would be natural, but it might be wishful thinking, to regard such ideas as confined to fanatical minorities unlikely to control the movements of warships. Governmental attitudes towards the use of violence in an international environment have undergone considerable modification since the days when pirates, for instance, were *hostes humani generis*. The Geneva Convention of 1958 on the Régime of the High Seas confined the pejorative description of piracy to violence 'committed for private ends'[10] and, if a political motive can be manufactured, there is probably no use of violence against foreigners which some governments will not pass over in silence, condone, connive at or even covertly commit. And it is hard to think of any government which has consistently condemned all such violence, irrespective of who used it or why.

It is conceivable, therefore, that the argument of this book – limited naval force is likely to be used only in a small minority of disputes – may ultimately prove unduly conservative. The Cuban landing of 1963 and the clash of Korean warships in 1969[11] might be the forerunners of other incidents in which governments would use their warships for missions which most of them still prefer to carry out by more clandestine means. It is surely too optimistic to apply to all existing, let alone future, governments, Mr Sulzberger's argument that:

it is obviously in the interest of all established régimes to frustrate the harming of each other's citizens or the seizure of each other's property.[12]

Today, admittedly, there are more governments which call themselves revolutionary than really are, but the idea of a régime dedi-
cated to the destruction, for destruction's sake, of the international
order, is no more inconceivable than the fact of revolutionary movements in more than one country committed to the purely nihilistic
overthrow of the domestic order. There might again be, as there
were in the seventeenth century, pirates in the English Channel enjoying governmental support.

These arguments are naturally too uncomfortable to be taken
seriously, because an irrational assailant, one who was indifferent to
advantage and concerned only to inflict injury, could deprive the
defence of many of the advantages considered in Chapter Three.
There are only seven or eight countries which maintain coastal defences on a scale capable of withstanding peace-time naval raids by
a reckless assailant. Britain is not among them. On 17 March 1970,
for instance, Rear-Admiral Morgan Giles told the House of Commons, without contradiction from the Under-Secretary of Defence
for the Royal Navy, that:

> last year a Russian squadron appeared unexpectedly off the North
> of Scotland and it was desirable to trail this Russian squadron . . .
> when the Commander-in-Chief wanted to do so, the only ship that
> he could make available was a civilian-manned naval tanker, the
> OLMEDA.[13]

Such incidents – 1968 and 1969 brought half a dozen press reports
of unexpected demands catching the Royal Navy short of ships[14] –
reflect the extent to which the increasing cost and sophistication of
British warships have compelled a reduction in their numbers and
availability. Preparation for war is becoming more difficult to reconcile with readiness in time of peace. War is outside the scope of this
book and others must argue the case for a British naval contribution
to the deterrence or conduct of war. But there is one point to bear in
mind: when choosing which dangers to guard against, their relative
magnitude may be less important than the chances of being able to
do anything effective about them. If the existence of the Royal Navy
in its present form is likely to tip the balance between successful
deterrence and general nuclear war or between victory and defeat in
whatever lesser war may be conceivable, then the Navy's suitability
for peace-time employment is necessarily a secondary issue. But the
importance of an objective is not enough to make it attainable or to
justify the pre-emption of resources if it is not. If the pincers of
technological development and financial stringency were to invest
the Navy's war-time rôle with the character of a forlorn hope, it

might be desirable to give priority to those lesser dangers which could actually be countered. That is why, even though the final choice must depend on questions not considered here, it seems worth asking whether, in the seventies and eighties, the size and shape of the Navy ought still to be determined by the needs of war.

On 15 August 1970, the world completed twenty-five years of violent peace. War no longer seemed inevitable: instability did. Few countries exhibited no symptoms among their peoples of the widespread desire for swift and radical change, but there was little agreement, within nations or among them, on the nature and direction of change. There was only a growing consensus that violence brought results and an emerging view that any change might be for the better, and best of all if it came by violent means.

Some peoples and some governments, however, clearly had – and may continue to have – greater incentives than others to control, to moderate, even to retard the impact on their own societies of the pace of change. They have something to lose and may wish to insulate their countries against those who see only the opportunities for gain. These are distinctions which cut across, but which unfortunately do not reconcile, the existing political divisions in the world. The United States and the Soviet Union are no nearer alliance because the government of each ardently desires to resist certain types of change; the lesser states who depend on these Super-Powers for protection against some threats cannot rely on their help against others. Indeed, there may be a tendency in both the Soviet Union and the United States for mounting domestic problems to produce a degree of detachment from disputes that affect neither their own authority nor the balance of power between them.

Other states could, therefore, find themselves exposed to more threats, yet enjoy less protection. Britain is, in this respect, at once peculiarly vulnerable – an overcrowded archipelago heavily dependent on imports – and, still a little insulated by the surrounding sea, potentially fortunate. In a situation of nominal peace, the ability to deploy a force that is locally and immediately superior may be decisive. In the Narrow Seas, this need not be, even if now perhaps it is, beyond British naval capacity. The conflicts in Indo-China and the Middle East have shown how far the Super-Powers will go – and they may in future be prepared to go further – at the expense of their clients, in order to avoid a direct confrontation. Britain too might be involved in a dispute, whether with the Soviet Union, or, more probably, with some lesser nation, which the United States did not regard as involving the central balance of power or justifying the intervention of the United States Navy. Preventing gun-running to

Ireland or ensuring seaborne access to Gibraltar, for instance, are possible naval tasks for which no American assistance might be forthcoming. The ability, in these or lesser confrontations, to deploy a convincing naval force might be a better deterrent, either to the other party or to outside intervention, than any invocation of alliances or brandishing of missiles. Nuclear war has never been a very convincing option for Britain.

Instead of measuring a navy by the yardstick of its war-time rôle, which is becoming ever more difficult to imagine, or define,[15] it might be better for Britain, perhaps for other countries as well, to formulate, and then plan to meet, the requirements of violent peace. The ability to achieve local superiority at key points or in vital sea areas might replace the one-, two-, three-power standards of an era that has probably vanished for ever. Calculating the new standard would naturally be a complex process, involving a choice of British political objectives as well as difficult assumptions about the nature of the international environment and the type of threat that might be encountered. The initial hypothesis might be that certain types or levels of major threat could be disregarded, because these would call in question the central balance of power. Either such threats would not be made by the Soviet Union or else they would evoke an American response. At the other extreme might be those threats, perhaps to distant colonies or overseas investments, to which British resistance would necessarily be isolated and, because of the difficulties involved, would probably be no more than token. In between, however, there would be a range of potential threats of importance to Britain, but of uncertain relevance to the central balance of power. At worst these would be disputes which Britain would have to handle on her own, at best the assistance of her allies might depend on the initial effectiveness of British exertions. During the Indonesian confrontation against Malaysia, even diplomatic support for British intervention waited upon the evidence of British military success in what was initially regarded as a hopeless, and consequently dubious, venture.[16] This gap between British and allied notions of what Britain can reasonably be expected to put up with is likely to widen further in the seventies and eighties.

In assessing the threat to British interests, it would be an error to regard the Soviet Union as Britain's only potential assailant, even perhaps as the most likely candidate for that rôle. But, in home waters, it is clearly the Soviet Navy that could pose the largest threat. The size of this should not be exaggerated: it cannot be so great that it alarms the United States, impairs Soviet readiness for major war or creates serious naval deficiencies for the Soviet Union in other areas. We are considering the possible use of limited naval force in peace-time by a government whose foreign policy is usually rational, predictable and cautious. Perhaps the maximum, though this is a rough guess for argument's sake and not a considered estimate, might be the fleet which passed the Orkneys in March 1969 on the way to Atlantic exercises west of Ireland: twenty-nine ships including one Sverdlov cruiser, two Krestas, two Kashins, two Kotlins and two Rigas.[17] This is a force which could doubtless be dealt with even in limited war, when fleet submarines and Royal Air Force bombers could be employed and assistance expected from allies, though there is occasionally a tendency to exaggerate the availability of the United States Navy. It was the American press – and not a disgruntled British admiral – who pointed out that H.M.S. EAGLE played the key part in the NATO exercise *Silver Tower* of September 1968, which, although planned nearly two years in advance, had to take place without an American strike carrier, all fifteen of these irreplaceable vessels being then otherwise engaged.[18] In time of peace, however, it might be politically important, if a Soviet fleet were employed expressively to reinforce Soviet diplomatic pressure by its ostentatious manœuvres[19] – to be able to reassure British public opinion by the equally visible deployment of an equivalent British fleet. Unless the British Government can appear capable at least of disputing the rule of the Narrow Seas, the conduct of British foreign policy could become uncomfortably dependent on detailed American approval – and the availability of American warships.

This need not be an impossibly expensive objective. What is required is not a surface force capable of winning a naval battle on its own, but one which cannot simply be shouldered out of the way. The inherent advantages of coastal defence are so great that even an inferior fleet can deprive an assailant's threat of credibility, let alone prevent him from achieving a *fait accompli*, whereas bombers and submarines cannot be presented as a counter without at least an implicit threat of escalation. But the fleet must exist and be ready to sail. And when it sails, there must still be something left to contain another low-level threat elsewhere – Spanish manœuvres off Gibraltar,[20] for instance, which might provide an incentive to a simultaneous Soviet naval demonstration off the coast of Ulster. The British Government might well believe that neither threat was intended to lead to war, but would British public opinion support a resolute policy without visible British warships to back it and to keep the dispute at a reassuringly low level of challenge and response? And, if the British Navy could not manage this, would the United States Government, which abstained in successive debates over

Gibraltar in the General Assembly, feel bound to take their place? American disapproval of escalation might be made clear, the Sixth Fleet might discourage any westward movement of the Soviet Mediterranean Squadron, but the reassurance of public opinion in Britain – and in Gibraltar – might strike Washington as demanding American mediation rather than American warships. It is not only the Gods who help those that help themselves.

These are only examples. But they do suggest that any assessment of future British naval requirements would demand a full analysis of Britain's 'pressure-points': the areas in which, failing adequate local defence, limited naval force might be employed to confront the British Government with a *fait accompli* or a low-level threat to which a satisfactory American response would be uncertain or even unlikely. Such an analysis – and none will be attempted here – would naturally be only one factor in a much more complicated equation, in which the inevitably excessive demands of naval defence would have to be adjusted to the resources British governments might be prepared to divert from other purposes. What proportion of total resources would be appropriate and which British overseas interests need – or deserve – independent defence are questions far beyond the scope of this book. So is the naval assistance, if any, which might be expected from other allies than the United States. But there is one additional factor which merits a passing mention, not least because it applies to other navies than that of Britain: it is arguable that such an approach would have its repercussions on the nature of warships as well as on their numbers and deployment. A capacity for the instant obliteration of a distant enemy, however desirable in nuclear war, might be less appropriate for the exercise of limited naval force. The ability to survive collision, for instance, might be more important than the possession of cruise missiles with a range of hundreds of miles. Some naval equivalent would be needed to the clubs and shields the British Army found so useful in Ulster, though this would have to be supplemented by a capacity for escalation. How far this should extend, indeed the whole concept of a limited warship, will present difficulties for naval tacticians and designers if gunboat diplomacy becomes more prevalent. As it is, there have been a number of instances in which the United States found their armoury too sophisticated even for limited war in Vietnam, where very high levels of violence and destruction were regarded as acceptable by American leaders.

Of course only the United States could afford to build a separate fleet for a single campaign or to keep in reserve a greater number and variety of ships than a dozen navies have in commission. Less richly endowed nations must make do with what they possess and, when they build, design one ship for several purposes. There is thus a logical argument to reinforce the human preference of naval officers for the utmost in fire power and technical sophistication: a ship fit for a war need only supplement her radar and missiles with an old-fashioned gun to do as well in peace, but the converse does not hold. Even if it is always true – and this is not the place to discuss the possible exceptions – this is an extravagant argument, unless it can be shown that the science-fiction type of naval battle is conceivable outside the context of general nuclear war (in which its outcome would be irrelevant) and, if conceivable, that such a battle could actually be won by a limited number of sophisticated ships. Otherwise Britain and France, for instance, might only be emulating, at the end of the century, the eccentricities committed during its early years by Argentina, Brazil and Chile, when they competed against one another in the purchase of Dreadnoughts as useless as they were expensive. Those of Brazil, for instance, bombarded only their own compatriots, who were sufficiently impressed by the performance to add to the two they already possessed an order for the largest battleship in the world, a gesture that would undoubtedly have won this singular contest if only Brazil had been able to pay for the completed vessel.[21]

The prize then was almost avowedly one of mere prestige, but very few countries, and only at certain periods of their history, have had genuinely practical reasons for trying to build bigger and better ships than their rivals. Even if it is attainable, victory over the enemy's fleet may not be the best way to win a war, but preparing for an obviously losing battle, as the German Navy did twice, is a mere waste of resources that, if directed towards different targets, might achieve success. If the money that can be spared is insufficient, then a policy of building only the best ships may simply mean building too few for success in war or availability in peace, whereas the same amount might provide enough cheaper ships, not to be any more use in war, but to serve in, even to help to keep, the peace. As the Foreign Office argued in 1907, when Admiral Fisher was sacrificing quantity to quality, gunboats to the battle-fleet,

> The opportune presence of a British ship of war may avert a disaster which can only be remedied later at much inconvenience and considerable sacrifice.[22]

A final chapter is not the place to argue the proposition that war may no longer afford opportunities for the employment of warships, which should accordingly be designed, as their commanders should be trained, for other duties. This is one of the many extensions which are conceivable, but not essential, to a more restricted thesis: the continuing utility of limited naval force. Its existence has been established, its various uses distinguished and some account given of the resources and doctrines that might support its employment. This is a sufficient start for a theory that is newer and less substantial than the practice. Its application, as this chapter has endeavoured to demonstrate, is a question, a series of questions, for others to consider. Whatever rôle the answers may finally assign to warships, the desirability, indeed the urgency of considering the use of limited force scarcely requires explanation or emphasis. Ours is an age which has raised to the heights of nightmare both man's capacity to kill and the subtlety of his speculations concerning slaughter. Obliteration is more than possible: it has become an academic discipline. Only recently and hesitantly have men begun to wonder whether the new learning makes common sense, if ultimate power is actually usable. Bishop Odo's Mace – a weapon permitted to ecclesiastics because its impact drew no blood – still seems medieval, but we no longer dare call the idea absurd. Our notions are worse – and not even funny.

The way towards megadeaths is well charted and straightforward. There is a single theory, properly worked out and coherent. Scientific man need only maintain his progress to reach his final destination. Turning aside means exploring one difficult and devious trail after another. Limited naval force is among them: an expedient with an uncertain future, neither intrinsically desirable nor generally applicable. If men were sensible, governments would resolve their disputes without the threat or use of force. If men accepted the logic of their own lunacy, there would be no limit to the force they employed. It is in the absurd world of real life that governments sometimes impose their will through the ritual confrontation of warships, by seizing vessels, landing marines or establishing a blockade. Such devices are of interest because they have actually been used; they are of importance because their employment might be repeated; their value derives from the existence of worse alternatives. That is the point of trying to find a pattern, to outline a theory, to urge questions on the attention of others.

This book is only a beginning, a contribution to the understanding of one element in a problem that is larger, more complex, but less academic than it seems. Already, outside the study windows, beyond the lawns of the Naval College, the doors of Embassies crumble before the battering of the mob; beneath the indifferent waves the silent submarines await the impulse from one distant capital to smash another. Time is short, civilization brittle.

NOTES

[1] *Hamlet* IV, iii 9.

[2] Samuel Johnson, *The Vanity of Human Wishes.*

[3] In a recent scenario of limited naval force (by Rear-Admiral Bagley in *USNIP* of February 1970) the space devoted to setting the scene, though not excessive, leaves little room for the incident and almost none for argument.

[4] William Kamman, *A Search for Stability*, Chapter 11, University of Notre Dame Press 1968.

[5] Robert Kennedy, *13 Days*, Macmillan 1968.

[6] For the theory of terminal situations and its application to the conduct of international disputes, see: Grant Hugo, *Appearance and Reality in International Relations*, Chapter 2, Chatto & Windus 1970.

[7] See Chapter 2.

[8] See Appendix.

[9] Peter Padfield, *An Agony of Collisions*, Chapter 9, Hodder & Stoughton 1966.

[10] See J. L. Brierly, *The Law of Nations*, Chapter VI, Sixth Edition, O.U.P. 1963.

[11] See Appendix.

[12] Article in *International Herald Tribune*, 8 April 1970.

[13] *Hansard*, Col. 289.

[14] For some of them see article by Desmond Wettern in the *Spectator* of 13 December 1969.

[15] 'The rôle of naval forces in total war is somewhat uncertain', *Defence: Outline of Future Policy*, Para 24, Command 124 of 1957, H.M.S.O. London.

[16] See, for instance, the article: 'President Sukarno Gains American Sympathy' in *The Times* of 20 January 1964.

[17] *Le Monde*, 3 April 1969.

[18] Article by L. Edgar Prina in *Navy Magazine* of October 1968.

[19] See Appendix 1968, for an actual example.

[20] Peace-time action against Gibraltar need not be confined to manœuvres. See Barry Wynne, *The Day Gibraltar Fell*, Macdonald 1969 for a detailed scenario of a bloodless capture of Gibraltar by Spanish forces.

[21] See Richard Hough, *The Big Battleship*, Michael Joseph 1966.

[22] Quoted in Arthur J. Marder, *From the Dreadnought to Scapa Flow*, Vol. 1, Chapter 4, O.U.P. 1961.

Appendix

FIFTY YEARS OF GUNBOAT DIPLOMACY

An Illustrative Chronology

THIS is not a complete list of all the examples of the application of limited naval force during the last fifty years. That would need a special book. The instances listed below have been chosen to show the different ways in which, year by year and for half a century, many governments have employed this expedient in various parts of the world. Because it is meant to illustrate the range of gunboat diplomacy, and to avoid tedious repetition, the choice made does not reflect the actual distribution of gunboat diplomacy in particular years or geographical areas. The number of incidents in China during the late twenties, for instance, was disproportionately large. This chronology does not, therefore, present a historically or geographically representative cross-section of the actual employment of gunboat diplomacy during the last fifty years and cannot be used as a basis for any of the mathematical conjectures fashionable among a certain school of writers on international relations.

The choice of examples included has been based on the definition reached in Chapter One:

the use or threat of limited naval force, otherwise than as an act of war, in order to secure advantage, or to avert loss, either in the furtherance of an international dispute or else against foreign nationals within the territory or the jurisdiction of their own state.

Naval action in time of war has been excluded unless this takes place against allies or neutrals and actions resulting in war (whether declared or not) have only been quoted as examples of failure and on the assumption that only limited force was originally intended.

The description 'assailant' is given to the government which used or threatened naval force, whether or not actual violence was employed and without any attempt to distinguish between offensive and defensive action. Similarly, the 'victim' is the other party to the dispute or, in the absence of a specific dispute, the government whose sovereignty was infringed, whether or not this government invited or acquiesced in the action taken. The classification of incidents is in accordance with Chapter Two: 'D' stands for definitive force, 'P' for purposeful, 'C' for catalytic and 'E' for expressive.

Finally, an attempt has been made in the summary of each incident to indicate whether the action taken was successful or unsuccessful. The only judgment implied by these epithets is whether or not the results actually achieved corresponded with the intention of the assailant, and no attempt has been made to take account of wider considerations. For instance, British action against Egypt on 30 April 1928, is described as successful because the objectionable Bill was withdrawn from the Egyptian Parliament. This does not imply any judgment that the long-term repercussions were advantageous to British interests or that the policy of employing limited naval force to achieve such ends was necessarily correct. The whole of this chronology is intended only to illustrate the uses of gunboat diplomacy as an instrument of governments and the merits of the foreign policies which seemed to require this employment are beyond the scope of this book.

The problem of documenting these incidents is a difficult one. The descriptions given have generally been compiled from a variety of secondary sources (which often differ on such details as the precise date). To quote them all would sometimes mean giving more space to footnotes than to the text. To quote none might be irritating to the serious student. The compromise usually adopted has been to give a single reference and readers insufficiently enlightened by this will have to resort to the bibliography at the end of the book.

Date	Assailant	Victim	Inciden	Type

1919

Date	Assailant	Victim	Inciden	Type
	Britain	Russia (Bolshevik and German forces in Baltic Area)	After the conclusion of the armistice with Germany in November 1918, a British naval squadron was sent to the Baltic 'to show the British flag and support British policy'. It was not finally withdrawn until 1921, having by then failed to overthrow the Soviet Government and having enabled Estonia, Latvia, Lithuania and to a lesser extent Finland to resist Russian and German attack and to consolidate their independence (see Chapter 2). Partially successful.	C
14 May	United States	Greece Turkey	U.S.S. ARIZONA lands marines to guard US Consulate at Constantinople during Greek occupation of that city.[1]	P

Note French, United States and Italian warships were also involved to a lesser extent and there were many other instances of the use of limited naval force against the Bolsheviks during this year.

[1] David M. Cooney, *A Chronology of the United States Navy 1775–1965*, Franklin Watt Inc., N.Y. 1965. This source lists seven other American naval interventions in various parts of the world during 1919.

1920

Date	Assailant	Victim	Inciden	Type
14 May	United States	Mexico	'Bandits in charge Manzanillo since 11 a.m. 14th. Destroyer THORNTON, Commander Stirling, arrived 4 p.m. and saved town from violence. Standing by.'[2]	P

[2] Telegram from US Consul at Manzanillo, *Papers Relating to the Foreign Relations of the United States* (henceforth *US Doc.*) 1920, Vol. III, p. 153. US Government Printing Office, Washington 1936.

177

Date	Assailant	Victim	Incident	Type
			1 9 2 0	
18 May	Soviet Union	Iran Britain	Bolshevik destroyer and coastal motor-boats seize White Russian ships in Enzeli harbour, bombard and occupy town and expel small British contingent. Although the subsequent creation of a 'Red Revolutionary Committee of Persia' proved an ephemeral achievement, the continued occupation of Enzeli, Resht and other parts of the province of Gilan gave the Soviet Union a bargaining counter which, after the seizure of the Persian throne by Reza Khan on 21 February 1921, resulted in the signature of an advantageous Russo-Persian treaty and the repudiation by Persia of the earlier Anglo-Persian Agreement. Partially successful.[3]	C
17 November	Britain	Greece	After the electoral defeat of the pro-British Greek Prime Minister, Venizelos, he leaves the country hurriedly on a yacht which was escorted by H.M.S. CENTAUR to prevent any attempt by the new Greek Government to arrest Venizelos. Successful.[4]	D

Note   British naval activities continued in the Baltic and elsewhere there were numerous instances of the use of limited naval force against the Bolsheviks.

[3] *Documents on British Foreign Policy 1919–1939* (henceforth *Brit. Doc.*) First Series, Vol. XIII. pp. 488–747, H.M.S.O. 1963.
[4] *Brit. Doc.*, First Series, Vol. XII, pp. 504 and 510, H.M.S.O. 1962.

Date	Assailant	Victim	Incident	Type
			1921	
28 February –19 March	Britain	Soviet Union	British warships evacuate British subjects and sympathizers from Batum before this capital of the ephemeral state of Georgia falls to the Bolsheviks. Successful.[5]	D
5 August	United States	China	The United States Navy establish a Yangtse River patrol 'to protect US interests, lives and property and to maintain and improve friendly relations with the Chinese people'. The success achieved in the first objective was more conspicuous than in the second.[6]	P
18 August	United States	Panama	400 United States marines embarked by u.s.s. PENNSYLVANIA to induce Panama to conform to American decision regarding her border dispute with Costa Rica.[7] Successful.	P
1 November	Britain	Austria Hungary	H.M.S. GLOWWORM and other British ships of the Danube Flotilla collect the ex-Emperor Karl of Austria–Hungary from Baja in Hungary after the failure of his attempt to regain the throne and convey him to Rumania, whence H.M.S. CARDIFF takes him to Madeira. This intervention by the Royal Navy was approved by the principal European governments and the use of naval force was necessary only to prevent the ex-Emperor being rescued by his partisans, or kidnapped by his opponents, while on his way to exile.[8]	D

179

---

[5] *Brit. Doc.* First Series, Vol. XII, pp. 675–8.
[6] Roskill op. cit., p. 271.
[7] 'American Relations in the Carribbean', *Council on Foreign Relations*, Chapter 5, Yale U.P. 1929.
[8] 'The Exiling of the Late Ex-Emperor Karl of Austria–Hungary, article in *Naval Review*, Vol. XI 1923.

Date	Assailant	Victim	Incident	Type
			1922	
14 August	Britain	China	President Sun Yat Sen rescued from Canton after his defeat by Chinese rebels and taken to Shanghai in British gunboat. Successful.[9]	D
September	Britain United States France Italy	Turkey	British and other warships (including battleships) sent to Smyrna (being evacuated by Greeks and occupied by Turks following armistice ending their war) to maintain order and protect foreign nationals and property in the town until Turkish authority fully established. Warships also protected and helped the evacuation of over 200,000 Greeks. Reasonably successful.[10]	P
September/ November	Britain	Turkey	British fleet sent to the Dardanelles and Bosphorus to help prevent Turkish forces (which had defeated the Greeks after the war in which Britain was neutral)[11] from crossing into Europe. Successful.	P
18 November	Britain	Turkey	The Sultan of Turkey rescued from his rebellious subjects by H.M.S. MALAYA and taken to Malta. Successful.[12]	D

[9] Arnold J. Toynbee, *Survey of International Affairs* (henceforth cited as Toynbee irrespective of editor for the particular year) O.U.P. 1925 Supplement, p. 41.

[10] See articles 'Smyrna and After' in *Naval Review*, Vol. XI 1923.

[11] The genuineness of British neutrality (declared on May 1921) is attested by an Admiralty telegram of 29 July 1922 to the C.-in-C. Mediterranean instructing him to be prepared to bombard the Piraeus, to seize Greek shipping and to blockade Greece. Fortunately it was never necessary to apply these Palmerstonian measures (see Roskill op. cit.).

[12] David Walder, *The Chanak Affair*, Chapter 10, Hutchinson 1969.

Date	Assailant	Victim	Incident	Type
			1923	
January	Britain and France	Lithuania	British cruiser and French gunboat sent to Memel after the Lithuanian seizure of that port (then under temporary French administration). Although they succeeded in rescuing the French garrison (which had surrendered) and in saving the face of the Allies, the Lithuanian *fait-accompli* had to be accepted and formalized. Only partially successful.[13]	P
27 August	Italy	Greece	Italian fleet bombarded and subsequently occupied the Greek island of Corfu in order to extract concessions from the Greek Government. (See Chapter 2.) successful.	P
6 December	Britain France Italy Japan Portugal United States	China	Warships sent by these governments to Canton to protect Customs House (the Chinese customs were then under foreign administration) against seizure by Chinese Government. Warships withdrawn the following April. Successful.[14]	P

[13] Toynbee op. cit., 1920–23, p. 259 O.U.P.
[14] Toynbee op. cit., 1925, Vol. II, p. 313.

Date	Assailant	Victim	Incident	Type
			1 9 2 4	
11 January	Britain	Mexico	H.M.S. CAPETOWN sent to Minatitlau in Mexico to protect a British oil refinery during a Mexican revolution. She was subsequently relieved by other British warships and, after the arrival of various Mexican gunboats, the commander of H.M.S. CONSTANCE informed the belligerents that he could not approve of the firing of the ships' guns in his vicinity, so that he suggested the battle should take place elsewhere. Successful.[15]	P
27 February	United States	Honduras	US marines landed at Puerto Ceiba to protect American interests in civil disturbances. Successful, but US warships had to intervene on other occasions in later months.[16]	P
18 December	Italy	Albania Yugoslavia	Three Italian destroyers sent to Albanian ports when the Albanian Government was threatened by insurrection allegedly sponsored by Yugoslavia. The insurrection succeeds and relations between Albania and Yugoslavia improve although the Yugoslavian Government continued to deny complicity. Unsuccessful.[17]	P

[15] 'Some Notes Upon a Visit to Mexico', article in *Naval Review*, Vol. XII 1924.
[16] *US Doc.*, 1924, Vol. II, pp. 300–324.
[17] Toynbee, Vol. II, p. 286.

Date	Assailant	Victim	Incident	Type
			1925	
23 June	Britain	China	An armed detachment landed by H.M.S. TARANTULA to protect the British concession at Shameen (from rioting students) opens fire when the bridge is attacked by Chinese troops. Successful.[18]	P
4 August	United States	Nicaragua	US marines withdrawn from many areas in that country. Within a month trouble breaks out, and at the request of the Nicaraguan Government the U.S.S. DENVER is sent to Corinto and the U.S.S. TULSA to Bluefields, both on 13 September. Their presence did not prevent a *coup d'état*. Unsuccessful.[19]	P
12 October	United States	Panama	US marines land in Panama at the request of the President of Panama to restore order after rioting. Successful.[20]	P
5 November	United States	France	Two US destroyers sent to Beirut for the reassurance of American nationals endangered by disturbance in the French mandated territory of Syria and the Lebanon. They stayed one month. Successful.[21]	C

---

[18] See Command 2636 (China No. 1) of 1926, H.M.S.O. London. This was only one of many similar incidents in 1925.
[19] William Kamman, *A Search for Stability*, University of Notre Dame Press 1968.
[20] Toynbee op. cit., 1925, Vol. II, p. 412.
[21] Toynbee op. cit., 1925, Vol. I, p. 431.

Date	Assailant	Victim	Incident	Type
			1926	
6 May	United States	Nicaragua	Cruiser U.S.S. CLEVELAND lands marines at Bluefields to protect US nationals and property from civil war.[22] This was the first of many instances and the marines were not finally withdrawn until 1933. Although successful in its immediate objective, this intervention developed into military occupation of the entire country.	P
4 September	Britain	China	British gunboats break an anti-British boycott at Canton and Swatow by clearing the harbour of the picket-boats maintained by the strike committee and landing marines to clear pickets from British-owned wharves. Successful.[23]	P
5 September	Britain	China	After persuasion by H.M. consul had failed, H.M. ships WIDGEON and COCKCHAFER rescue British Merchant Navy officers from two ships captured by the Chinese and inflict severe damage on the city of Wanhsien. Subsequent negotiations lead to recovery of ships as well. Successful but substantial casualties.[24]	P

184

Note In 1926, fifteen British, nine American, ten Japanese and six French gunboats regularly patrolled the Yangtse River. These and other warships were constantly in action during 1926.

[22] Kamman op. cit.
[23] Toynbee op. cit. 1926, p. 289.
[24] Toynbee op. cit. 1926, pp. 307–14.

Date	Assailant	Victim	Incident	Type
			1927	
January/ February	Britain France Italy Japan The Netherlands Portugal Spain United States	China	British expeditionary force and US marines land at Shanghai to protect International Concession after the British concession at Hankow had been seized (the intervention of a British cruiser enabled the foreign community to be evacuated). Other powers also sent warships to Shanghai. Altogether thirty-five warships were concentrated off this Chinese port (nine of them British) and 40,000 troops and marines (half of them British and Indian) were landed or held in readiness offshore. Most of them were withdrawn when the immediate threat was over, but small garrisons were retained for many years. No serious fighting took place and the threatened attack by the Chinese Revolutionary armies was successfully deterred.[25]	P
23 February	Britain	Nicaragua United States	Having received no satisfactory reply to their request for American protection of British subjects in Nicaragua, the British Government announce the dispatch of the cruiser COLOMBO to Corinto. This elicits the desired undertaking and COLOMBO leaves again a few days later.[26] Successful.	P

Date	Assailant	Victim	Incident	Type
			1927	
24 March	Britain United States	China	British and US warships bombard Nanking to cover the evacuation of foreign nationals after attacks by Chinese troops on foreign consulates and nationals in Nanking. Successful and Chinese apologies later received.[27]	P
30 May	Britain	Egypt	Battleships sent to Alexandria and Port Said to reinforce the British High Commissioner's representations to the Egyptian Government. Latter eventually give satisfaction on 14 June. Successful.[28]	P

Note Minor instances of naval intervention to protect or rescue British subjects in China during 1927 were far too numerous to be listed, but one unusual incident deserves to be rescued from oblivion. On 20 October the British submarine L4 sank a Chinese pirate ship in Chinese territorial waters. In their subsequent protest the Chinese Government complained, *inter alia*, that excessive force had been used and that some of the victims of the pirates had perished together with the latter. This illustrates the relative clumsiness of the submarine as an instrument of naval diplomacy. Nevertheless enough pirates were rescued to be taken to Hong Kong and hung.[29]

[25] Toynbee op. cit. 1928, p. 240.
[26] Kamman op. cit.
[27] *The China Year Book 1929–30*, pp. 843–7. Tientsin Press Ltd.
[28] Toynbee op. cit., p. 240.
[29] *The China Year Book 1929–30*, pp. 795–8.

Date	Assailant	Victim	Incident	Type
			1928	
5 January–30 June	Britain	China	Royal Navy operate a weekly convoy system for British shipping using the Yangtse River. Successful.[30]	P
10 April	Japan	China	Japanese warships, which had already assembled at Tsingtao, landed marines to protect Japanese interests threatened by Chiang Kai Shek's invasion of the Shantung province in the course of Chinese civil war. Landing soon develops into full-scale expeditionary force, much fighting takes place and original objective is lost sight of. Japanese forces eventually withdrawn. Unsuccessful.[31]	C
30 April	Britain	Egypt	The British High Commission having demanded the withdrawal from the Egyptian parliament of an objectionable Bill and Egypt's compliance being delayed, five warships are demonstratively dispatched from Malta. Successful.[32]	P

187

[30] Other countries did much the same. See *The China Year Book 1929–30*, pp. 771–803.
[31] Toynbee op. cit. 1928, pp. 407–13.
[32] Toynbee op. cit. 1928, p. 273.

Date	Assailant	Victim	Incident	Type
			1929	
March	United States	Canada	US Coast Guard cutter DEXTER sinks Canadian ship I'M ALONE (a rum smuggler) by gunfire in international waters. A long legal wrangle ensued.[33]	D
23 April	United States	Mexico	'Commander (of US destroyer ROBERT SMITH) and Consul have conferred with officers of the Federal gunboat BRAVO and have obtained promise not to bombard Guayamas.' One of many naval interventions in 1929 to protect US nationals and property during an insurrection in Mexico.[34]	P

Note Because of the rarity of incidents affecting the Soviet Navy it is worth recording that, on 12 October, the Soviet gunboats LIEBKNECHT, KALMUK, BATRAK, ARACHANIN and LENIN sank three Chinese gunboats, captured another and thus enabled Soviet troops to take the town of Tungkiang at the confluence of the Amur and Sungari rivers. This was not, however, an act of limited naval force, but part of an undeclared war that lasted months and involved many thousands of troops.[35]

[33] H. R. Kaplan, 'A Toast to the Rum Fleet', *USNIP*, May 1968.
[34] *US Doc.* 1929, Vol. III, p. 400.
[35] Peter S. H. Tang, *Russian and Soviet Policy in Manchuria and Outer Mongolia*, Chapter 5, Duke University Press 1959.

Date	Assailant	Victim	Incident	Type
			1930	
January	Soviet Union	Turkey	The unobserved entry into the Black Sea of the Soviet battleship PARIZHSKAYA COMMUNA and the cruiser PROFINTERN alters the naval position to the advantage of the Soviet Union 'and to this may be traced the acceptance by Turkey of the protocol on naval armaments concluded between the two countries on 7 March 1931'.[36]	C
16 July	Britain	Egypt	Warships sent to Alexandria, Port Said and Suez in readiness to protect foreign nationals and interests after rioting (the Italian Government had said they would send their ships if the British Government did not). Warships withdrawn 29 July. Successful.[37]	P
27 July–2 August	Britain Italy Japan United States	China	Gunboats evacuate foreign nationals from Changsha during fighting in course of civil war. Successful.[38]	D

[36] Max Beloff, *The Foreign Policy of Soviet Russia*, Vol. 2, Chapter. 3, O.U.P. 1949.

[37] Toynbee op. cit. 1930, pp. 217–18.

[38] 'Communism on the Yangtse', Article in *RUSI Journal*, Vol. LXXVI, 1931.

Date	Assailant	Victim	Incident	Type
			1931	
11 April	United States	Nicaragua	U.S.S. ASHEVILLE sent to Puerto Cabezas to protect American (and British) nationals endangered by local disturbances which had arisen after the reduction of the forces of US marines which had occupied the country for many years. Successful.[39]	P
			1932	
29 January	Japan	China	Japanese warships (including aircraft carrier) bombard Chapei (a suburb of Shanghai) and land sailors after attacks on Japanese subjects and a boycott of Japanese goods. The Japanese described their own action as 'drastic measures in a possible minimum degree'.[40] Japanese ambitions proved to be rather more ambitious but Chinese resistance was greater than expected and the incident developed into weeks of large-scale fighting before Japanese forces were largely withdrawn. Unsuccessful.	C

[39] Kamman op. cit.

[40] *Documents on British Foreign Policy*, second series, Vol. 9, Doc. 143, H.M.S.O.

190

Date	Assailant	Victim	Incident	Type
			1932	
February	Britain and United States	Japan and China	A British cruiser squadron and the US Asiatic Fleet sent to Shanghai to protect the International Concession, to secure the cessation of hostilities and the withdrawal from the vicinity of Chinese and Japanese forces. Soon after his arrival, Admiral Sir H. Kelly 'told the Japanese Admiral he was to give orders forthwith to stop his aircraft flying over my ships and that I would open fire if they did so . . . he has promised to help me in every way to obtain peace'.[41] After discussion in Geneva and elsewhere as well as in Shanghai itself, a cease-fire was negotiated by Chinese and Japanese representatives aboard Admiral Kelly's flagship, H.M.S. KENT, and this came into force on 3 March. Although British writers attribute this result to Admiral Kelly's intervention, Mr Stimson, US Secretary of State, subsequently declared that the decisive factor had been the concentration of the US Main Fleet at Hawaii.[42] French and Italian warships were also sent to Shanghai but were not involved in the settlement of the Sino-Japanese dispute. Successful.	C

191

---

[41] *Ibid.*, p. 371, 5 February.
[42] Ferrel, *American Diplomacy in the Great Depression*, Yale University Press 1957.

Date	Assailant	Victim	Incident	Type
			1 9 3 3	
13 August	United States	Cuba	Two U.S. warships sent to Havana (and others, with marines embarked, held in readiness off the coast) so that the 'moral effect' of their presence would assist President Roosevelt's special envoy, Mr Sumner-Welles, to replace President Machado by a Cuban administration more inclined to protect American interests. Successful, but not for long.[43]	P
5 September	United States	Cuba	Following a *coup d'état* (which overthrew the government arranged by Mr Sumner-Welles) the concentration of the Atlantic Fleet (including the battleship MISSOURI) in Cuban waters begins. After protracted negotiations a reasonably conservative Cuban Government is achieved and naval withdrawal begins on 23 January 1934. Successful.[44]	P

Note On 2 January the last US marines were withdrawn from Nicaragua after many years of occupation.[45]

[43] Robert F. Smith, *The United States and Cuba*, Chapter 10, C.S.V. Press, New Haven 1960.
[44] Toynbee op. cit., pp. 380–90.
[45] Kamman op. cit.

192

Date	Assailant	Victim	Incident	Type
			1934	
January	United States	China	U.S.S. TULSA lands marines to protect American Consulate at Foochow. Successful.[46]	P
23 June	Italy	Albania	Nineteen Italian warships sent to make a demonstration at Durazzo to induce the Albanian Government to make concessions to Italy. Only partially successful.[47]	P

Note On 15 August US marines were finally withdrawn from Haiti after many years of occupation.[46]

[46] Cooney op. cit.
[47] Toynbee op. cit., 1934, p. 536.

Date	Assailant	Victim	Incident	Type
			1935	
March	Britain	Greece	Battleship H.M.S. ROYAL SOVEREIGN sent to Phaleron Bay to protect British interests after Greek Monarchist revolt. No action required.[48]	C
20 September	Britain	Italy	The British Government formally notified the Italian Government of the reinforcement of the British Fleet in the Mediterranean (by a substantial part of the Home Fleet and some ships from the China Station). The British Government had no intention of going to war, so this can be regarded either as an expressive use of naval force or as a threat intended to influence Italian conduct towards Abyssinia. The Italian Government treated it as a bluff and countered it by an equally demonstrative reinforcement of their troops in Libya. This led to Italian proposals for mutual de-escalation which were eventually tacitly accepted. Unsuccessful.[49]	E or P

Note During the mid-thirties the Royal Navy maintained thirteen gunboats and a cruiser on the Yangtse, five gunboats on the Canton River and an anti-piracy patrol of destroyers to the northward of Hong Kong. These warships could call on substantial reinforcements from the British China Fleet. See Admiral Sir Frederic C. Dreyer, *The Sea Heritage*, Museum Press Ltd. 1955.

[48] Kenneth Edwards, *The Grey Diplomatists*, Rich & Cowan 1938, Chapter 8.
[49] Toynnee op. cit., Vol. II, pp. 254–7.

Date	Assailant	Victim	Incident	Type
			1 9 3 6	
4 May	Britain	Italy	H.M.S. ENTERPRISE demonstrated British sympathy for the defeated Emperor of Abyssinia by taking him to safety in Palestine. H.M.S. CAPETOWN subsequently took him to London.[50]	E
3 August	Germany	Spain	*Panzerschiff* DEUTSCHLAND and Torpedo Boat LUCHS visit Ceuta in Spanish Morocco to demonstrate Hitler's support for Franco's rising. Successful. (See Chapter 2.)	E
19 August	Spain	Britain and others	Interference with foreign shipping in the seas around Spain begins and is continued by Spanish warships on both sides in the Civil War. British and other foreign warships intervened on many occasions, but these practices were partially successful in reducing the flow of supplies to Spain.[51]	P

195

[50] Toynbee 1935, Vol. II, p. 357.
[51] See Appendix to *International Law and Diplomacy in the Spanish Civil Strife*, Norman J. Padelford, N.Y., Macmillan 1939, for a useful list of incidents.

Date	Assailant	Victim	Incident	Type
			1936	
1 December	United States	Argentina and others	President Roosevelt arrives at Buenos Aires in the cruiser INDIANAPOLIS escorted by the U.S.S. CHESTER to attend the first session of the Inter-American Conference for the Maintenance of Peace, where one of the main points at issue was American reluctance to accept the Argentinian doctrine prohibiting intervention in other countries. On paper it was Argentina who was successful.[52]	E

Note 1936 produced far more instances of the use of limited naval force in connection with the Spanish Civil War than can be listed here. Two points, however, are worth recording: on 17 November the Spanish Nationalists proclaimed a blockade of Republican ports and announced their readiness to attack foreign ships making for these ports. On 3 December the British Government prohibited the export of arms to Spain in British ships. The second point is that Soviet naval weakness made it impossible for them to prevent eighty-four Soviet ships being stopped and searched by Spanish Nationalists between October 1936 and April 1937. The Soviet Merchant ship KOMSOMOL was actually sunk on 14 December 1936.

(See Hugh Thomas, *The Spanish Civil War*, Chapter 40, Eyre and Spottiswoode 1961.)

---

[52] *Franklin D. Roosevelt and Foreign Affairs*, Vol. III, Harvard University Press 1969.

Date	Assailant	Victim	Incident	Type
			1937	
8 March	Britain France Germany Italy	Spain	A 4-power naval patrol is agreed to prevent outside intervention in the Spanish Civil War. As only Britain really believes in non-intervention, this fails in its ostensible purpose but its existence helps to placate British public opinion.	E
6 April	Spain	Britain	Spanish Nationalist cruiser ALMIRANTE CERVERA stops a British ship bound for Bilbao. British Government initially acquiesce in the blockade thus inaugurated, but British warships eventually intervene to protect the passage of British vessels carrying food. For the time being the Spanish blockade fails, and the Royal Navy succeeds.	P
31 May	Germany	Spain	A German cruiser and four destroyers bombard Almería in retaliation for a Spanish air attack on DEUTSCHLAND. The incident is then skilfully exploited by the German Government to obtain an implicit Franco-British endorsement of the right of retaliation in these circumstances. No German warships seem to have been bombed subsequently, though this happened to several British warships and there were 150 air attacks on British merchant vessels. As the British Government confined themselves to protests, these attacks continued throughout the war. Successful.	P

Date	Assailant	Victim	Incident	Type
			1937	
August	Italy	Spain Britain France and others	'Unknown' (actually Italian) submarines start sinking ships bound for Republican ports. On 1 September H.M.S. HAVOCK was unsuccessfully attacked and on 2 September the tanker WOODFORD was sunk (see below).	P
14 September	Britain and France	Italy	At the Nyon Conference Britain and France agreed that their warships would attack and destroy unidentified submarines in areas where merchant ships had been attacked. This threat was temporarily successful and submarine attacks were suspended.	P

Note 1 See Hugh Thomas op. cit. for all these incidents.
Note 2 On 30 June three Soviet gunboats were again in action on the Amur, this time against the Japanese, who sank one of them, Max Beloff, *The Foreign Policy of Soviet Russia 1929–41*, Vol. II, p. 167.

Date	Assailant	Victim	Incident	Type
			1938	
11 January	Italy	Spain and others	Italian submarines resume the sinking of merchant vessels bound for ports in Republican Spain (see below).[53]	P
1 February	Britain	Italy	After the sinking by an 'unknown' submarine of the British ship ENDYMION off Cartagena the Italian ambassador was told that the Royal Navy reserved the right to destroy all submerged submarines in its patrol zone. No further sinkings by submarines were reported and the Italian Government acquiesced. Successful.[53]	P

198

[53] Hugh Thomas op. cit.

Date	Assailant	Victim	Incident	Type
			1938	
December	Argentina	United States and others	Imitating President Roosevelt (see 1936) the Argentinian foreign minister arrives at Lima aboard the cruiser LA ARGENTINA to attend the Pan/American conference, a gesture that symbolized an increasingly independent policy followed by Argentina on this occasion and in subsequent years.[54]	E

[54] Raz and Ferrari, *Argentina's Foreign Policy 1930–1962*, University of Notre Dame Press 1966.

Date	Assailant	Victim	Incident	Type
			1939	
9 February	Britain	Spain Germany Italy	H.M.S. DEVONSHIRE evacuates 450 Spanish Republicans from Minorca as part of a deal (negotiated on board this cruiser) whereby this Republican island was surrendered to the Nationalists on condition that no German or Italian forces were allowed to occupy it. Successful.[55]	P
23 March	Germany	Lithuania	Having successfully demanded the cession of Memel, Hitler emphasizes the forceful character of this transaction by sailing into that harbour that very day in DEUTSCHLAND. Successful.[56]	E

199

[55] Hugh Thomas op. cit., p. 580.
[56] Leonard Mosely, *On Borrowed Time*, Chapter 7, Weidenfeld & Nicolson 1969.

Date	Assailant	Victim	Incident	Type

1939

Date	Assailant	Victim	Incident	Type
17 May	Britain France United States	Japan	Warships land sailors at Kulangsu to protect international settlement against incursion by Japanese forces. Although British and French contingents are withdrawn on outbreak of European war, US sailors do not leave until Japanese do so simultaneously on 18 October. Successful.[57]	P

[57] Toynbee, *The Eve of War 1939*, pp. 634–6.

1940

Date	Assailant	Victim	Incident	Type
21 January	Britain	Japan	H.M.S. LIVERPOOL stops the Japanese ship ASAMU MARA thirty-five miles off Tokyo and removes twenty-one German passengers. In spite of strong Japanese protests this results in Japanese agreement to refuse passage on Japanese ships to German reservists on their way home to Germany.[58]	D P
6 February	Britain	Norway	H.M.S. COSSACK enters Norwegian territorial waters and, in defiance of Norwegian protests, liberates 299 British prisoners from the German ship ALTMARK. (See Chapter 2.) Successful.	D

[58] Nicholas R. Clifford, *Retreat from China*, Longmans, Green & Co. Ltd. 1967.

Date	Assailant	Victim	Incident	Type
			1940	
10 May	Britain	Iceland	British cruisers BERWICK and GLASGOW and destroyers FEARLESS and FORTUNE land troops to occupy Iceland in case the Germans should be tempted to do so. The initial reaction of the Icelandic Prime Minister was to protest that the neutrality and independence of Iceland had been flagrantly violated, but he changed his mind during the day and made a broadcast that evening asking the Icelandic nation to treat British soldiers as their guests. Successful.[59]	C

[59] Donald E. Nuechterlein, *Iceland: Reluctant Ally*, Chapter 2, Cornell University Press, 1961.

Date	Assailant	Victim	Incident	Type
			1941	
19 January	Britain	United States	'In order to clothe the arrival of our new Ambassador, Lord Halifax, in the United States with every circumstance of importance, I arranged that our newest and strongest battleship, the KING GEORGE V, with a proper escort of destroyers should carry him and his wife across the ocean.'[60] From a nation in Britain's desperate straits this was indeed an expressive gesture. Successful.	E

[60] Winston S. Churchill, *Grand Alliance*, Cassell & Co. 1950, Chapter 2.

Date	Assailant	Victim	Incident	Type
			1941	
12 April	United States	Denmark	The Governor of South Greenland 'greatly disturbed and resentful' at the agreement concluded by the United States Government with the Danish Minister in Washington (who was disavowed and dismissed by his government) for the establishment of American defence facilities in Greenland, informs the United States Consul at Godthaab that he would only be prepared to admit it as inevitable 'when faced with the *fait-accompli*'. This is provided by the US Coastguard cutters CAYUGA, NORTHLAND and MODOC (the last of which was to be twice mistaken, a month later, by the Royal Navy for the German battleship BISMARCK).[61] On 19 April the US Consul was to report that the Governor 'has exhibited a very co-operative attitude and a very realistic understanding of the situation in Greenland'.[62] Successful.	P

[61] Russell Grenfell, *The Bismarck Episode*, Faber & Faber 1958.
[62] *Foreign Relations of the United States*, Vol. 2, p. 46–54, US Government Printing Office 1959.

Date	Assailant	Victim	Incident	Type
			1941	
19 July	United States	Germany	The US Navy ordered to escort shipping of any nationality to and from Iceland. When US warships engaged in this un-neutral practice came into conflict with German submarines, President Roosevelt seized the opportunity to denounce German action as 'piracy', to describe their warships as 'the rattlesnakes of the Atlantic' and to say 'we have wished to avoid shooting. But the shooting has started and history has recorded who fired the first shot.'[63] Whatever historians may think of this pronouncement, it suggests a dual motive for the President's original intervention, which was purposeful in so far as it assisted Britain and catalytic in so far as it brought the US nearer war with Germany.	P and C
24 December	Free France	United States	A French submarine and three corvettes under Admiral Muselier seize Saint Pierre and Miquelon in defiance of American opposition (see Chapter 1).	D

[63] Pratt, *The American Secretaries of State and their Diplomacy*, Cooper Square, New York 1964, Chapter 13.

Date	Assailant	Victim	Incident	Type
			1942	
6 November	United States	France	A British submarine H.M.S. SERAPH under nominal American command picks up General Giraud (who had escaped from German captivity) from La Fosette on the French coast and takes him to Gibraltar so that his influence can be used to reconcile his compatriots to the Allied landing in French North Africa. The operation was successful but the General's influence did not come up to American expectations.[64]	D

[64] Anthony Heckstall-Smith, *The Fleet that Faced Both Ways*, Anthony Blond 1963, Chapter 28.

Date	Assailant	Victim	Incident	Type
			1943	
8/9 September	Italy	Germany	Italian fleet sails for Malta to surrender, a manifestation of the Royal Government's change of allegiance that prompted immediate German air attack, but earned future British diplomatic support '. . . when the Italian fleet loyally and courageously joined the Allies, I felt myself bound to work with the King of Italy and Marshal Badoglio . . . the surrender of the Italian fleet was solid proof of their authority'.[65] Successful.	E and P

[65] Winston S. Churchill, *Closing the Ring*, Cassell & Co. 1952, Chapters 6–11. This view also has Italian support, see Marc Antonio Bragadin, *The Italian Navy in World War II*, US Naval Institute 1957.

Date	Assailant	Victim	Incident	Type
			1945	
October	United States	Soviet Union and China	In an effort to assist the Chinese Nationalists to establish control of Manchuria before the Communists can, the US navy transport nationalist troops to Dairen, Hulutao and Yingkow but, when refused permission to land by the local Soviet commanders and fired on by Communist Chinese, Vice-Admiral Bailey did not persist. The delay entailed enabled the Chinese Communists to build up their forces and gain control of Manchuria. Unsuccessful.[66]	D

[66] Max Beloff, *Soviet Foreign Policy in the Far East 1944–51*, p. 42, O.U.P. 1953.

Date	Assailant	Victim	Incident	Type
			1946	
5 March	United States	Soviet Union	To encourage the Turkish Government to resist Soviet territorial demands, the body of the deceased Turkish Ambassador to Washington is sent home in the battle-ship MISSOURI.[67] The US Secretary of State thought this demonstrative gesture persuaded the Soviet Union to relax their pressure on Turkey.[68]	E
6 March	France	China	In the course of a dispute over the withdrawal from North Vietnam of Chinese occupation troops, the French cruiser EMILE BERTIN opens fire on Chinese troops at Haiphong. Results uncertain but Chinese do withdraw.[69]	P
18 July	Britain	Iran Soviet Union	H.M.S. NORFOLK and H.M.S. WILD GOOSE sent to Basra (Iraq) after rioting at the British oil refinery at Abadan (Iran) had been fomented by the Soviet-backed Tudeh party. The dispatch of these warships was followed in August by the landing of troops and, although actual intervention in Iran did not prove necessary, eventual outcome was satisfactory to British interests and entailed a setback to the growth of Soviet influence in Iran. Successful.[70]	P

205

---

[67] Rear-Admiral John D. Hayes, 'The Sea 1956–1967', article in *Naval Review 1969*, US Naval Institute.
[68] In fact the pressure continued and menacing manœuvres by the Soviet Black Sea Fleet during the summer had to be countered by American and British naval visits to Istanbul, see Kirk *The Middle East 1945–1950*, O.U.P. 1954.
[69] *Keesing's Contemporary Archives.*
[70] *Ibid.*

Date	Assailant	Victim	Incident	Type
			1946	
30 September	United States	Soviet Union	US Government announce that units of the US Navy will be permanently stationed in the Mediterranean to carry out American policy and diplomacy. They are still there, and, on balance, their presence has been beneficial to American interests. Successful.[71]	C
22 October	Britain	Albania	An attempt to over-ride Albanian objections and assert the right of innocent passage through the Corfu Straits (where H.M.S. ORION and H.M.S. SUPERB had been shelled by Albanian coastal batteries in May of that year) results in severe damage and loss of life to the British destroyers H.M.S. SAUMAREZ and VOLAGE, in a freshly-laid minefield. Although most of these mines were subsequently removed by British minesweepers (protected by a substantial British fleet) in November, the initial use of force was unsuccessful and attempts (through negotiation, the Security Council and the International Court) to obtain redress all failed.[72]	P

[71] *Ibid.*
[72] Leslie Gardiner, *The Eagle Spreads His Claws*, William Blackwood & Sons 1966.

Date	Assailant	Victim	Incident	Type
1947				
	Britain	The future state of Israel and others	For most of this year British naval patrols in the Eastern Mediterranean intercepted and seized ships carrying Jewish illegal immigrants to Palestine, thereby hoping to placate Arabs and facilitate the agreed solution of the Palestine problem. Although many ships were intercepted, some got through and the diplomatic effort was a complete failure.[73]	P
18 March	United States	Greece Soviet Union	On the same day that Congressional authorization was sought for President Truman's programme of aid to Greece against Communism, the US Government announced that a strong naval squadron (including the carrier LEYTE) would visit Greek ports.[73]	E

[73] *Keesing's Contemporary Archives.*

Date	Assailant	Victim	Incident	Type
1948				
28 February	Britain	Guatemala	Cruisers H.M.S. SHEFFIELD and H.M.S. DEVONSHIRE sent to Belize to deter Guatemala from prosecuting by force her claim to British Honduras. Successful.[74]	P

[74] *Keesing's Contemporary Archives.*

Date	Assailant	Victim	Incident	Type
			1948	
24 June	United States	Israel and Arab States	Three American destroyers assigned to Count Folke Bernadotte, UN Mediator for Palestine, 'to maintain peace between Arab and Israeli forces'. They did not succeed in this impossible task, but they did evacuate the UN team from Haifa in July 1948.[74]	C
November	United States	China	1,500 marines landed to re-inforce US naval base at Tsingtao (which was abandoned in February 1949). Temporarily successful.[75]	P
November	Britain and United States	China	Two American cruisers and a British destroyer sent to Shanghai to protect their nationals there. Temporarily successful.[75]	P

[74] Cooney op. cit.
[75] *Keesing's Contemporary Archives.*

Date	Assailant	Victim	Incident	Type
			1949	
19 April	Britain	China	H.M.S. AMETHYST attempts to ascend Yangtse to continue mounting guard on H.M. Embassy at Nanking, but is driven aground by Communist artillery fire. Attempts to rescue her by H.M.S. CONSORT the same day and by H.M.S. LONDON and BLACK SWAN on 21 April failed, but H.M.S. AMETHYST finally escaped to rejoin the fleet on 31 July. Nevertheless the objective (to protect H.M. Embassy, the need for which was lamentably demonstrated in 1967) was not attained and never again attempted. Unsuccessful.[76]	P

Date	Assailant	Victim	Incident	Type
			1949	
April	Britain United States	China	Additional British and US cruisers sent to Shanghai for protection of their Nationals. Temporarily successful.[77]	P
26 June	China	Britain United States	Nationalist Chinese proclaim a blockade of the Chinese coast, and in spite of American and British protests, attack and occasionally seize British and American vessels. Not very successful.[77]	P

[76] *Survey of International Affairs 1949–50, pp. 322–4.*
[77] *Keesing's Contemporary Archives.*

			1950	
March	United States	Vietnam	Two US destroyers were sent to Saigon to demonstrate American support for Bao Dai's government, but his opponents organized a protest against the destroyers' visit which led to serious rioting on 19 March. Not very successful.[78]	E
27 June	United States	China	US Seventh Fleet ordered to patrol Taiwan Straits to prevent Communists from invading Formosa or Nationalists from invading China. Successful.[79]	P

[78] *Keesing's Contemporary Archives.*
[79] Cooney op. cit.

209

Date	Assailant	Victim	Incident	Type
			1950	
7 December	China	Japan	Japanese fishing vessel DAI-ICHI-UNZEN MARU seized by Communist Chinese warship – the first of 158 vessels captured during the four years that followed before Japanese fishermen agreed to respect Chinese prohibited zones. Successful.[80]	D and P

[80] Ohira, Z. and Kuwahara, T., 'Fishing Problems between Japan and the People's Republic of China', article in *The Japanese Annual of International Law*, No. 3, 1959.

Date	Assailant	Victim	Incident	Type
			1951	
26 June	Britain	Iran	Cruiser H.M.S. MAURITIUS sent to Abadan for protection to British subjects during dispute with Iran (in which force was *not* employed). British subjects evacuated by this cruiser (which had meanwhile been reinforced by destroyers) on 3 October. Successful in its limited objective.[81]	P and D
1 July	Egypt	Britain and Israel	Egyptian corvette stops, plunders and damages British merchant ship in Gulf of Akaba as part of an attempted Egyptian blockade of Israel. British and other protests are unavailing as is discussion in the Security Council.[81]	P
14 July	Britain	Egypt	British destroyer flotilla sent to Red Sea to prevent further incidents of this kind. Agreement on future procedures for British ships using the Gulf of Akaba reached with Egypt on 26 July.[81]	P

[81] *Keesing's Contemporary Archives.*

Date	Assailant	Victim	Incident	Type
			1951	
24 October–31 December	Britain	Egypt	British warships (altogether twenty-seven but usually two cruisers at any one time) employed to keep Suez Canal open to shipping when Egyptian labour was withdrawn and clearance denied to British merchant ships. The cruisers provided a protected labour force and the Egyptians finally resumed normal working in February/March 1952. Successful.[82]	P and D
			1952	
26/27 July	Britain Canada	Egypt	After a *coup d'état* in Egypt, a large British naval force (including two carriers – one of them Canadian) assembles off the Egyptian coast in case intervention is needed to protect British nationals in Egypt. Successful.[82]	C
12 September	United States	Soviet Union	President Tito goes to sea in the U.S.S. CORAL SEA to observe a fire-power demonstration during the visit to Split of this American carrier, together with the cruiser SALEM and four destroyers.[83] Although naval visits do not usually count, this demonstration that American help was available – and acceptable – to Yugoslavia carried an obvious message for Marshal Stalin.[84]	E

[82] *Ibid.*

[83] Information kindly supplied by the US Naval Attaché in London.
[84] A similar demonstration had been arranged for the Spanish Government in January and was followed by fleet visits and the negotiation of an agreement for American bases in Spain, Cooney op. cit.

Date	Assailant	Victim	Incident	Type
			1953	
January	Argentina	Britain	Argentine naval vessel lands a party and erects buildings to signify occupation of the disputed British territory of Deception Island. On 16 February the buildings are demolished and the intruders arrested and expelled by H.M.S. SNIPE. Unsuccessful.[85]	E and D
September	South Korea	Japan	South Korean naval vessels start seizing Japanese fishing boats crossing the so-called 'Rhee Line' which was not recognized by any other country.[85] This practice continued for two years, the captive fishermen being exploited as hostages to secure concessions from Japan on other issues.[86]	E and D

[85] *Keesing's Contemporary Archives.*

[86] Even larger numbers of Japanese vessels and fishermen were seized by Soviet patrol ships from 1945 to 1969, but the extent to which Japanese fishermen have been excluded from the Sea of Okhotsk and even parts of the Sea of Japan, while Soviet trawlers have continued to operate south of Tokyo, cannot altogether be regarded as the result of Soviet naval superiority. Other factors, including the prolonged retention in the Soviet Union of Japanese prisoners of war, played an important part in the protracted Soviet–Japanese negotiations. The Soviet–Japanese maritime controversy is thus less of a precedent than the potential basis for some scenario of the future. See Ohira, Z., 'Fishing Problems between Soviet Russia and Japan', article in *The Japanese Annual of International Law*, No. 2, 1958.

Date	Assailant	Victim	Incident	Type
			1954	
May	United States	Britain Guatemala and others	In order to prevent the Guatemalan Government from importing arms to resist a revolution organized by the C.I.A., the US Government threaten a naval blockade and air-sea patrols were established in the Gulf of Honduras from 20 May to 7 June.[87] The British Government are induced to discourage British ships from carrying arms. Successful.[88]	P
July	South Korea	Japan	A South Korean force is landed on the Takeshima Islands, long disputed between South Korea and Japan. The islands are henceforth occupied by South Korea. Successful.[89]	D
26 July	United States	China	After six US nationals are killed on a British airliner shot down by Chinese fighters, two US aircraft carriers (HORNET and PHILIPPINE SEA) are sent to the scene of the incident and the C.-in-C. of the US Pacific Fleet announces that all of his ships and aircraft have orders to be 'quick on the trigger'. Two Chinese aircraft were shot down but the US Government (unlike the British who confined themselves to negotiations) got no apology nor compensation. Unsuccessful.[90] from the Chinese,	C

213

[87] Cooney op. cit.
[88] Anthony Eden, *Full Circle*, Chapter 6, Cassell & Co. 1960.
[89] *Keesing's Contemporary Archives.*
[90] *Ibid.*

Date	Assailant	Victim	Incident	Type
			1954	
August	Japan	South Korea	A Japanese patrol boat was sent to investigate the South Korean seizure of the Takeshima Islands, but withdrawn when fired on. Unsuccessful.[91]	P
16 November	Peru	Panama and others	Peruvian warships captured five whaling ships registered in Panama within 200 miles of the Peruvian coast, an extent of territorial waters not recognized by other countries. Similar incidents involving other South American countries took place fairly frequently and even when major powers were the victims they confined themselves to protests. Successful.[92]	D
			1955	
6–13 February	United States	China	US Seventh Fleet (including five carriers) evacuate Chinese nationalists from the Tachen islands, successfully deterring the Communists from interference.[93]	D and P
18 May	United States	North Vietnam	US Navy complete the evacuation (begun on 16 August 1954) of 300,000 refugees from North Vietnam, which had come under Communist control as a result of the Geneva Agreement of 1954.[94]	D

214

91 *Ibid.*
92 *Ibid.*

93 Cooney op. cit.
94 *Ibid.*

Date	Assailant	Victim	Incident	Type
			1 9 5 5	
3–9 August	South Korea	Japan	South Korean warships capture eleven Japanese fishing vessels, the crew of which are kept as hostages. (See 1953.) Successful.[95]	P and C

[95] *Keesing's Contemporary Archives.*

Date	Assailant	Victim	Incident	Type
			1 9 5 6	
October	United States	Britain and France	Harassing tactics employed by the US Sixth Fleet against British and French warships to demonstrate American disapproval of the Anglo-French intervention at Suez. The point was made but carried less conviction than other measures.[96]	E
18 October	France	Germany	French warships arrest in international waters German freighter HELGA BOGE carrying arms to Algerian rebels, the first of many German ships thus intercepted.[97]	D
31 October	United States	Egypt Britain and France	US Sixth Fleet lands marines at Alexandria and other points in Middle East to protect the evacuation of 2,000 Americans and other foreign nationals during fighting between Egypt and Britain and France. Successful.[98]	D

[96] A. J. Barker, *Suez: The Seven Day War*, pp. 90–91. Faber & Faber 1964.
[97] Jean Bernigaud, 'Les Aspects Maritimes de la Guerre d'Algérie', article in *Revue de Défense Nationale*, October 1968.
[98] Captain Daniel J. Carrison, *The United States Navy*, p. 39, Prager N.Y. 1968.

Date	Assailant	Victim	Incident	Type
			1957	
20 April	United States	Egypt Jordan Soviet Union[99] and Syria	US naval transports with 1,800 marines aboard anchor off Beirut in readiness for intervention in Jordan (whose independence and integrity were regarded as threatened by Nasserist subversion) while the Sixth Fleet carried out maneuvres in the Eastern Mediterranean. King Hussein succeeded in re-establishing his authority. Successful.	C
February–April	United States	Egypt	American destroyers patrol Straits of Tiran and Gulf of Aquaba to prevent Egyptian interference with American merchant vessels bound for Israel. Successful.[100]	P

[99] The US Government regarded the opposition in Jordan to King Hussein as Soviet inspired but the main evidence for this is the subsequent Soviet protest, on 29 April, against the movement of the Sixth Fleet as 'an open military demonstration against the countries of the Arab East'. See *Keesing's Contemporary Archives*.
[100] Cooney op. cit.

Date	Assailant	Victim	Incident	Type
			1958	
12–17 January	United States	Indonesia	Destroyer Division 31 asserts right of innocent passage through Lombok and Mahassai Straits after these had been claimed as territorial waters by Indonesia. Successful.[101]	E
18 January	France	Yugoslavia	Yugoslav ship carrying arms to Algerian insurgents intercepted on high seas by French Navy. Arms seized. Successful.[102]	D

[101] Cooney op. cit.
[102] *Keesing's Contemporary Archives*.

216

Date	Assailant	Victim	Incident	Type
			1958	
15 July	United States	Lebanon Syria Egypt Soviet Union	US Sixth Fleet lands marines in the Lebanon. (See Chapter 2.) Successful.	C
1 September	Britain	Iceland	Royal Navy begins a campaign to nullify the Icelandic ban on British fishing within twelve miles of the Icelandic coast by protecting British trawlers thus engaged. From 1 September 1958 to 14 March 1959 the Royal Navy foiled sixty-five Icelandic attempts to arrest British trawlers, but H.M.G. finally had to concede the Icelandic case. Unsuccessful.[103]	P and C
7 September	United States	China	US Seventh Fleet ordered to escort Chinese Nationalist convoys to within three miles of Quemoy so as to prevent Chinese Communist Navy from making their blockade effective. Successful and no fighting between Chinese and Americans. Among the aircraft carriers employed was the U.S.S. ESSEX, dispatched via the Suez Canal from the Mediterranean, where she had participated in the Lebanon operation.[104]	P

[103] See Frank Goldsworthy, 'More Fun than Fury in the Fish War', *USNIP* February 1961, and *Keesing's Contemporary Archives*.

[104] Elward F. Baldridge, 'Lebanon and Quemoy', article in *USNIP* February 1969.

Date	Assailant	Victim	Incident	Type
			1959	
12 February	South Korea	Japan	The South Korean Government react to Japanese repatriation of certain Koreans to North Korea by threatening to resume seizure of Japanese fishing vessels and to extend detention of hostages they had previously undertaken to release (see 1953). Partially successful.[105]	P
26 February	United States	Soviet Union	U.S.S. R.O. HALE sends a party aboard the Soviet trawler NOVOROSSISK in international waters after a series of breaks in the submarine cables in the Atlantic. The trawler denied responsibility, but no further breaks occurred. Successful.[106]	P
7 April	France	Morocco and Czechoslovakia	French Navy intercept a Czech freighter carrying arms to Morocco and confiscate arms as really destined for the Algerian rebels. Successful.[107]	P
24 April–4 May	United States Colombia	Cuba	US and Colombian warships patrol Caribbean coast off Panama to prevent any further landing of Cuban guerrillas in that country. Superfluous as Cubans surrendered meanwhile and Cuban Government disavow them.[108]	D

218

[105] *Keesing's Contemporary Archives.*
[106] Cooney op. cit.
[107] During the Algerian War the French Navy also stopped and searched on the high seas (even outside the Mediterranean) British, Bulgarian, Danish, German, Italian, Panamanian, Polish, Rumanian, Swedish and Yugoslav vessels. See Jean Bernigaud, 'Les Aspects Maritimes de la Guerre d'Algérie', article in *Revue de Défense Nationale*, October 1968.
[108] Cooney op. cit. and *Keesing's Contemporary Archives.*

Date	Assailant	Victim	Incident	Type
			1960	
5 April	Netherlands	Indonesia	To deter attacks by Indonesia on New Guinea, the Netherlands Government announce the dispatch of the aircraft carrier KAREL DOORMAN and two destroyers to the colony. No attacks are made, but reactions from Indonesia (which breaks off relations and retaliates against Dutch embassy, nationals and property) and from various neutral governments are adverse. On balance, unsuccessful.[109]	P
July	United States	Congo	American carrier WASP arrives off coast in readiness to evacuate Americans. While there she delivers petrol to the forces sent to the Congo by the United Nations.[110]	C
17 November	United States	Cuba	After armed uprisings allegedly inspired by the Castro régime in Cuba against the governments of Guatemala and Nicaragua, the carrier U.S.S. SHANGRI-LA and US destroyers patrolled the Caribbean coasts of these two countries until 10 December 'to prevent intervention on the part of Communist-directed elements . . . through the landing of armed forces or of supplies from abroad'. Successful.[111]	P

219

[109] *Keesing's Contemporary Archives.*
[110] Cooney op. cit.
[111] *Keesing's Contemporary Archives.*

Date	Assailant	Victim	Incident	Type
			1961	
15 April	United States	Cuba	Visible presence offshore of US fleet encourages the group of Cuban exiles organized by the C.I.A. to attempt the overthrow of the Castro régime by a landing at the Bay of Pigs, but, as actual naval support is not given, the attempt fails. Unsuccessful.[112]	C
29 June	Britain	Iraq	Landing of marines and troops together with naval concentration help to deter Iraqi invasion of Kuwait. (See Chapter 2.) Successful.[113]	P
21 July	France	Tunisia	After an initial bombardment by aircraft from the carrier ARROMANCHES, the cruisers COLBERT, BOUVET and CHEVALIER-PAUL force the entrance to the Lake of Bizerta and, with the help of French troops, break the Tunisian blockade of the Bizerta naval base complex and re-establish French control. Successful in its immediate objectives, though France later made concessions.[114]	C
19 November	United States	Dominican Republic	Visible presence offshore of US fleet (including carriers FRANKLIN D. ROOSEVELT and VALLEY FORGE with 1,800 marines aboard) enables President Kennedy's representative to secure the expulsion of the Trujillos (the family of the late dictator) and the establishment of a government acceptable to the United States. Successful.[115]	P

[112] Haynes Johnson, *The Bay of Pigs*, Hutchinson 1965.
[113] Lt.-Com. James Stewart, 'East of Suez', *USNIP*, March 1966.
[114] *Keesing's Contemporary Archives*.
[115] John Bartlow Martin, *Overtaken by Events*, Chapter 4, Doubleday & Co., N.Y. 1966.

Date	Assailant	Victim	Incident	Type
			1962	
15 January	Indonesia	Netherlands	A flotilla of Indonesian motor-torpedo-boats attempts to land infiltrators in Netherlands New Guinea, but is intercepted by the Netherlands Navy, who sink one vessel and put the other two to flight. Unsuccessful.[116]	C
16 May	United States	North Vietnam Laos Thailand	Carrier covers disembarkation of US marines in Thailand, an operation intended to demonstrate American readiness to intervene if Communists push their military successes in Laos too far. Successful.[117]	E and P

[116] *Keesing's Contemporary Archives.*
[117] *Naval Review* 1964, US Naval Institute.

Date	Assailant	Victim	Incident	Type
			1963	
21 February	France	Brazil	French destroyer TARTU sent to fishing grounds off north-east coast of Brazil after three French lobster boats had been seized by Brazilian warships sixty miles off the coast. The Brazilians countered with a cruiser, five destroyers and two corvettes, TARTU was soon withdrawn and the effect of these naval moves on the compromise settlement ultimately reached in 1964 is uncertain. (See also Chapter 4.)	C and E

P

221

Date	Assailant	Victim	Incident	Type
			1963	
26 February	United States	Dominican Republic	US aircraft carrier BOXER anchors off Santo Domingo ready to send helicopters to rescue Vice-President Johnson in case of trouble during the latter's visit to the Dominican Republic. Nothing happens.[118]	P and D
27 April	United States and Britain	Haiti	An American naval task force (including the carrier BOXER and 2,000 marines) cruises off Haiti in readiness to protect US nationals threatened by conflict between Haiti and the Dominican Republic, possibly also to intervene if government of Haiti is overthrown, but crisis blows over without naval intervention being required.[119] A British destroyer and frigate also stand by. US but not British nationals subsequently evacuated. Successful.	C
13 August	Cuba	Britain	Two Cuban warships land a party on a British island in the Bahamas to seize nineteen Cuban refugees and two fishing boats. When H.M.S. LONDONDERRY investigated, it was found out that this normally uninhabited island had been used as a base by Cuban exiles from the United States for their attacks on Cuba. Steps were accordingly taken by the British Government to discourage the use of British territory for this purpose. Successful.[120]	D and P

222

[118] Martin op. cit., Chapter 13.
[119] Martin op. cit., Chapter 18.
[120] *The Times*, 16, 17 and 21 August.

Date	Assailant	Victim	Incident	Type
			1964	
3–7 January	Britain and United States	Zanzibar	U.S.S. MANLEY, H.M.S. OWEN and R.F.A. HEBE evacuate US and British nationals from Zanzibar following the revolution there. Successful.[121]	D
25 January	Britain	Tanganyika	Royal Marines landed from H.M.S. CENTAUR to suppress the mutiny in the Tanganyikan army. Successful.[122]	P
29 January 15 February 13 March	Turkey	Cyprus N.A.T.O. U.N.	To reinforce their threat of armed intervention failing the adoption of satisfactory measures for the protection of the Turkish minority in Cyprus: Turkish fleet assembles off Iskanderun. The fleet sails. The fleet embarks troops. All these threats brought an immediate concession but they did not achieve a lasting solution which had to be sought by other means.[123]	P
2–5 August	North Vietnam	United States	American destroyers patrolling in the Gulf of Tongking are attacked by North Vietnamese torpedo-boats.[124] Much about this incident is still obscure, but, if the objective was to discourage American naval activity, the attempt was unsuccessful and American retaliation can be regarded as marking the moment when the conflict in Vietnam first assumed the character of war between the United States and North Vietnam.[125]	P

[121] *Keesing's Contemporary Archives.*
[122] Lt.-Col. T. M. P. Stevens, 'A Joint Operation in Tanganyika', *RUSI Journal*, February 1965.
[123] Philip Windsor, 'NATO and the Cyprus Crisis', *Adelphi Paper No. 14*, November 1964, Institute for Strategic Studies, London.
[124] *Keesing's Contemporary Archives.*
[125] Joseph C. Goulden, *Truth Is The First Casualty*, David McNally & Co. 1969.

Date	Assailant	Victim	Incident	Type
			1 9 6 5	
28 April	United States	Dominican Republic	536 US marines landed from aircraft carrier to protect US citizens during the civil war (evacuation by unarmed marine helicopters had begun the previous day but on the 28th armed marines were landed ready to meet opposition). The objective was later extended (and the participation of the Organization of American States obtained) to include the prevention of Communist influence in the Dominican Republic Government. By 6 May the United States had 22,000 men ashore and 9,000 afloat. By 3 September a provisional government acceptable to the United States had been established, but the final withdrawal of US forces actually took place on 20 September 1966. Although its necessity was disputed this was a successful operation but expensive financially (it cost 150 million dollars though US casualties were low). Forty ships of the US Navy were involved.[126]	C
1 December	Britain	Rhodesia	Pending the arrival of British troops and military aircraft in Zambia, the aircraft carrier H.M.S. EAGLE cruises off the coast of Tanzania to reassure the Zambian Government that Rhodesian air attacks on Zambia (which the latter government feared) would be prevented. Successful.[127]	C

224

[126] Captain James A. Dare, 'Dominican Diary', *USNIP* December 1965.
[127] *Keesing's Contemporary Archives.*

Date	Assailant	Victim	Incident	Type
			1966	
10 April	Britain	Rhodesia	As authorized by the Security Council's resolution of 9 April 1966, H.M.S. BERWICK boards the Greek tanker MANUELA and persuades her not to continue her voyage to Beira. British naval patrol continues throughout the year to turn back tankers believed to be carrying oil for Rhodesia. Apparently successful in its limited objective. (See Chapter 4.)	P and E
September	Britain	Argentina	H.M.S. PUMA sent from Cape Town to Port Stanley (Falkland Islands) following a 'symbolic' invasion of that colony by a group of private Argentinian citizens and anti-British demonstrations in Argentina itself. The problem was solved by negotiation and naval force was not employed.[128]	E

225

[128] *Ibid.*

Date	Assailant	Victim	Incident	Type
			1967	
24 May	Britain and United States	Egypt	After a speech by the British Prime Minister stating that Her Majesty's Government would join with other governments to assert the right of passage by vessels of all nations through the Straits of Tiran (which Egyptian land forces had just closed as part of Egyptian measures against Israel) the Admiralty announced that H.M.S. VICTORIOUS and other warships were being held in the Mediterranean 'in readiness against any eventuality' and the US Sixth Fleet was concentrated in the Eastern Mediterranean. This threat of purposeful force (described by the Egyptian Foreign Minister as gunboat diplomacy) was not pursued and, in the event, did more harm than good to British and American interests. Unsuccessful.[129]	P and C
8 June	Israel	United States	Israeli torpedo-boats attack and drive off the U.S.S. LIBERTY, a so-called 'technical research' ship apparently monitoring Israeli transmissions during the war with Egypt. If the attacks were deliberate, this was an expensive success: the Israelis have already had to pay more than three million dollars in compensation with more claims to come.[129]	D

226

[129] *Ibid.*

Date	Assailant	Victim	Incident	Type
			1967	
10 July	Soviet Union	Israel	Soviet naval squadron visits Port Said (eight ships) and Alexandria (four ships) and its commander declares 'we are ready to co-operate with Egyptian armed forces to repel any aggression'.[130] It is uncertain whether the Israelis intended any further advance, but they did not make one, and the gesture was, in any case, welcome to Arab opinion and helped to relieve Arab disappointment at the absence of earlier and more effective Soviet support.	E and P
29 November	Britain	South Yemen	The naval concentration, originally planned for other purposes, assembled off Aden to cover the withdrawal of British troops, is retained in case British civilians have to be protected or evacuated from the newly independent republic. The necessity did not arise and the fleet was dispersed on 31 January 1968. (See Chapter 4.)	C

---

[130] *The Times*, 11 July 1967.

Date	Assailant	Victim	Incident	Type
			1968	
23 January	North Korea	United States	North Korean naval craft put a stop to the use of American vessels for close electronic surveillance of their coast by capturing the u.s.s. PUEBLO and bringing the ship and her crew into port before US forces could intervene. US Government later have to make humiliating concessions to obtain the release of crew. (See Chapter 2.) Successful.	D and P

227

Date	Assailant	Victim	Incident	Type
			1968	
25 January	United States	North Korea	American naval task force including three carriers assembles in Sea of Japan as part of American response to seizure of PUEBLO. It begins to disperse, without doing anything, on 6 February. Unsuccessful.[131]	C
January	Soviet Union	United States	Soviet force of sixteen ships manœuvres between American warships and coast of North Korea. (See Chapter 5.) Not enough is known about this incident to permit any judgment of the degree of success achieved.	E
	Britain	Rhodesia	Beira patrol continues although Rhodesia is by now obtaining oil by other routes. (See Chapter 4.)	E
July	Soviet Union	Norway	A major amphibious force supported by escort destroyers, missile-carrying destroyers, supply vessels, etc. sailed from the Baltic Sea along the entire Norwegian coast to the Kola Peninsula.[132] This was explained by the Soviet press as a reply to the NATO naval exercises of the previous month – 'needless to say, such a show of bellicosity in the immediate vicinity of our frontiers could not be ignored by the Soviet Union'.[133] Once again, it is too early to assess the results of a move presumably intended to support the Soviet press campaign against Norwegian membership of NATO.	E

[131] *Keesing's Contemporary Archives.*
[132] Statement of Norwegian Minister of Defence quoted in NATO letter of January 1969.
[133] 'NATO: Northern Flank', article by Major-General Boris Tephinsky in Soviet weekly *New Times* No. 36 of 11 September 1968.

228

Date	Assailant	Victim	Incident	Type
1969				
22 April	Iran	Iraq	Iranian warships escort an Iranian merchant ship from Khorramshahr to the Persian Gulf in successful defiance of an Iraqi threat to stop any ships flying the Iranian flag from sailing through waters claimed by Iraq. For lack of warships Iran had been compelled to give way to a similar threat in 1961, but naval action now secured her purpose.[134]	P
22 April	United States	North Korea	American battleship NEW JERSEY and a large task force including carriers sent to the Sea of Japan following the destruction of a US surveillance aircraft by North Korean aircraft on 15 April. There was no reaction from North Korea and the fleet was eventually withdrawn without achieving anything.[135]	E
13 June	South Korea	North Korea	An armed North Korean vessel sent to pick up a spy from the South Korean island of Huksando is intercepted at sea and sunk by a South Korean destroyer.[136]	D
29 November	Spain	Britain	After changes in the Spanish Government had prompted newspaper speculation that Spanish claims to Gibraltar might now be no longer pressed so vigorously, the Spanish helicopter carrier DEDALO and twelve other Spanish warships were sent to Algeciras Bay, apparently to demonstrate continued Spanish determination. (See Chapter 2.)	E

229

[134] *Keesing's Contemporary Archives.*
[135] *The Times*, 23 April 1969.
[136] *The Times*, 14 June 1969 (similar incidents took place in September and October of the same year).

BIBLIOGRAPHY

THE list of books that follows has been arranged in two main sections. GENERAL comprises works of which the relevance is not confined to any one episode, period or geographical area, whereas the PARTICULAR list has been subdivided into categories of this kind. A list of useful periodicals is included in the first part, but the references to specific articles made in earlier footnotes are not repeated in the bibliography unless the whole article is both relevant and important. Nor does the bibliography list every book earlier mentioned as the source of some incidental quotation or passing reference. Broadly speaking these are works that offer the reader additional information or opinions.

Their relevance, however, can seldom be more than partial. The political application of limited naval force, in so far as it constitutes a subject at all, is one that tends to elude the grasp of writers on naval and diplomatic problems alike. This is particularly true of historians, who have yet to attempt any account of the twentieth-century use of gunboat diplomacy. The archives have still not been ransacked and, with the honourable exception of a few books devoted to specific episodes, the secondary sources scarcely exist. Libraries of miscellaneous writing must be dredged for passing references or for the footnotes to which the subject is usually consigned, even by diplomatic and naval historians. The present work thus contains a greater accumulation of relevant historical material than is available elsewhere, but not all of it comes from the purest sources or has passed the filter beds of expert scrutiny and analysis. The trouble is that the use of warships in peace-time has been scantily recorded and sometimes with a certain inattention to detail. Diplomatic historians are liable to regard 'battleship' as just another synonym for 'warship'; their naval colleagues to display an occasional breeziness over dates or political factors. Both tend to hurry over these trivia in their eagerness to arrive at greater things: a treaty or a war.

Many of the books listed below should accordingly be consulted with caution.

I – GENERAL

1. *Diplomatic History*

(a) *Basic Books*

The following works are probably the major source of published information in English. Although many of their myriad volumes are barren and there are surprising omissions from them all, no student of gunboat diplomacy can afford to neglect their lists of contents or restrain a sigh at the inadequacy of their indexing.

Documents on British Foreign Policy 1919–1939, H.M.S.O. London.
Documents on German Foreign Policy, H.M.S.O. London and Government Printing Office, Washington.
Keesing's Contemporary Archives, Bristol (from 1945).
Papers relating to the Foreign Relations of the United States, U.S. Government Printing Office Washington.
Survey of International Affairs, Royal Institute of Internaional Affairs, Chatham House, London.

Further volumes are still appearing in each series except that on German Foreign Policy.

(b) *Background Reading*

CALVOCORESSI, Peter, *World Politics Since 1945*, Longmans 1968.
CHURCHILL, Winston S., *The Second World War* (6 vols.), Cassell 1948–1954.
HIGGINS, Rosalyn, *United Nations Peace-Keeping 1946–1967* (3 vols.), R.I.A.A., O.U.P. 1969–1970.
HUDSON, G. F., *The Hard and Bitter Peace*, Pall Mall 1966.
JANSEN, G. H., *Afro-Asia and Non-Alignment*, Faber & Faber 1966.
KNAPP, Wilfred, *A History of War and Peace 1939–1965*, O.U.P. 1967.
MORRIS, James, *Pax Britannica*, Faber & Faber 1969.
MYDANS, C. S. S., *The Violent Peace*, Atheneum, N.Y. 1968.
RICHARDSON, R. P., *An Analysis of Recent Conflicts 1946–1964*, Center for Naval Analyses, Arlington Va, USA. 1970.
WOOD, David, *Conflict in the Twentieth Century*, Adelphi Paper No. 48, Institute for Strategic Studies, London. June 1968.

WOODWARD, Llewellyn, *British Foreign Policy in the Second World War*, H.M.S.O. London 1970.

WORSLEY, Peter, *The Third World*, Univ. of Chicago Press 1964.

2. Naval History

There is no history of gunboat diplomacy since 1919 and none of the books listed below do more than throw an occasional sidelight, sometimes with many omissions and inaccuracies, on the events of the period.

(*a*) *Relevant pre-1919 History*
PRESTON and MAJOR, *Send a Gunboat*, Longmans 1967.

(*b*) *American Naval History*
CARRISON, Capt. David J., *The United States Navy*, Praeger, N.Y. 1968.

COONEY, David M., *A Chronology of the United States Navy 1775–1965*, Franklin Wait Inc., N.Y. 1965.

MITCHELL, D. W., *History of the Modern American Navy*, 1947.

MORISON, Samuel Eliot, *History of US Naval Operations in World War II*, Little Brown & Co. 1947 and later.

SPROUT, H. and M., *Toward a New Order of Sea Power*, Princeton U.P. 1943.

(*c*) *British Naval History*
EDWARDS, Kenneth, *The Grey Diplomatists*, Rich & Cowan 1938.

GARBUTT, Paul E., *Naval Challenge 1945–1961*, Macdonald 1961.

MARTIN, L. W., *British Defence Policy: The Long Recessional*, Adelphi Paper No. 61, Institute for Strategic Studies, London 1969.

ROSKILL, Stephen, *Naval Policy Between the Wars, Vol. 1, 1919–1929*, Collins 1968.
The War at Sea, H.M.S.O. 1954.

(*d*) *Miscellaneous*
HEZLET, Vice Admiral Sir Arthur, *Aircraft and Sea Power*, Peter Davies 1970.

POLMAR, Norman, *Aircraft Carriers*, Macdonald 1969.

3. Naval Strategies, Strengths and Technical Factors

BOOTH, Richard, *The Armed Forces of African States*, Adelphi Paper, No. 67, Institute for Strategic Studies, London 1970.

BROWN, Neville, *Strategic Mobility*, Chatto & Windus 1963 'Deterrence from the Sea' Article in *Survival*, for June 1970, I.S.S. London.

CLARK, Admiral J. J. C. and BARNES Capt. D. H. B., *Sea Power and its Meaning*, Franklin Watts Inc., N.Y. 1966.

GRETTON, Sir P., *Maritime Strategy*, Cassell 1965.

KUENNE, Robert E., *The Attack Submarine*, Yale U.P. 1965.

MARTIN, L. W., *The Sea in Modern Strategy*, Chatto & Windus 1967.

MOULTON, J. L., *British Maritime Strategy in the 1970s*, R.U.S.I., London 1969.

PADFIELD, Peter, *An Agony of Collisions*, Hodder & Stoughton 1966.

POLMAR, Norman, *Aircraft Carriers*, Macdonald 1969.

ROSKILL, Stephen, *Strategy of Sea Power*, Collins 1962.

SANGUINETTI, *Atome et Batailles Sur Mer*, Hachette, Paris 1965.

SKAAR, BLENNER and OHRELIUS (editors), *The Royal Swedish Navy*, Hörsta Förlag, Stockholm 1957.

4. *Periodicals* (other than daily and weekly newspapers)

Annual Register of World Events, Longmans, London.

Armed Forces Management (monthly), Washington.

Brassey's Annual, London.

Current History (monthly), Philadelphia.

Foreign Affairs (quarterly), New York.

International Affairs (quarterly), R.I.A.A., London.

International Defence Review (quarterly), Geneva.

Keesing's Contemporary Archives (weekly), Bristol.

Jane's Fighting Ships (annual), Sampson, Low, Marston & Co., London.

Journal of the Royal United Service Institution (quarterly), London.

Marine Corps Gazette (monthly).

Military Balance, The (annual), Institute for Strategic Studies, London.

Military Review, The (monthly), Fort Leavenworth, Kansas.

NATO Letter (monthly), Brussels.

Naval News Summary, Ministry of Defence, London.

Naval Review (quarterly), London.

Naval Review (annual), US Naval Institute.

Navy (monthly), Wimbledon.

Navy News (monthly), Portsmouth.

New Times (English language weekly), Moscow.

Revue de Défense Nationale (monthly), Paris.

Revue Maritime (monthly), Paris.
Soviet Military Review (monthly in English), Moscow.
Statements on the Defence Estimates (annual), H.M.S.O. London.
Strategic Survey (annual), Institute for Strategic Studies, London.
Survey of British and Commonwealth Affairs (fortnightly), C.O.I. London.
Survival (monthly), Institute for Strategic Studies, London.
The World Today (monthly), R.I.I.A., London.
United States in World Affairs (annual), Council on Foreign Relations N.Y. Harper.
United States Naval Institute Proceedings (monthly), Annapolis.

5. *Theoretical Works on Force and International Relations*

BARNET, Richard J., *Intervention and Revolution*, World Publishing Co. N.Y. 1968.
BUCHAN, Alastair, *War in Modern Society*, C. A. Watts 1966.
CARR, E. H., *The Twenty Years Crisis*, Macmillan 1940.
HUGO, Grant, *Britain in Tomorrow's World: Principles of Foreign Policy*, Chatto & Windus 1969.
—*Appearance and Reality in International Relations*, Chatto & Windus 1970.
KNORR, Klaus, *On the Uses of Military Power in The Nuclear Age*, Princeton U.P. 1966.
LUTTWAK, Edward, *Coup d'État*, Allen Lane 1968.
MCNAMARA, Robert S., *The Essence of Security*, Hodder & Stoughton 1968.
PENROSE, E. F., *The Revolution In International Relations*, Frank Cass 1965.
SCHELLING, Thomas C., *Arms and Influence*, Yale U.P., 1966.
VITAL, David, *The Inequality of States*, O.U.P. 1967.

II – PARTICULAR

Unlike those listed earlier, many of the books that follow are directly relevant, being detailed accounts of particular applications of limited naval force. Those marked with an asterisk are recommended.

1. ALTMARK (1940)

BROOKES, Ewart, *Prologue to a War*, Jarrolds 1966.
DERRY, T. K., *The Campaign in Norway*, H.M.S.O. 1952.
Documents on German Foreign Policy 1918–1945, Series D. Vol. VIII, US Government Printing Office, Washington, 1954.

H.M.S.O., *Correspondence Respecting the German Steamer 'ALTMARK'*, Command 8012 of 1950, London.
INSTILLING FRA UNDERSØKELSESKOMMISJONEN AV 1945, *Altmark Saken*, Oslo 1947.
MOULTON, J. L., *The Norwegian Campaign of 1940*, Eyre & Spottiswoode 1966.
*OMANG, Reidar, *Altmark Saken 1940*, Gyldendal Norsk Forlag 1953.
ROSKILL, S. W., *The War at Sea*, H.M.S.O. 1954.
VIAN, Sir P., *Action This Day*, Frederick Muller 1960.

2. Baltic (*1919–1921*)

AGAR, A. W. A., *Baltic Episode*, Hodder & Stoughton 1963.
BENNETT, G., *Cowan's War*, Collins 1963.
JÄGERSKIÖLD STIG, *Riksföreståndaren Gustaf Mannerheim 1919*, Holger Schildts Förlag Helsingfors 1969.
MERCER, David M., 'The Baltic Sea Campaign', article in *USNIP*, September 1962.
PAASIVIRTA, Juhau, *The Victors in World War I and Finland*, Finnish Historical Society, Helsinki 1965.
PAGE, S. W., *The Formation of the Baltic States*, Harvard University Press 1959.
PRIDHAM, Francis, *Close of a Dynasty*, Allen Wingate 1956.
*ULLMAN, Richard H., *Britain and the Russian Civil War*, Princetown University Press 1968.

3. Caribbean (*1919–1969*)

ABEL, Elie, *The Missiles of October*, MacGibbon & Kee 1966.
AGUILAR, Alonso, *Pan-Americanism from Monroe to the Present* tr. Asa Zata, Monthly Review Press, N.Y. 1968.
BEMAN, Lamar T., *Intervention in Latin America*, H. W. Wilson Co. N.Y. 1928.
BEMIS, Samuel Flagg, *The Latin American Policy of the United States*, N.Y. Harcourt, Brace 1943.
COUNCIL ON FOREIGN RELATIONS, *American Relations in the Caribbean*, Yale U.P. 1929.
DALE, Capt. J. A., 'Dominican Diary', article in *USNIP* 1965.
GALVÃO, Henrique, *The Santa Maria*, Weidenfeld & Nicolson 1961.
HOWLAND, Charles P., *American Relations in the Caribbean*, Yale U.P. 1929.
JOHNSON, H. P. and others, *The Bay of Pigs*, W. W. Norton & Co. 1964.

*KAMMAN, William, *A Search for Stability*, Univ. of Notre Dame Press 1968.

MARTIN, John Barlow, *Overtaken by Events*, Doubleday & Co., N.Y. 1966.

PERKINS, Dexter, *The United States and the Caribbean*, Harvard 1966.

SLATER, Jerome, *The O.A.S. and US Foreign Policy*, Ohio State University Press 1967.

SMITH, Robert F., *The United States and Cuba*, College and University Press, New Haven 1960.

STUART, Graham, *Latin America and the United States*, Fifth Edition, Appleton, Crofts Inc., N.Y. 1955.

SZULC, T. and MEYER, K. E., *The Cuban Invasion: The Chronicle of a Disaster*, Frederick A. Praeger N.Y. 1962.

WOOD, Bryce, *The Making of the Good Neighbor Policy*, Columbia, U.P. 1961.

4. *China and the Far East (1919–1969)*

China Year Book, The (irregular annual of the twenties and thirties), Tientsin Press Ltd.

CHRISTOPHER, S. W., *Conflict in the Far East*, Leiden, E. J. Brill 1950.

CLIFFORD, Nicholas, *Retreat from China: British Policy in The Far East 1937–1941*, Longmans 1967.

DREYER, Admiral Sir Frederic C., *The Sea Heritage*, Museum Press 1955.

FERRELL, R. H., *American Diplomacy in the Great Depression*, Yale U.P. 1957.

GWYNN, Gen. Sir Charles, *Imperial Policing*, Macmillan 1934.

HAMILTON, Commander Louis, *Manuscript Journal* in National Maritime Museum, Greenwich, London.

HEWLETT, Sir W., *Forty Years in China*, Macmillan 1943.

H.M.S.O., *Papers relating to the Settlement of the Nanking Incident of March 24, 1927*, Command 3188 of 1928, London.

MORSE and MACNAIR, *Far Eastern Inernational Relations*, Houghton Mifflin, Boston 1931.

NAVY DEPARTMENT, Tokyo, *On the Shanghai Incident*, March 1932.

OHIRA, Z. and KUWAHARA, T., 'Fishery Problems Between Japan and the Peoples Republic of China', article in the *Japanese Annual of International Law*, No. 3, 1959.

PANIKKAR, K. M., *Asia and Western Dominance*, Allen & Unwin 1953.

PERRY, Hamilton Derby, *The Panay Incident*, Macmillan, Toronto 1969.

Q

POLLARD, Robert T., *China's Foreign Relations 1917-1931*, N.Y. Macmillan 1933.

SALISBURY, Harrison E., *The Coming War Between Russia and China*, Secker & Warburg 1969.

STATE DEPARTMENT, *United States Relations with China, 1944-1949*, US Govt. Printing Office 1949.

*TANG, PETER S. H., *Russian and Soviet Policy in Manchuria and Outer Mongolia*, Duke University Press 1959.

TANG TSOU, *America's Failure in China 1941-1950*, Univ. of Chicago Press 1963.

TULEJA, Commander T. V., *Statesmen and Admirals: The Quest for a Far Eastern Naval Policy (1922-1941)*, 1963.

TWEEDIE, Admiral Sir Hugh, *The Story of a Naval Life*, Rich & Cowan.

WALEY, Arthur, *The Opium War through Chinese Eyes*, Allen & Unwin 1958.

WHEELER, Commander G. E., *Prelude to Pearl Harbour: the US Navy and the Far East (1921-1931)*, 1963, Missouri U.P.

5. *Iceland (1940-1960)*

BEARD, Charles A., *President Roosevelt and the Coming of the War 1941*, Yale U.P. 1948.

GRIFFITHS, John C., *Modern Iceland*, Pall Mall Press 1969.

HISTORICAL DIVISION HQ US MARINE CORPS, *The US Marines in Iceland 1941-1942*, Washington 1970.

NUECHTERLEIN, Donald E., *Iceland: Reluctant Ally*, Cornell Univ. Press 1961.

6. *Lebanon (1958)*

CHAMOUN, Camille, *Crise Au Moyen Orient*, Paris Gallimard 1963.

COPELAND, Miles, *The Game of Nations*, Weidenfeld & Nicolson 1969.

EISENHOWER, Dwight D., *The White House Years*, Vol. III, Waging the Peace, London, Heinemann 1966.

HEINL, D., *Soldiers of the Sea*, US Naval Institute 1962.

KIRK, George E., *Contemporary Arab Politics*, N.Y. Praeger 1961.

MARINE CORPS HISTORICAL BRANCH, G.3. Division, *Marines in Lebanon 1958*, Washington 1966.

MCCLINTOCK, Robert, 'The US Intervention in Lebanon', article in *USNIP*, October 1962.

MURPHY, Robert, *Diplomat Among Warriors*, Collins 1964.

QUBAIN, Fahim I., *Crisis in Lebanon*, Middle East Institute, Washington 1961.
THAYER, Charles W., *Diplomat*, N.Y. Harpers 1959.

7. LIBERTY, MADDOX and PUEBLO (*1964–1968*)

ARMBRISTER, Trevor, *A Matter of Accountability*, Barrie & Jenkins 1970.
BRANDT, E., *The Last Voyage of U.S.S. PUEBLO*, W. W. Norton & Co., N.Y. 1969.
*GOULDEN, Joseph C., *Truth Is the First Casualty: The Gulf of Tonkin Affair–Illusion and Reality*, Rand McNally & Co., Chicago 1969. (Also touches on LIBERTY and PUEBLO.)
TULLY, Andrew, *The Super Spies*, Arthur Baker Ltd. 1970.

8. *Mediterranean (1919–1969)*

ALBION, R. G. and CONNERY R. H., *Forrestal and the Navy*, Columbia, U.P. 1962.
*BARROS, James, *The Corfu Incident of 1923*, Princetown Univ. Press 1965.
BRAGADIN, Marc Antonio, *The Italian Navy in World War II*, US Naval Institute 1957.
CHALMERS, W. S., *Max Horton and the Western Approaches*, Hodder & Stoughton 1954.
EDWARDS, Kenneth, *The Grey Diplomatists*, Rich & Cowan 1948.
*GARDINER, Leslie, *The Eagle Spreads His Claws*, William Blackwood & Sons 1966.
GASTEYGER, Curt, *Conflict and Tension in the Mediterranean*, Adelphi Paper No. 51, Institute for Strategic Studies, London 1968.
HECKSTALL-SMITH, Anthony, *The Fleet That Faced Both Ways*, Anthony Blond, 1963.
MARDER, Arthur, 'The Royal Navy and the Ethiopian Crisis of 1935–36', *American Historical Review*, Vol. LXXV, No. 5, June 1970.
REITZEL, William, *The Mediterranean: It's Rôle in America's Foreign Policy*, Kennihat Press Inc., Port Washington, N.Y. 1948.
WINDSOR, Philip, *NATO and the Cyprus Crisis*, Adelphi Paper No. 14, Nov. 1964, Institute for Strategic Studies, London.
WYNNE, Barry, *The Day Gibraltar Fell*, Macdonald 1969.

9. *Middle East (1919–1969)*

BARKER, A. J., *Suez: The Seven Day War*, Faber & Faber 1964.

CHURCHILL, Randolph S. and Winston S., *The Six Day War*, Heinemann 1967.

COPELAND, Miles, *The Game of Nations*, Weidenfeld & Nicolson 1969.

EDEN, Anthony, *Full Circle*, Cassell 1960.

HUNTER, Robert E., *The Soviet Dilemma in the Middle East*, Adelphi Papers No. 59 and 60, Institute for Strategic Studies, London.

MONROE, Elizabeth, *Britain's Moment in the Middle East 1919–1956*, R.I.I.A., O.U.P. 1963.

NOVO, J. A. de, *American Interests and Policies in the Middle East 1900–1939*, Univ. of Minnesota 1963.

PAGET, Julian, *Last Post: Aden 1964–1967*, Faber & Faber, 1969.

THOMAS, Hugh, *The Suez Affair*, Weidenfeld & Nicolson 1966.

WALDER, David, *The Chanak Affair*, Hutchinson 1969.

10. *Miscellaneous*

BEARD, Charles A., *President Roosevelt and the Coming of The War 1941*, Yale U.P. 1948.

BROOK-SHEPHERD, Gordon – *The Last Hapsburg*, Weidenfeld & Nicolson 1968.

MACARTNY, C. A., *October Fifteenth: A History of Modern Hungary 1929–1945*, Edinburgh Univ. Press 1956.

MOSELEY, Leonard, *On Borrowed Time*, Weidenfeld & Nicolson 1969 (for Memel 1939).

PAZ and FERRARI, *Argentina's Foreign Policy 1930–1962*, Univ. of Notre Dame Press 1966.

11. *Saint Pierre et Miquelon* (*1941*)

*ANGLIN, Douglas C., *The St. Pierre and Miquelon Affair of 1941*, Univ. of Toronto Press 1966.

AUPHAN and MORDAL, *The French Navy in World War II*, tr. Sabalot, U.S. Naval Institute 1959.

GAULLE, Charles de, *Mémoires de Guerre: L'Appel 1940–1942*, Paris Librairie Plon.

MUSELIER, Vice-Admiral, *De Gaulle Contre le Gaullisme*, Editions du Chêne 1946.

WOODWARD, *British Foreign Policy in the Second World War*, H.M.S.O. 1970.

12. *Soviet Union* (*1919–1969*)

BELOFF, Max, *The Foreign Policy of Soviet Russia*, O.U.P., 1949; *Soviet Foreign Policy in the Far East 1944–1951*, O.U.P. 1953.

BUTLER, William E., *The Law of Soviet Territorial Waters*, N.Y., Praeger 1967.

CATTELL, David T., *Soviet Diplomacy in the Spanish Civil War*, Univ. of California Press 1957.

CENTER FOR STRATEGIC AND INTERNATIONAL STUDIES, *Special Report on Soviet Sea Power*, Georgetown University, Washington, June 1969.

COX, Lt.-Com. David R., 'Sea Power and Soviet Foreign Policy', Article in *USNIP*, June 1969.

ELIOT, George Fielding, 'The Kremlin Builds a Cold War Fleet', article in *US Marine Corps Gazette*, June 1969.

HAYTER, Sir William, *Russia and the World*, Secker & Warburg 1970.

HERRICK, Robert Waring, *Soviet Naval Strategy*, US Naval Institute, Annapolis 1968.

HORELICK, A. L. and RUSH, M., *Strategic Power and Soviet Foreign Policy*, Univ. of Chicago Press, 1966.

ISAKOV, Admiral of the Fleet I. S., *The Red Fleet in the Second World War*, Hutchinson.

McCGWIRE, Commander M. K., *The Background to Russian Naval Policy*, article in Brassey's Annual 1968.

MITCHELL, Mairin, *The Maritime History of Russia*, Sedgwick and Jackson 1949.

OHIRA, Z., 'Fishery Problems Between Soviet Russia and Japan', article in *The Japanese Annual of International Law*, No. 2., 1958.

SALISBURY, Harrison E., *The Coming War Between Russia and China*, Secker and Warburg 1969.

SAUNDERS, M. G., *The Soviet Navy*, Weidenfeld & Nicolson 1958.

SCHMIDT, Helmut, 'The Brezhnev Doctrine', article in *Survival*, October 1969.

WHETTON, Laurence L., 'The Mediterranean Threat', article in *Survival*, August 1970.

WOLFE, Thomas W., *Soviet Power and Europe 1965–1969*, RAND Corporation Memorandum Rm-5991-PR of July 1969.

13. *Spanish Civil War (1936–1939)*

CERVERA, Valderrama, Almirante Juan, *Memorias de Guerra*, Editorial Nacional Madrid 1968.

EDEN, Anthony, *Facing the Dictators*, Cassell 1962.

EDWARDS, Kenneth, *The Grey Diplomatists*, Rich & Cowan 1938.

H.M.S.O., *Documents on German Foreign Policy Series D,* Vol. III, London 1951.

H.M.S. ROYAL OAK 1936–1938 Commission: Executive Officer's Log, Manuscript in National Maritime Museum, Greenwich.

JACKSON, Gabriel, *The Spanish Republic and The Civil War,* Princeton U.P. 1965.

MORENO, Fernández, Almirante D. Francisco, *La Guerra en e Mar,* Editorial Ahr, Barcelona 1959.

PADELFORD, Norman J., *International Law and Diplomacy in The Spanish Civil Strife,* N.Y. Macmillan 1939.

PUZZO, Dante A., *Spain and The Great Powers 1936–1941,* Columbia U.P. 1962.

STEER, G. L., *The Tree of Gernika* Hodder & Stoughton 1938.

THOMAS, Hugh, *The Spanish Civil War,* Eyre & Spottiswoode 1961.

TOYNBEE, Arnold J., *Survey of International Affairs 1937,* Vol. II, R.I.I.A. and O.U.P. 1938.

INDEX

Names of ships are in capital letters, thus – BOXER. Theoretical classifications and concepts are listed primarily under Gunboat Diplomacy and Limited Naval Force.

*These assailants were NOT also victims.